WINSTON
CHURCHILL
AN ILLUSTRATED BIOGRAPHY

WINSTON CHURCHILL

AN ILLUSTRATED BIOGRAPHY

R G GRANT

GALLERY BOOKS
An imprint of W.H. Smith Publishers Inc.
112 Madison Avenue
New York, New York 10016

Published by Gallery Books
A Division of W H Smith Publishers Inc.
112 Madison Avenue
New York, New York 10016

Produced by
Brompton Books Corp.
15 Sherwood Place
Greenwich, CT 06830

ISBN 0-8317-9458-5

Printed in Portugal

10 9 8 7 6 5 4 3 2 1

CONTENTS

CHAPTER ONE
Inheritance

On 12 August 1873, Lord Randolph Churchill, the younger son of the Duke of Marlborough, met American heiress Jennie Jerome at a ball held on board the cruiser *Ariadne* at Cowes. Jennie was only 19 years old, a high-spirited girl whose sensual beauty had already won many admirers. The young English aristocrat, impulsive and headstrong by nature, proposed to her on the third night after their first encounter.

An American marriage was to become a classic manoeuvre for Old World artistocrats prepared to trade blue blood for hard cash. But the practice was not yet common, and the engagement provoked much adverse comment. Jennie's father, Leonard Jerome, had come from nowhere, making his million on Wall Street as a financial adventurer; on her mother's side there was believed to be some Indian

blood. Lord Randolph was a descendant of John Churchill, the first Duke of Marlborough, one of the greatest military heroes in English history, repeatedly victorious over the armies of the Sun King, Louis XIV, in the time of Queen Anne. Not surprisingly, there was opposition to such an unequal match from Lord Randolph's father. But despite his unimpressively slight build and foppish appearance, Lord Randolph was forceful, obstinate and devious. All opposition was beaten down and in April 1874 the couple were married in the chapel of the British Embassy in Paris. The birth of a son followed within the year.

Winston Leonard Spencer-Churchill was born on 30 November 1874 at his grandfather's Oxfordshire seat, Blenheim Palace, the imposing edifice designed by Sir John Vanbrugh for the first Duke of Marlborough. Winston was, from the very start, both impatient and inconvenient to others, arriving almost two months prematurely and putting his mother into labour on a Sunday, when only a local country doctor was available to tend her. It was fortunate, in an age of high infant mortality, that the premature birth passed off without complications. The baby was small but healthy and robust. A wet nurse was found for him, Mrs Elizabeth Everest; it was with this warm-hearted servant that he would form his closest attachment throughout his infancy and childhood.

Blenheim was not the home of Winston's parents, nor did they stand to inherit it. As a younger son of the ducal family, Lord Randolph had to be content with a much more modest establishment in London. There the baby Winston was left to the care of his beloved Mrs Everest. No Victorian father involved in the important business of the world would be more than an occasional visitor to the nursery, and no mother of any standing would sacrifice her social life to the drudgery of child rearing. Yet even by the standards of their class and time, Winston's parents showed a remarkable lack of interest in their young child. In a famous phrase, Churchill wrote of his mother: 'She shone for me like the Evening Star. I loved her dearly – but at a distance.' The distance from his father was even greater. As he grew up, the young Winston was deeply hurt by his failure to establish any close relationship with Lord Randolph or even to win his respect. If Lord Randolph ever did turn his attention to his son, it was to criticize his failings and deride his achievements. Yet despite this harsh neglect – or perhaps rather because of it – Winston idolized his father beyond all measure.

Winston's family was not rich. Like so many English aristocrats, the Duke of Marlborough was not wealthy enough to provide a handsome allowance for a younger son. Lord Randolph's swift plunge into matrimony may well have been free of mercenary motive; it certainly failed to solve his financial problems, which remained chronic to the end of his life. He always lived in high style, however, and ignored the irritating gap between his means and his expenditure.

At the time of Winston's birth, Lord Randolph moved in the same circles as the Prince of Wales,

BELOW: *The infant Winston with his mother, Lady Randolph Churchill, née Jennie Jerome. The child rarely benefitted from such maternal solicitude.*

RIGHT: *The seven-year-old Winston poses with all the arrogance and self-importance of a child brought up by servants, acutely aware of his family's high ancestry and social standing.*

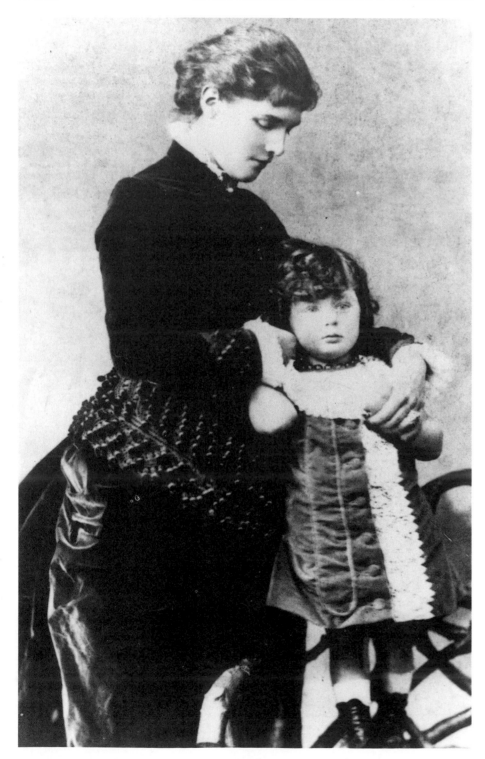

the future King Edward VII, an elegant but rather empty-headed society that took its amoral pleasures at the racetrack, Cowes regattas, London balls, country house parties and fox-hunts. He was also a newly elected Member of Parliament, representing Woodstock, a constituency that had for generations been in the gift of the Duke of Marlborough. But this agreeable situation was soon cast to the winds by Lord Randolph's own rash and high-handed behaviour.

Lady Aylesford, a married woman, had successively become the mistress of the Prince of Wales and of Lord Randolph's elder brother, the Marquis of Blandford. When the Prince apparently encouraged Lord Aylesford to divorce his wife and to cite Blandford as co-respondent, Lord Randolph counter-attacked by obtaining intimate letters from the Prince to Lady Aylesford and threatening to publish them if a scandal broke. Blackmailing the heir to the throne was, by any standards, a reckless proceeding. The matter was patched up without undue publicity, but the Prince's anger was not appeased. He effectively banned Lord Randolph from London society. To save everyone embarrassment, Prime Minister Benjamin Disraeli appointed Lord Randolph's father Lord-Lieutenant of Ireland, and the Duke took his reprobate son with him to Dublin as a personal secretary. The two-year-old Winston went into exile with his parents; his earliest memories were of Ireland.

From their home next to the viceregal lodge, Mrs Everest took her young charge for donkey rides in Phoenix Park. Once all three – nurse, child and animal – were so panicked by a suspected sighting of

ABOVE: *Blenheim Palace, Winston's birthplace, was built at public expense as a gift of the nation for his great military ancestor, John Churchill, the first Duke of Marlborough.*

FAR LEFT: *Jennie's looks had a boldness and sensuality that marked her out among the usually paler, more passive beauties of her time.*

LEFT: *The Prince of Wales, future King Edward VII, Victoria's rumbustious son whose more relaxed morals altered the tone of British high society.*

ABOVE: *Jennie poses elegantly in her riding habit for a society photographer.*

believed – though far from certain – that Lord Randolph had contracted syphilis soon after Winston's birth, possibly from a Blenheim housemaid. Whether or not this was the cause, marital relations were evidently curtailed. Jennie was young, beautiful and full of life; she sought her pleasures elsewhere. In 1879 she bore a second son, but Lord Randolph was almost certainly not his father. The child was christen~~~ ~~~~~nge Churchill, after one of ~~~~~~~ admirers, Colonel John ~~~~~~ ot to see the choice of na~~~ ~~~~~ternity.

The exile of the Churchills was ended by the general election of 1880, which brought to power a new Liberal government under William Ewart Gladstone. The Duke of Marlborough, a Conservative appointee, lost his place as Lord-Lieutenant and returned to England. With his family back in London, in 1882 Winston was taken from the maternal care of his much-loved Mrs Everest and sent away to preparatory school. It was a hateful initiation to the outside world. The school, St George's Ascot, was fashionable, expensive, and blessed with such unusual modern facilities as electric lighting. But the headmaster, the Reverend Mr Sneyd-Kynnersley, was an unbridled sadist. He delighted to flog the boys until they bled. Winston received more than his fair share of the attentions of this odious man. He irritated his teachers by displaying a precocious intelligence in his reading of English classics, yet still contriving to come bottom of the class in all other subjects. A school report concluded: 'He has no ambition.' His conduct was described as 'very bad – a constant trouble to everybody.'

The birch failed to break the will of this rebellious young boy, but two years of brutality and misery did eventually affect his health. Probably at the recommendation of the family doctor, he was removed to a far gentler school run by two elderly spinsters in Brighton. There he remained up to the age of 13, a still pugnacious but relatively happy child. 'The impression of those years makes a pleasant picture in my mind,' he later wrote, 'in strong contrast to my earlier schoolday memories.'

While Winston was enduring these mixed fortunes at school, his father had quite unexpectedly become one of the most prominent political personalities in the country. Politics had not preoccupied Lord Randolph unduly before 1880; he owed his seat in Parliament to his powerful family connections and during six years as an MP he had made only one speech of any note. But in an extraordinarily short time thereafter, he transformed himself into the bright rising star of the Tory party and one of the most talked-of men in Britain. During his childhood Winston rarely met his father and could only follow his political fortunes in the newspapers. Yet Lord Randolph's meteoric career was to obsess him well into manhood. He was to repeat many of its most striking aspects with extraordinary fidelity during his own rise to power two decades later. This second-hand experience had more formative influence on Winston's life than anything that happened to him personally in his childhood or youth.

Fenian terrorists that Winston was thrown off his mount and landed on his head, suffering 'concussion of the brain.' He was imperious toward servants, unruly and uncontrollable: one of the naughtiest of infants. At the age of five he accidentally scarred another child for life by striking him across the face with a toy whip. Although there had been no Churchill of great public renown since the first Duke of Marlborough, even in childhood the young Winston must have been acutely aware of the importance of his family and its glorious military ancestry. His most prized possession was a collection of toy soldiers over a thousand strong which he delighted to manoeuvre and command in mock battle.

Meanwhile his parents found what pleasure they could in fox-hunting and provincial society. Their marriage was already a failure. It is generally

LEFT: *Winston (right) and his brother Jack affectionately photographed with their mother in 1889.*

The background to Lord Randolph's rise to prominence was the disastrous Tory defeat in the 1880 general election. The much depleted Tory ranks in the House of Commons were thoroughly demoralized. Faced with the towering presence of Gladstone at the head of the Liberal front bench, their own team led by the courteous Lord Northcote looked paltry and thin. The field was open for an

BELOW: *Wearing a straw hat, Winston perches alongside his mother at a garden party in the mid-1880s. Even at this young age, he manages to occupy the centre of the picture.*

ABOVE: *Lord Randolph's handlebar moustache, melancholy features and dandyish dress gave political caricaturists plenty to play with.*

Rosebery, commented on 'his tinge of violent eccentricity.' But he had a genuine gift for personal invective and sustained carping rhetoric that counted for much at a time when reports of political speeches were read by the public with an avidity that is today unknown. Despite his sometimes caddish behaviour and barely concealed cynicism, he did, in fact, win genuine popularity in the country at large.

Lord Randolph's rallying cry was 'Tory Democracy.' This was the stick with which he intended to beat the 'old guard' of the Tory leadership. It was not an original idea: Disraeli had already envisaged a Conservative Party that would embrace the inevitable rise of democracy, exploiting the role of the aristocracy as the 'natural' leadership of the nation, dazzling the common people with the glories of Empire and a modicum of social reform. Nor did it make Lord Randolph in any sense a lover of the masses. A letter he wrote during his first election campaign at Woodstock is often quoted against him:

I heard one of the lower orders, who were there in crowds, say 'there is a rum specimen,' evidently alluding to me. I was so angry and would like to have been an Ashantee King for the moment and executed him summarily.

But despite his patrician attitudes, Lord Randolph was in his way a genuine rebel against the stuffy complacency of his class. He detested humbug and pomposity – his own disdain for pretention led to the dropping of the hyphen from the family name, 'Spencer-Churchill.' He was a foe to respectability and described the aristocracy and the working class as bound together by 'a common bond of immorality.' He had also grasped realities of his times that eluded most contemporaries. He appreciated that the future lay with mass organizations and an appeal to a mass public. He was one of the first politicians after Gladstone to stump the country addressing public meetings.

ambitious man to seize the initiative in the Commons. Lord Randolph Churchill began an assault on both Liberal and Tory leaders in the House almost as soon as Parliament opened and pursued it relentlessly thereafter. With three Tory colleagues he formed a Conservative ginger group which was baptized 'the Fourth Party' (the Irish MPs were the third). Pouring scorn both on Gladstone (characterized as 'the Moloch of Midlothian') and on Lord Northcote ('the Goat'), he adopted a series of provocative postures on issues of the day that compelled public attention.

Of slight build and hesitant lisping speech, with bulging eyes and twirled moustache, Lord Randolph was an unprepossessing figure. His strange cackling laugh and the wild flailing of his arms as he delivered an oration expressed a sometimes violent, always unpredictable personality. His enemies saw him as an unprincipled adventurer and opportunist – the Earl of Derby dismissing him as 'thoroughly untrustworthy; scarcely a gentleman, and probably more or less mad.' Even a friendly observer, Lord

RIGHT: *Lord Northcote, the feeble leader of the Conservatives in the House of Commons, was ridiculed by Lord Randolph as 'the Goat.'*

His critics were certainly right when they pictured him as an adventurer driven by personal ambition. He had a gambler's love for the sheer excitement of politics. His stand on public issues was unpredictable and randomly opportunist. He toyed with the Catholic Irish nationalists, then backed the Ulster Protestants, coining the famous phrase 'Ulster will fight and Ulster will be right.' He stood out against imperial expansion in Egypt as an abuse of power, but was later personally responsible for the annexation of Burma. Yet for all his inconsistency and boyish irresponsibility, he possessed such 'spirit and go' that in 1884 an Irish MP recognized in 'this dashing, irrepressible and, at first sight, frivolous youth the one man of unblemished promise in his party.'

He was given much of the credit for turning the tide against the Liberals by the middle of the decade, and the Tory 'old guard' could not afford to ignore his influence in Parliament and in the country. When the Tories formed a government in 1885, he was appointed Secretary of State for India. The following year he rose still further, to become Chancellor of the Exchequer and Leader of the Commons at the precocious age of 37, recognized as second-in-command to the prime minister, Lord Salisbury.

Yet Lord Randolph's fall was even faster than his rise. His restless energy irritated his cabinet colleagues, as he repeatedly interfered in issues that were no concern of his department – a characteristic that Winston was to reproduce infallibly when himself a minister two decades later. His personal rudeness won him many enemies. Once when dining at Hatfield House, the home of Lord Salisbury, he is

said to have grumbled openly: 'Bad dinner, cold plates, beastly wine.' Such casual insults were not forgotten. But what totally undid him was his overweening vanity and ambition. He believed himself indispensable and would brook no opposition. It is typical of the man that, wildly spendthrift in his personal life, he should as Chancellor insist on rigorous economies. Just before Christmas 1886, five months after taking over the Exchequer, he resigned on the relatively trivial issue of cuts in Army spending. In Lord Randolph's own words, Lord Salisbury jumped at the resignation 'like a dog at a bone.' It must have been Lord Randolph's expectation that he would be recalled to office with renewed powers. But Lord Salisbury did not want this

ABOVE: *Gladstone, the Grand Old Man of British politics, was another butt of Lord Randolph's malicious wit.*

LEFT: *Lord Salisbury, the prime minister under whom Lord Randolph served his brief ministerial career.*

RIGHT: *Winston as a 15-year-old at Harrow. His highest wish was to be allowed to aid his father in his political career.*

troublesome colleague back. 'Did you ever know a man,' Salisbury asked, 'who, having got rid of a boil on the back of his kneck, wants another?' Lord Randolph would never serve in government again.

It was not immediately clear that Lord Randolph's ambitions lay in ruins. He had re-established his place in the best society. In 1887 he was able to present the 12-year-old Winston to a placated Prince of Wales on board the royal yacht *Osborne*. His speeches were still reported at length in the newspapers and when he travelled abroad he was greeted as an important statesman. Whether through syphilis or some other hidden cause, his physical health and mental faculties were already in decline, but his reputation remained high. When Winston went to Harrow in 1888, he was pointed out to visitors to that prestigious school as the son of an especially famous father.

Winston's admission to Harrow, despite a failure to write anything at all in the Latin paper of the entrance examination, was itself a tribute to the influence of his family. He was placed in the lowest form in the school, the Third Fourth, along with the other dunces. His housemaster was impressed by his unpunctuality, carelessness and 'phenomenal slovenliness.' The headmaster, Dr Welldon, was sharp enough to recognize latent gifts in an apparently hopeless pupil, and tried to bring them out with frequent application of the rod. This was a failure: after his early training at the hands of the iniquitous Sneyd-Kynnersley, Winston was impervious to physical intimidation. In the subjects he disliked – especially the all-important Latin and Greek – he remained obstinately null.

In those areas where he was prepared to exert himself, the young Winston did score some notable

BELOW: *The scene in the lobby of the House of Commons in 1886. The group in the foreground comprises, left to right, Joseph Chamberlain, the Irish leader Charles Stewart Parnell, Gladstone, Lord Randolph Churchill and the Duke of Devonshire.*

ABOVE: *Although the young Winston poses proudly enough in his Harrow dress, he was both bored and miserable during his time at the school – 'the only barren and unhappy period in my life.'*

successes. He already had an exceptional grasp of the English language and his memory was remarkable: he won a prize for the faultless recitation of 1200 lines from Macaulay's *The Lays of Ancient Rome*. His interest in history was marked. And he developed a passion for fencing, eventually winning the Public School championship in the sport. These were small things, however, to set against the general trend of failure. As he later wrote, with only slight exaggeration: 'The only comments which had ever been made upon my work at school had been "Indifferent," "Untidy," "Slovenly," "Bad," "Very

bad," etc.' Hints of future greatness were hard to discern.

Winston's parents viewed his present behaviour with irritation and contemplated his future with something approaching despair. The only thing he seemed good at was spending money, of which he always wanted more. By rights, Winston should have followed in his father's footsteps by going up to Oxford, but plainly university would be wasted on such a dullard. So what was he to do? Lack of a university education would block many paths of advancement. The Church was briefly considered, then

wisely ruled out. That only left the Army. Winston still cherished his collection of toy soldiers and spent most of his holidays constructing fortifications or playing at battles with his brother, Jack. When tackled by his father on the subject, he proved not averse to a military career. So the boy was put into the Harrow Army Class, which prepared pupils for the entrance examination to the Royal Military Training College at Sandhurst.

In all, Winston spent nearly five years at Harrow. He loved the school songs; the rest he hated. He was not especially unpopular or subject to bullying. He simply found the whole experience a stultifying bore. To blossom, his nature required the centre of the stage, and at school this was denied him. His energy merely made him disruptive and his inordinate self-confidence and ambition manifested themselves as arrogance and conceit. Above all, school kept him from the one place he really wanted to be – at his father's side. Not surprisingly Winston judged his school years to have been 'not only the least agreeable, but the only barren and unhappy period in my life.' He looked forward to Sandhurst as the path out of 'discomfort, restriction and purposeless monotony' into the mysterious joys of adulthood.

Examinations for the Army, as for other areas of government employment, were a quite recent innovation, designed to introduce an element of meritocracy into the established culture of privilege and nepotism. They almost brought Winston's military career to a very premature conclusion. Twice he attempted the exam in 1892 and twice he failed, despite valuable special coaching from the obliging Dr Welldon. To prepare for the third attempt, Winston's parents sent him to the best London 'crammer,' a retired officer who virtually guaranteed a pass to those who could afford his services. It worked, but only to a degree. Winston passed the exam with too low a mark to qualify for the infantry. He would have to settle for the less intellectually demanding cavalry.

This in no way dissatisfied the budding officer, already a keen horseman with a taste for dash and show. But Lord Randolph was outraged. The cavalry was far more expensive than the infantry because of the cost of upkeep of a horse. This was money the family could ill afford. What is more, following the old ways of patronage, he had already arranged a future place for his son in the 60th Rifles. It was humiliating that this could not now be taken up. In his anger, Lord Randolph fired off a withering blast of invective in Winston's direction. He denounced his lack of application, his 'slovenly, happy go lucky, harum scarum style of work,' and his bragging overconfidence in his own abilities. In Lord Randolph's opinion, his son was well on the way to becoming 'a mere social wastrel.' Deeply hurt, the young man promised to reform.

Winston was much happier once accoutred in the ceremonial scarlet and gold of an officer cadet. He accepted discipline in uniform as he never had at school. Although poor at infantry drill, he performed well in the relentless horseback training and showed an unwonted diligence in the study of the military curriculum. His extracurricular activities were less controlled. His father raged at his extravagance and carelessness – although Lord Randolph's rages were by this time more the symptom of a disease than a rational response to misbehaviour.

On one strange occasion Winston drew the public eye with a mixture of cadet rowdiness and precocious political oratory. A dispute arose over arrangements at the Empire Theatre, Haymarket, which attracted the ire of a moral reformer, Mrs Ormiston Chant. At her instigation, the drinking area of the theatre was separated from the promenade, where ladies of easy virtue paraded, by a canvas screen. The Empire was much frequented by Sandhurst cadets and, Winston prominent amongst them, they took up the cause of freedom against prudery. One unbridled evening, the cadets tore down the offending screen and Winston delivered his first political speech, a rousing oration on the ruins of the moral barricade. He was clearly enjoying integration into his new, sometimes boisterous milieu.

Despite periodic parental disapproval, his new status did bring Winston a modicum of respect from his father. He was now thought fit to be introduced to Lord Randolph's circle of acquaintances, ranging

LEFT: *Winston (left) with two fellow cadets at Sandhurst in 1894. He found military training and camaraderie a breath of fresh air after the stifling enclosure of life at school.*

BELOW: *This late photo-portrait makes painfully clear Lord Randolph's premature physical and mental decline.*

from the leading lights of high society and prominent Conservative politicians to the more disreputable individuals whose lives centred on the Turf. But his father would not permit the relationship to blossom into greater intimacy. When his son offered to assist Lord Randolph in his work, his advance was met with a frosty refusal.

Winston had already been many times to the House of Commons, a rapt onlooker as his father and other great politicians of the day, such as the octogenarian Gladstone, deployed their oratorical skills. He was deeply imbued with what might be termed the family myth: that his father's Tory Democracy had rescued the Conservatives in their darkest hour of defeat, only to be cast aside by the ungrateful 'old guard' once victory was gained. But even to so partisan an observer, it was now painfully obvious that Lord Randolph's powers had deserted him. His speeches had become a torture, stumbling and incoherent, as he wrestled with the advancing disease that held him in its iron grip. His friend Lord Rosebery summed up the melancholy spectacle of his decline in a memorable phrase: 'He was the chief mourner at his own protracted funeral, a public pageant of gloomy years.' In the summer of 1893 he had been diagnosed as suffering from 'general paralysis of the insane' – a euphemism for tertiary syphilis. This was a death sentence.

In June 1894 Lord Randolph unadvisedly embarked on a world tour, dragging his wife away from her current lover, Lord Wolverton, to accompany him. Haggard and incoherent, he struggled from country to country in the Far East, dealing the final blow to his fast-waning health. He had always been subject to fits of rage, but now his violent swings of mood veered towards insanity. In December he was brought home to his mother's house in Grosvenor Square to die. England was in the grip of one of the coldest winters for years and there were ice floes on the Thames. Early on the bleak frozen morning of 24 January 1895, death mercifully released Lord Randolph from the torpor of premature senility. He was 45 years old.

The awful manner of his father's decline and death carried a powerful admonition for Winston. The diagnosis of syphilis was unreliable – it was the fashionable medical explanation for any disease affecting the brain and nervous system. But Winston would have believed it, and the terrible spectacle of his father's last years must have influenced his future behaviour. As far as can be discovered, he had little or no involvement with sex until his marriage at the age of 33. Also, under the influence of his father's early death, Winston had no expectation of longevity. One of the most striking characteristics of his early career was to be his haste: a lot of living had to be crammed into a short time.

His father had died owing Lord Rothschild £60,000 (as a measure of this enormous sum, £1000 was at the time a very comfortable annual income for a prosperous middle-class household). When the family finances were sorted out, Winston could expect no more than a small allowance to live on. The rest of his legacy from Lord Randolph was more difficult to assess. It is impossible to distinguish the warp and weft of genetic inheritance and filial imitation, but by one or the other, Winston grew up to reproduce his father's rashness and ambition, his feverish energy, his dependence on rhetoric and bold gesture, a tendency to bully if he could not get his way. The family contacts at the highest levels of government and society were another form of inheritance, almost worth the fortune Lord Randolph never had.

But the most valuable patrimony was his father's name. It was, on the face of it, an ambivalent legacy. Probably more important people had disliked and distrusted Lord Randolph than had admired and

THE ILLUSTRATED
LONDON NEWS

REGISTERED AT THE GENERAL POST OFFICE FOR TRANSMISSION ABROAD.

No. 2911.—VOL. CVI.   SATURDAY, FEBRUARY 2, 1895.   With Supplement: The late Lord Randolph Churchill   SIXPENCE. By Post, 6½d.

FUNERAL OF LORD RANDOLPH CHURCHILL: THE SCENE IN WOODSTOCK CHURCH.

respected him. His detractors could all too easily transfer their accusations of instability, irresponsibility and lack of principle from the father on to the son. Yet the advantages for Winston were much greater. As son of the notorious Lord Randolph, he was sure to attract attention whatever he did. This was a powerful springboard for a vigorous and ambitious young man.

However sincerely grieved, Lord Randolph's death was a liberation for his son. The dream of Winston's youth had been to win acceptance from his father, to grow into his constant companion and eventually stand alongside him in the House of Commons. The best he could imagine was to be permitted to live in his father's shadow. Now suddenly he stood alone and his energies were free to express themselves without the constraint of filial respect or parental rebuke. His mother was a youthful 40-year-old absorbed in her own affairs and not inclined to interfere with any decisions her son might take. Winston had just passed out of Sandhurst with a very respectable performance (twentieth out of 130 candidates). He was fully independent; his life was in his own hands.

CHAPTER TWO
Imperial Adventures

LEFT: *Churchill at the age of 21, a supremely ambitious young cavalry officer, eager for military glory. He wears the full dress uniform of a subaltern in the 4th Queen's Own Hussars.*

A T the age of 20, Churchill's overriding ambition was to sit in the House of Commons as his father had before him. But this was not an objective to be seized direct. He had to acquire a few more years' experience and a good deal more money before he could successfully embark on a political career. With supreme self-confidence, Churchill assumed he would win a few medals in soldiering before moving on to the conquest of Parliament. In February 1895 he joined the 4th Hussars as a second lieutenant. The commander of this fashionable cavalry regiment, Colonel John Brabazon, was a friend of Churchill's mother. It was the first of many occasions on which the far-ranging contacts of that self-centred but sociable woman were to serve his turn.

The British Army at this period was not, by European standards, a very serious fighting force. Historian Eric Hobsbawm has written that for officers it represented 'a children's game played by adults, the symbol of their superiority to civilians, of virile splendour and of social status.' In 80 years Britain had been involved in only one major war, in the Crimea, and expert opinion held that the Army would in all probability never fight against a fellow 'civilized' country again. Yet in this apparently pacific world the value of heroism in battle was drummed into schoolboys by their teachers and naively celebrated in prose and verse – like *The Lays of Ancient Rome* Churchill had learnt by heart at Harrow. The stoicism and courage of the warrior were contrasted favourably with the corrupting softness of a decadent civilization. The fantasy of war as a romantic adventure had never so predominated over the harsh reality of suffering and death.

As usual in a long peace, a taste of battle was highly prized among officers. It had scarcity value; it promised excitement; and it conferred status. Although Churchill was not exceptional in his enthusiasm to 'see action,' no one else could have pursued this end with quite the energy and persistence that he tirelessly displayed. This was partly a function of the naked ambition that impressed, startled or shocked so many people who met him in his twenties. But it was also the expression of an incorrigible taste for excitement that made him thirst for danger, forgetful of all physical fear. Before going to Sandhurst, Churchill had sustained a serious injury – a ruptured kidney – by jumping off a bridge to avoid capture in a children's game. In battle, too, his physical courage was sometimes to prove foolhardy or reckless.

Churchill's first encounter with armed conflict was a holiday jaunt. A subaltern's holidays were substantial, lasting most of the five winter months. With barely more than half-a-year's service behind him, Churchill decided he would rather dedicate this spare time to war than to fox-hunting. As it happened, the only war to hand was in Cuba, where Spanish regulars were fighting highly effective local guerrillas. A subaltern colleague agreed to accompany him and the necessary arrangements were made with typical Churchillian panache. Shamelessly trading on his father's name and contacts, he not only elicited a letter of introduction to Spanish General Martinez de Campos, but also had himself entrusted with an official mission by British army intelligence. To help finance the venture, he obtained an agreement from the *Daily Graphic* newspaper – which had once published articles written by Lord Randolph during a visit to South Africa – to pay him £5 a letter as a war correspondent. For Army permission, this newly commissioned second lieutenant applied direct to Lord Wolseley, the Commander in Chief of the Army. Churchill had learnt from his father: always deal with the man at the top.

Travelling via the United States, Churchill reached Havana on 20 November 1895. Welcomed by the Spanish as if he were an official British army observer, he joined a column of troops on the march. Ten days later, on his twenty-first birthday, he came under fire for the first time, from Cuban guerrillas. The fighting was slight and scrappy, and

BELOW: *A typical illustration of the romance of war from a popular boys' magazine of the 1890s. Churchill partly moulded himself on such naive images of heroism and tales of derring-do.*

Churchill took no active part, but on the whole he was delighted with the experience. Only much later would he reflect on the absurdity of risking death in a distant corner of the world just for the fun of it. His articles were published in the *Daily Graphic* and his escapade was commented on, in general unfavourably, by other newspapers. He was back in England by the New Year, bringing with him a lifelong taste for Havana cigars, a firm faith in the virtues of the siesta, and also the small beginnings of a public reputation.

There was always the risk for Churchill that his military career would shunt him into a siding off the main line of his ambition. In 1896 he was busily consolidating his position as a junior but familiar figure at the dinners, balls and country house parties of the social and political élite, to which his name and parentage gave him ready access, when his regiment was ordered to Bangalore in southern India, a posting that offered neither social excitements nor hope of military glory. This time his contacts failed him, and in September he reluctantly embarked on the 21-day voyage to Bombay. Arrival brought further misfortune: in his haste to land, Churchill slipped awkwardly and dislocated his right shoulder. This injury was to plague him on and off for the rest of his life.

Churchill did not succumb to the undemanding charm of Bangalore, where a subaltern could slumber away his days in pampered idleness. Instead, he devoted his drive and energy to two great objectives: compensating for the awesome deficiencies of

ABOVE: *A scene from the Spanish campaign against Cuban guerrillas in 1895, in which Churchill received his baptism of fire.*

BELOW: *Posted to Bangalore in India, Churchill sought excitement in polo tournaments. Most of his money – far more than he could afford – was spent on these fine polo ponies.*

ABOVE: *Sir Bindon Blood,
commander of the Malakand Field
Force.*

RIGHT: *Churchill in his Hussar's
uniform, Bangalore, 1897.*

commonplaces of the camp – contempt for female suffrage, for example, as bound to lead to that patently ludicrous consequence, female MPs. In the future Churchill was to reveal very considerable mental powers, but the fertility of his brain would never be tempered by the discrimination that characterizes a true thinker. On the surface, he threw out ideas and inspirations in a maddening firework display mixing duds and colourful explosions. His few bedrock beliefs, on the other hand, were emotional, instinctive, impervious to reasoned argument.

After only eight months in India, Churchill took his first leave in England. Still restless, he was on the lookout for an escape from return to the torpor of Bangalore, when his attention was drawn to an outbreak of unrest among warlike Pathan tribesmen on the frontier between British India and Afghanistan. In command of the three brigades organized to quell the Pathan, later called the Malakand Field Force, was one of Churchill's social acquaintances, the splendidly named General Sir Bindon Blood. Churchill fired off a telegram to Sir Bindon requesting permission to join the expedition and set off back to India without waiting for a reply.

When the answer came, it was disappointing. There was no room for another officer, but Churchill was welcome to come along as a war correspondent if he liked. The rules governing war correspondents and their relation to the military were totally unclear at this time. Churchill's commanding officer in Bangalore was eventually persuaded that since, by a combination of his mother's efforts and his own, Churchill had been engaged to write articles for the *Pioneer Mail* in Allahabad and the *Daily Telegraph* in London, he should be given leave to go. Hence Churchill joined the Malakand Field Force as a correspondent in September 1897.

This punitive expedition ranks no more than a footnote in the history of the British Empire. Once more the army of the Raj tramped through the valleys, burning crops, driving off cattle, destroying villages and filling in wells, as a proof of racial superiority and a lesson to the Pathan not to misbehave again. But by the standard of the time the fighting was quite substantial. The mountain tribesmen were fearsome warriors on their own terrain. In the first action where Churchill was involved, in the Mamund valley, the Field Force lost 150 dead or wounded in a day, more than 10 percent of the troops engaged. Despite his observer status, Churchill was after a medal and deliberately placed himself in the thick of the fighting, taking extraordinary risks. He was with a small party of British officers and Sikh soldiers who advanced up the valley too far in front of the main body of troops. The detachment pulled back very late and was almost engulfed. At one point Churchill hesitated to retreat and became a one-man rearguard, firing his pistol at a tribesman who had advanced to within 20 yards. He wrote to his mother afterwards: 'I play for high stakes and given an audience there is no act too daring and too noble.' Only a thin line distinguished the man of action from the actor.

his formal education and winning polo trophies for the regimental team. Avidly through the hot afternoons he consumed voluminous works of history and philosophy – Gibbon, Macaulay, Malthus, Darwin, Schopenhauer, along with now-forgotten writers such as the materialist Winwood Reade. His enthusiasm easily brushed aside the disapproval of fellow officers, disturbed by such unsuitable intellectualism. Yet an intellectual Churchill was never to be; he was always in his essence a man of action. What he gained most from this crash course of reading was a formidable idiosyncratic prose style, out of Gibbon by Macaulay, and a sense of history as an unfolding drama, the clash of empires in which great men played their decisive parts. A conviction of his own predestined role as a leading actor on the stage of history was to be an important source of strength for Churchill, the foundation of his personal myth.

As for philosophy and religion, Churchill was convinced by the arguments of materialism, but was content to remain an emotional believer, calling upon God for protection in moments of greatest peril. This was a view that recommended itself to most officers: religious enthusiasm was frowned upon, but atheism smacked of revolution. Indeed, most of Churchill's ideas at this time remained the

There was no medal for Churchill, but he was delighted to be mentioned in dispatches, where he was praised for his 'courage and resolution' and commended, somewhat bathetically, for having 'made himself useful at a critical moment.' With the deaths of other British officers clearing the way, he was temporarily attached to the 31st Punjab Infantry Regiment, giving him his first chance to command troops in battle. But his hopes of staying on the Northwest Frontier were quickly dashed. Senior officers had taken note of this strange subaltern who seemed to think he could move about where he liked in the Army. After six weeks Churchill was ordered back to his regiment at Bangalore.

Nothing daunted, Churchill now set out to write his first book, *The Story of the Malakand Field Force*. It was completed in a mere seven weeks and emerged to excellent reviews – although thanks to an eccentric uncle entrusted with seeing the book into print, it appeared with appalling spelling and even worse punctuation. The book sold well, presumably because it combined a boyish enthusiasm for colonial warfare, recommended as a healthy all-male open-air activity, with a detailed lingering precision in the description of gruesome wounds and violent death. Graver readers were struck by the author's high literary style and precocious pose of wisdom and experience. The Prince of Wales and the prime minister, Lord Salisbury, both expressed praise of the book. This was heady stuff indeed for a 23-year-old to absorb.

Unable to get back to the Northwest Frontier, Churchill decided to continue his writing career.

Having nothing particular to write about, he turned to the novel. *Savrola* is, as Churchill himself quite rightly later judged, best forgotten, a feeble and lifeless political romance, its philosopher-statesman hero an embarrassingly naive projection of the author's egoistic fantasies. Fortunately, news of war quickly rescued him from this false direction, throwing up fresh visions of real-life action, fame and adventure.

Thirteen years before, at Khartoum in the Sudan, the eccentric but much revered General George Gordon had been speared to death on a staircase by the Dervish forces of the Mahdi in the most celebrated of all Victorian imperial melodramas. Now Britain's revenge was at hand. General Sir Herbert Kitchener, the Sirdar of Egypt, was leading an Anglo-Egyptian Army down the course of the Nile to retake the Sudan. Public excitement was at a high pitch. Here surely was one of those epic moments of history in which Churchill so keenly desired to play a part. Yet there existed an immovable obstacle to his participation in the Sudan: Kitchener would not allow it.

Churchill's Malakand book had spread the author's reputation far and wide; this was not now to his advantage. Once the book's success focussed attention on this unruly subaltern, opinion in the Army tended to turn very much against him. Soldiers did not like journalists; a soldier-journalist was a perverse hybrid. A second lieutenant had no business criticizing generals. And how was it that Churchill could gad about to any battlefield that took his fancy? His behaviour smacked of presumption and disrespect. The word 'bumptious' was the most common epithet applied to this excessively well-connected 'medal-hunter.' Kitchener took an especially dim view of such irregularities; he would not have Churchill serve with his army.

Kitchener's impassive willpower was a considerable force to reckon with. But so was Churchill's dynamic persistence. He had soon taken leave to visit London, where he could marshall all his high-placed contacts in support of his cause. His mother gave dinner to everyone who might remotely influence the case. Churchill even persuaded the prime minister, Lord Salisbury, to plead on his behalf direct to Kitchener. The refusal was dry and explicit. Just when all seemed lost, Churchill learnt that a friend of the family, Lady Jeune, had managed to persuade the Adjutant General, Sir Evelyn Wood, that Kitchener's pretension to pick and choose officers for the British contingent of his Anglo-Egyptian force was presumptuous. This was by rights a War Office prerogative. Within two days Churchill had orders from the War Office to join the 21st Lancers in Cairo for the Sudan campaign. With an added commission from the *Morning Post* to act as war correspondent at £15 a column, he arrived in Cairo on 2 August 1898.

Churchill still feared that the 21st Lancers would arrive in the Sudan too late for the battle, but the fine system of river steamers and railways organized by Kitchener transported them the 1400 miles south to Atbara in just a fortnight. Here they took to their

BELOW: *A contemporary depiction of the opening stage of the battle of Omdurman. The Dervish horde advances straight into the concentrated fire of the British infantry.*

horses and by 28 August were advancing cautiously on Omdurman with the other 25,000 men of the Anglo-Egyptian Army in full battle order. On 1 September advanced patrols at last sighted the army of the Dervishes. Ironically, Churchill was instructed to carry a report of the situation back to Kitchener himself, and so had a brief face-to-face encounter with the man who had tried so hard to keep him out of the Sudan. Kitchener showed no sign at all of recognition.

The battle came the following day, 2 September. It was, for Churchill, 'the last link in the long chain of those spectacular conflicts whose vivid and majestic splendour has done so much to invest war with glamour.' At sunrise the 50,000-strong Dervish army, chanting the praises of Allah under their white and yellow banners, advanced across open ground straight at the solid ranks of the British infantry. Many Dervishes were armed only with spears, swords or muskets; the British had Lee Enfield rifles, Maxim guns, and the support of gunboats on the Nile. 'The weapons, the methods and the fanaticism of the Middle Ages,' Churchill wrote, 'were brought by an extraordinary anachronism into dire collision with the organisation and inventions of the 19th century.' It was a dire collision indeed. The Dervish fell in their thousands, mown down without inflicting more than a few minor casualties on the infidel enemy.

Somewhat prematurely, Kitchener now ordered an advance on Omdurman along the Dervishes' right flank. Commanded by Colonel Rowland Martin, the 21st Lancers thrust forward to mop up enemy strag-

glers attempting to flee back to the town. At a certain moment, the regiment came under fire from about 150 Dervishes at 300 yards range and a few men were hit. Without hesitation, Colonel Martin ordered right wheel and charge. Churchill's troop was on the right of the line. As the lancers galloped to the crest of the slope where the riflemen were crouched, there was suddenly revealed a mass of several thousand Dervishes hidden in a dry water course behind them. The centre of the charging cavalry plunged straight into the midst of the enemy and was brought to a halt, stabbed and hacked at from all sides. Fortunately for Churchill, the right of the line passed to the side of the main body of Dervishes. Nonetheless, he was assailed at close quarters by three sword-wielding enemies, whom he dispatched with his Mauser – because of his injured shoulder, he chose not to draw his sword in the charge but to use his pistol, and this decision may have saved his life. By the time the regiment regrouped and drove the Dervishes off with carbine fire, 21 officers and men had been killed and 49 wounded – almost a quarter of the regiment. The rest of the Anglo-Egyptian Army had lost only 27 dead and 379 wounded in the entire battle.

The charge was undoubtedly a military blunder. Kitchener was furious with the Lancers and sent them back to Cairo as soon as he could. Churchill recognized the futility of the action but publicly extolled its heroism and martial spirit. Personally he was jubilant at having ridden in a real cavalry charge, one of the last ever executed by the British Army. It was typical of Churchill to have taken part in the only incident in the battle that conformed to his own romantic notions of warfare. He had an extraordinary talent for being in the right place at the right time – and for surviving unscathed from mortal risk.

Almost as soon as the battle was over, Churchill began work on his second book, *The River War*. This was to be much more than simply an account of his personal experiences in the Sudan campaign. Through extensive reading and interviews with leading personalities in Egypt, Churchill built up a picture of the whole background to the fighting, adding breadth and weight to his personal observations. There was criticism of Kitchener, both for the Sirdar's brutal attitude to the Dervish wounded and his desecration of the Mahdi's mortal remains after the victory. There was also much proud patriotic celebration of British courage and military valour. Completed by the summer of 1899, the two-volume work bore the hallmarks of mature Churchillian history: verbose and pretentious in parts, lacking depth of perception, but infused with a winning sense of vitality. It was a product of willpower, self-confidence and verbal energy, rather than insight or reflection, yet altogether an extraordinary achievement for a young man who was still only in his mid-twenties.

By the time *The River War* was delivered to its publisher, Churchill had left the army. The decision was apparently taken during his two months leave in England on return from Cairo. He had already attracted the attention of the Tories as an up-and-coming young man who would make a good MP; his close acquaintances included the prime minister's son, Lord Hugh Cecil. All that held him back was lack of money. MPs were not only unpaid, but also expected to pour substantial sums into their constituencies. He could never accumulate the necessary money by staying in the army. A subaltern earnt 14 shillings a week, out of which horses and uniforms had to be paid for, apart from expensive diversions such as polo. Even with his personal allowance, Churchill was always in debt. But now his writing was bringing in good money, he might earn enough from books and journalism to finance himself as an MP, although there would be little to spare. He returned to Bangalore for the last time in the winter of 1898-99, just staying long enough to help the 4th Hussars win the inter-regimental polo cup. By the end of March he had sent in his papers and was on the way back to England, no doubt believing he had turned his back on soldiering for life.

In the event, Churchill's first immersion in politics was to prove but a brief interlude. He was put up as a candidate for a by-election in Oldham, a prosperous mill town with a largely working-class electorate. Both seats had fallen vacant in this double constituency, and Churchill found himself standing with a 'Tory Socialist' – strange phenomenon – against two well-liked local Liberals. The inexperience of the Tory candidates told heavily against them and, after a hard-fought campaign, both were defeated. Churchill returned to London temporarily deflated, consoling himself by working on the proofs of his book. In October, war broke out in South Africa.

There was a long history of confrontation and conflict between the fiercely independent Boers, in the republics of the Orange Free State and the Transvaal, and the British in their neighbouring colonies, Cape Colony and Natal. The Boers stood in the way of British expansion in Africa; a showdown was felt by both sides to be almost inevitable. After a long build-up of tension, on 8 October 1899 the Transvaal issued an ultimatum to the British; this was the signal for the Boer War to begin. Of course, Churchill had to be involved. As an experienced and successful war correspondent he was courted by both the *Daily Mail* and the *Morning Post*. Playing one off against the other, he induced the *Morning Post* to offer the excellent terms of £250 a month, all expenses paid, to cover the war as he saw fit. No war correspondent had ever been so highly paid before. With just time enough to pack a copious supply of liquor in his luggage, on 11 October Churchill sailed from Southampton aboard the *Dunottar Castle*, which was also carrying the British army corps and its commander, Sir Redvers Buller.

The liner proceeded to Cape Town at a leisurely rate that infuriated the ever-impatient Churchill, who raged at Buller's placid complacency. Once

ABOVE: *Aged 24, Churchill set out on his political career as a Conservative candidate for the Oldham constituency.*

RIGHT: *Churchill photographed in October 1899, when he had metamorphosed into a war correspondent once more. The* Morning Post *offered him £250 a month with all expenses paid to cover the Boer War.*

his India days, Captain Aylmer Haldane. The events that followed were to make Churchill a national hero.

On 15 November, Haldane was ordered to carry out a reconnaissance towards Ladysmith on board an armoured train. He was well aware of the folly of this mission, since the train would be vulnerable to ambush by the highly mobile Boers. Still, he was keen for a fight and invited his friend Churchill to come along. The train steamed out with about 300 troops on board, but it had only gone 14 miles when Boers were spotted in the surrounding hills. Haldane ordered the retreat and, when the Boer field guns opened fire, the driver put on full speed. A trap had been set: as the train careered around a bend, it smashed into a pile of boulders on the line. Three trucks were derailed but the engine remained on the track, although the driver had been wounded.

Churchill seized this God-given chance for a public display of heroism. Leaving Haldane to organize counter-fire, he ran to the front of the train to direct operations clearing the track. Moving about in the open for long periods with complete disregard for the shrapnel and bullets that flew thick about him, he inspired the engine driver and uninjured troops to courageous efforts. Unfortunately, it proved impossible to reconnect the engine to those trucks remaining on the rails. It was finally decided to load the wounded on to the tender and start the engine moving at walking pace; the rest of the troops would have to retreat on foot, sheltering behind the engine as best they could. In the event, the engine soon gathered too much speed. Churchill, who was in the cab with the driver, got off and went back to contact Haldane, leaving the engine to steam to safety with the wounded. But the

BELOW: *A group photograph of British war correspondents setting off for South Africa. Churchill (middle row, second from left) is distinguished from his more relaxed colleagues by a look of fierce concentration.*

ashore, Churchill left the unhurried army corps behind and hastened north to Natal, where the fighting was already well under way. The mounted Boer riflemen were having by far the better of it. They had besieged Ladysmith and were advancing towards the coast. Churchill ended up in the small town of Estcourt, between Durban and Ladysmith, where inadequate British forces anxiously awaited a Boer onslaught. Here he met an old colleague from

rest of the British force had already surrendered; Churchill himself was rounded up by a mounted Boer and taken prisoner. He later convinced himself that the Commando who led him in at rifle-point was none other than Louis Botha, the future prime minister of the Union of South Africa. But it appears the honour actually fell to an obscure field-cornet called Oosthuizen.

ABOVE: *The British garrison at Ladysmith, besieged at an early stage of the war and only relieved much later after putting up a prolonged and heroic resistance.*

LEFT: *Taken prisoner by the Boers, Churchill seems to stand slightly apart from his fellow captives. According to the rules of war, as a civilian captured while taking part in military operations, he could legitimately have been shot.*

RIGHT: *Churchill's escape from the officers' prison in Pretoria was a humiliation for the Boers and they made strenuous efforts to recapture him. The price of £25 placed on his head, however, appears in retrospect surprisingly modest.*

£ 25.—.—

(vijf en twintig pond stg.)
belooning uitgeloofd door
de Sub-Commissie van Wijk V
voor den Specialen Constabel
dezer wijk, die den ontvluchte
Krijgsgevangene
Churchill
levend of dood te dezer kanten
aflevert.—

Namens de Sub-Comm.
Wijk V

Sec

Translation.

£25
(Twenty-five Pounds stg.) REWARD is offered by the Sub-Commission of the fifth division, on behalf of the Special Constable of the said division, to anyone who brings the escaped prisoner of war

CHURCHILL,
dead or alive to this office.
For the Sub-Commission of the fifth division.
(Signed) LODK. de HAAS, Sec.

NOTE.—The Original Reward for the arrest of Winston Churchill on his escape from Pretoria, posted on the Government House of Pretoria, brought to England by the Hon. Henry Massham, and is now the property of W. R. Burton.

BELOW: *Arriving back in Durban to a hero's welcome on 23 December 1899, Churchill addresses an enthusiastic crowd of local citizens and journalists from the steps of the town hall.*

Churchill did not take kindly to imprisonment. Conditions in the State Model School in Pretoria, where the British officers were held, conformed to the highest standards of treatment for prisoners of war. But to Churchill's wilful, restless nature, con-

finement was unbearable. He first tried to wheedle his way out by claiming release as a non-combatant civilian – an appeal that could be allowed little credence, given his prominent role during the train ambush (by the rules of war, the Boers could legally have shot him as a civilian engaging in military action). When it seemed the authorities would not accept Churchill's non-combatant status, he turned to plans of escape. Haldane and a colleague had already worked out how to slip out of the laxly guarded prison at a corner of the compound behind the latrines. To cope with the more difficult problem of reaching friendly territory – the Portuguese colony of Mozambique was 300 miles distant – they had assembled money and a map. Churchill forced his way into the escape plot and finally stole it. Frantically impatient, on the night of 12 December he seized the opportunity of a moment and climbed out of the camp. His colleagues were unable to follow, so he went on alone. Although this solitary escape was not intended, Haldane never forgave him for it.

Churchill's position once outside the camp was precarious. He had no map and spoke no Afrikaans. During the night, before the alarm was raised, he ambled casually out of Pretoria and jumped a ride on a goods train which he guessed was heading east towards Mozambique. Before dawn, he disembarked and took refuge in a clump of trees where he hid up during the daylight hours, watched, he later claimed, by 'a gigantic vulture, who manifested an extravagant interest in my condition.' The following

HOW I ESCAPED.

MR. WINSTON CHURCHILL TELLS HIS STORY.

SIX DAYS OF ADVENTURE AND MISERY.

The 'Morning Post" have most courteously supplied us with the following story from their special war correspondent, Mr. Winston Churchill, relating how he escaped from Pretoria and found his way to Delagoa Bay, which he subsequently left by sea for Durban.

Lorenco Marquez, Dec. 21 (10 p.m.).

On the afternoon of the 12th the Transvaal Government's Secretary for War informed me that there was little chance of my release. I therefore resolved to escape.

The same night I left the State Schools Prison at Pretoria by climbing the wall when the sentries' backs were turned momentarily.

I walked through the streets of the town without any disguise, meeting many burghers, but I was not challenged.

In the crowd I got through the piquets of the Town Guard and struck the Delagoa Bay Railroad.

I walked along it, evading the watchers at the bridges and culverts.

The out 11.10 goods train from Pretoria arrived, and before it had reached full speed I boarded with great difficulty, and hid myself under coal sacks.

I jumped from the train before dawn, and sheltered during the day in a small wood in company with a huge vulture, which displayed a lively interest in me.

I walked on at dusk.

There were no more trains that night.

The danger of meeting the guards of the railway line continued, but I was obliged to follow it, as I had no compass or map.

I had to make wide detours to avoid the bridges, stations, and huts, and in the dark I frequently fell into small watercourses.

My progress was very slow, and chocolate is not a satisfying food.

The outlook was gloomy, but I persevered with God's help for five days.

The food I had to have was very precarious.

I was lying up at daylight and walking on at night time, and meanwhile my escape had been discovered and my description telegraphed everywhere.

All the trains were searched.

Every one was on the watch for me.

Four wrong people were arrested.

But on the sixth day I managed to board a train beyond Middelburg, whence there is a direct service to Delagoa.

I was concealed in a railway truck under great sacks.

I had a small store of good water with me.

I remained hidden, chancing discovery.

The Boers searched the train at Komati Poort, but did not search deep enough, so after sixty hours of misery I came safely here.

I am very weak, but I am free.

I have lost many pounds in weight, but I am lighter in heart, and I avail myself of this moment, in the condition in which I find myself—which is a witness to my earnestness—to urge an unflinching and uncompromising prosecution of the war.

Chieveley Camp, Dec. 26 (10.30 a.m.).

Mr. Winston Churchill is once more in the British camp.—Central News.

night, unable to find another train to ride and wandering through the darkness, tired, hungry and hopelessly lost, he had the extraordinary good fortune to stumble upon the house of a British-born colliery manager who was anti-Boer. Churchill was fed and then hidden down a mine for days, while the Boers combed the land above for their famous escapee – there was a price of £25 on his head. The rest of Churchill's getaway was entirely organized by the manager and other miners, at great personal risk. They hollowed a space for him in a load of wool on a goods train destined for Mozambique. Churchill remained in this ingenious hiding-place until he was sure the border was past. On arrival in Lourenço Marques, he introduced himself to the British Consul, and after bathing and dining well took ship that night for Durban.

Churchill's bravery during the train ambush and his subsequent capture had been extensively covered in the British press. His escape caused a sensation. He arrived in Durban on 23 December, just after 'Black Week,' a dismal and humiliating series of British defeats. Here at last was something to cheer about in the general gloom. He received a

Churchill's escape from Pretoria made him famous. His own first account of the event, published in the Morning Post *(left), necessarily excluded mention of those people who had helped him get away, since they would have been exposed to reprisals from the Boer authorities. One of the most popular details of the escape story, the menacing vulture (dramatically rendered by a contemporary illustrator, above) was almost certainly invented, or at least exaggerated, by Churchill for its sensational effect.*

RIGHT: *Churchill on board the ship that brought him from Mozambique to Durban, his features glowing with the relief of escape and the euphoria of popular acclaim.*

BELOW: *A more sober Churchill serving as a lieutenant in the South African Light Horse. During the first six months of 1900 he witnessed some heavy fighting, especially during the battle for Spion Kop, where British casualties were heavy.*

hero's welcome, complete with brass band, and addressed cheering crowds from the steps of Durban town hall. Back in Britain there were a few questioning voices: the *Daily Nation* informed its readers that 'Mr Churchill's escape is not regarded in military circles as either a brilliant or honourable exploit'. But the general tone of the press was adulatory. Churchill had made his reputation.

The rest of Churchill's war in South Africa was an extended postscript to this first, decisive adventure. Sir Redvers Buller agreed to give him a lieutenant's commission in the South African Light Horse, despite a specific War Office prohibition on combining the activities of war correspondent and officer – a new regulation that had, indeed, been directly provoked by Churchill's earlier exploits. Buller salved his conscience by keeping Churchill off the Army payroll; he thus became probably the only British officer ever to fight exclusively in the pay of a newspaper.

During the first six months of the year 1900, Churchill saw action aplenty. He was present at the terrible battle for Spion Kop, where the British suffered heavy casualties. In February he took part in the relief of Ladysmith, although he was not among the first to ride into the liberated town – the moving description of this event in his autobiography is a work of imagination. Next the focus of the war shifted to the Orange Free State, where the British forces were commanded by Lord Roberts. By now a past-master at internal army manoeuvres, Churchill took leave of the Light Horse and attached himself to Lord Roberts' forces – the general's opposition was deftly brushed aside. The army took Johannesburg and then advanced on Pretoria. On 5 June, Churchill was one of the first British officers to enter that town, the site of his captivity. With a conscious sense of the theatrically apt, he sought out the officers' prison camp (no longer located in the State Model School). Accompanied by his cousin 'Sunny,' the Duke of Marlborough, he rode into the camp, disarmed the guards and hoist the Union Jack to the cheers of the liberated prisoners.

Throughout this time, Churchill's dispatches to the *Morning Post* were read with avid interest by the British public, although they provoked a good deal of controversy. His expression of admiration for the Boer fighting man – 'worth from three to five regular soldiers' – gave considerable offence, and his appeal for magnanimity after the relief of Ladysmith – 'I earnestly hope and urge that a generous and forgiving policy be followed' – ran directly counter to the tide of jingoistic public sentiment. But the general patriotic tenor of his writing confirmed his status as a wartime hero of the Empire.

By July the war seemed virtually over. Only scattered guerrilla forces maintained the spirit of Boer resistance. Keen to resume his political career, Churchill resigned his temporary commission and set sail from Cape Town, homeward bound. This time his period of imperial adventures was truly at an end. Through a mixture of luck, physical bravery, literary flair and sheer pushiness, he had transformed himself from the son of a famous father into a renowned public personality in his own right. His considerable talent for self-publicity would now be devoted to exploiting this heroic reputation for financial and political profit.

There is no doubt that Churchill enjoyed himself outrageously in the pursuit of war. He was not indifferent to the cruel sufferings war entailed, but they in no way spoilt the intoxicating excitement of the game. Churchill was seduced by the enormous simplification of life in the field. He wrote of the Ladysmith campaign as one of his happiest memories:

We lived in great comfort in the open air, with cool nights and bright sunshine, with plenty of meat, chickens and beer. . . . One lived entirely in the present with something happening all the time. Carefree, no regrets for the past, no fears for the future.

Fearlessness was encouraged by a sense of personal invulnerability. Through the most dangerous circumstances, Churchill time and again escaped totally unscathed. At one moment, for instance, he was unhorsed within rifle range of the Boers in the middle of the open veldt and must surely have been shot but for the providential arrival of a brave trooper who rode up and carried him away to safety. His brother Jack, on the other hand, who came out to join Winston in February 1900, was shot in the calf during his very first skirmish. Churchill came to believe that he was preserved from harm by a special destiny which was preparing him for some high mission (a belief that his future adversary Hitler was also to hold about himself).

A young manhood spent on colonial battlefields confirmed Churchill in a lifelong devotion to the British Empire. He had been born at a time when, as he put it, 'the realisation of the greatness of our Empire and of our duty to preserve it was ever growing stronger.' He witnessed the great Jubilees of 1887 and 1897, when the symbolic trophies of Empire were paraded with matchless arrogance and pomp; he imbibed the late Victorian creed that Empire was a sacred duty, undertaken in the cause of civilization. He would have agreed with his compatriot Cecil Rhodes that 'we are the first race in the world, and that the more of the world we inhabit, the better it is for the human race.' Churchill's deeply emotional attachment to the British Empire was to survive undimmed through the years; although the Empire changed beyond recognition, he always saw it from the enchanted perspective of his youth.

LEFT: *Dressed as a war correspondent, Churchill chats to Colonel Byng, his commanding officer in the South African Light Horse. Churchill's flamboyant exploitation of his twin role as officer and journalist was highly unpopular in the Army and led to a rewriting of the rules, banning serving officers from acting as war correspondents.*

CHAPTER THREE

The Young Politician

O N his return from South Africa in July 1900, Churchill was much feted and admired. He processed in state through the streets of Oldham, his potential constituency, cheered by enthusiastic crowds. With the fighting still in progress and a general election in the offing, he was once again very much the right man for the moment.

The 'Khaki election' of 1900 was a very one-sided contest. With the Liberals split between supporters and opponents of the war, the Conservatives capitalized on the jingoistic spirit stirred up by recent military successes. The electorate was told in no uncertain terms that a vote for the Liberals was a vote for the Boers. In Oldham, electioneering started in mid-September and lasted a hectic two weeks. Churchill's election posters carried the crude message: 'Be it known that every vote given to the Radicals means 2 pats on the back for Kruger [the Boer leader] and 2 smacks in the face for our country.'

Under the circumstances the Oldham result on 1 October was surprisingly close: both Tory candidates were elected, but Churchill was only 222 votes ahead of his nearest Liberal rival. Still, it was enough. This was one of the first results announced

BELOW: *The photograph of Churchill that appeared on advertisements for his lecture tour in the winter of 1900-01.*

in a general election spread over a period of weeks, and the Tory leadership pronounced it a triumph. Churchill was invited to speak in support of other Tory candidates around the country, becoming, as he put it, a 'star turn' in the election. He had initially been very nervous about the reception he might receive as a public speaker, since he had a slight speech defect, being unable to pronounce the letter 's' correctly. But he had both an inspired journalist's knack for striking phrases and an actor's ability to project his personality to a large audience. His speeches were a great success and, by the end of the campaign, he could claim to have made a substantial personal contribution to the 134-seat Tory majority.

When the new Parliament first met briefly at the start of December, Churchill did not immediately take his seat. After five weeks of electioneering during which he had made a speech every night, he embarked directly on an extensive lecture tour of Britain and North America. The motive behind this tour was purely mercenary. Churchill's books and his dispatches to the *Morning Post* had enabled him to amass a not inconsiderable capital, but still insufficient for an MP of his extravagant tastes, who would want to mix on equal terms with the aristocracy and the business élite. Little was to be expected from his mother. After numerous love affairs she had recently scandalized society by marrying a handsome Guards officer, George Cornwallis-West, who was 20 years younger than herself and totally impecunious (the new stepfather was just 16 days older than his stepson Winston). The lecture tour was a brilliant ploy to make an adequate sum of money in the shortest possible time, so that Churchill could be fully independent and devote himself single-mindedly to his political ambitions.

It was an exhausting experience: over a period of more than ten weeks, Churchill addressed at least one meeting a day, except Sundays, rarely sleeping in the same place twice and frequently travelling overnight. In Britain and Canada his talk on the war in South Africa and his own spectacular adventures there, accompanied by a magic-lantern show, attracted large and appreciative audiences. The United States, generally pro-Boer in sentiment, provided a more patchy response, ranging from enthusiasm through indifference to downright hostility – especially in Chicago, described by Churchill as 'this strange place of pigs.' But financially the success was outstanding. Churchill generally earnt more than £100 a night, and on occasions over £300. By the time he returned to England he had built up his capital to a very substantial £10,000, entirely by his own efforts. It was not the least remarkable of his achievements.

On 14 February 1901 Churchill took his seat in the first parliamentary session of a new century and a new reign (Queen Victoria had died the previous month). With only a brief interruption, he was to remain in the House of Commons for the next 63 years. His object in entering politics was to emulate his father – 'to pursue his aims and vindicate his memory.' This was the only political programme to which he subscribed. He was, like his father before him, a Tory by birth and upbringing, rather than by reasoned choice. Indeed, in 1901 he can hardly be said to have had political ideas of any clear kind, beyond the generalities of attachment to British interests, the British Empire, and the existing order of British society and political institutions, which were the stock-in-trade of Conservatism. His father had stood for 'Tory Democracy' and this would therefore be his banner also. But infusing the term with any precise content was not easy. At first he confined his speeches to debates on the war in South Africa and issues relating to the Army, both subjects on which he could claim special knowledge.

Lord Randolph had been luckier in the parliamentary situation of his day. Then the Tories had been in opposition, weak in numbers and leadership, providing excellent opportunities for an energetic backbencher to make his mark. Churchill, on the other hand, took his place in a large Tory majority ranked behind a seasoned government that had been in power almost continuously for 15 years. It was hard for an ambitious newcomer to make an impression when all that was required of him was to troop through the division lobbies at the end of debates. Defending government policy from such a position of strength was an unexciting activity; attacking the well-entrenched Tory leadership was likely to prove ineffectual and block the path to promotion, which would be open only to those who curried favour.

ABOVE: *Chicago in the 1890s, described by Churchill as 'this strange place of pigs.'*

BELOW: *Ageing Tory Prime Minister Lord Salisbury (seated, with hat), leader of the 'old guard.'*

ABOVE: *With his high Anglican views, Lord Hugh Cecil was an unlikely ally for Churchill, yet the two MPs worked harmoniously together in their dissident Tory grouping, the 'Hughligans.'*

RIGHT: *Churchill's mother, now Mrs Cornwallis West. At 50 she was still a formidable and attractive woman – her second husband was almost the same age as her eldest son.*

tion of filial loyalty could have been found. Churchill embraced the cause of economy in a powerful speech that specifically referred to his father's example – 'this is a cause I have inherited, and a cause for which the late Lord Randolph Churchill made the greatest sacrifice of any minister of modern times.' Government speakers were quick to point out the inconsistency between Churchill's love of Empire and his parsimonious stance on military spending, accusing him of wanting 'to run Imperialism on the cheap'. But for Churchill there was a higher form of consistency: fidelity to his father's example.

The next step was to engineer a new version of Lord Randolph's 'Fourth Party.' Churchill joined a small group of Tory MPs who were dissatisfied with the government; led by Lord Hugh Cecil, they were nicknamed the 'Hughligans' or 'Hooligans' – a sobriquet their parliamentary behaviour occasionally merited. Lord Hugh was a devout Anglican, more of a Tory fundamentalist than a Tory democrat, but he and Churchill found temporary common cause in their readiness to take up cudgels against their own leaders. Lord Hugh's influence was predominant when the Hooligans opposed the Deceased Wife's Sister Bill, an eminently sensible measure to allow a widower to marry his sister-in-law, but counter to strict Anglican canon law; and Churchill was to the fore in criticizing a case of unjust punishment at Sandhurst. On these and other scattered issues, the Hooligans made themselves a notable nuisance to their own front bench.

It was at around this time Churchill discovered the interest in social reform that was to dominate his political career through the next decade. Given the extreme contrasts of ostentatious wealth and bleak poverty in Edwardian society, it is not surprising that the welfare of the poor became a major political issue. Nor is it especially surprising that Churchill, a young and active MP out to make his mark on the political scene, should have embraced the issue. His conversion dated from the winter of 1901, when he read Seebohm Rowntree's immensely influential book *Poverty: a Study of Town Life*, describing conditions in the city of York. This harrowing study inspired him to give some real content to Tory Democracy: the condition of the people must be improved, he concluded, or imperial glory was a sham. He made a serious effort over the following years to develop a coherent attitude toward the problem. He had conversations with the Fabian socialist Beatrice Webb and tried to define his own principles of non-socialist reform.

There was always an underlying egotism in Churchill's enthusiasm for the masses, as Liberal MP Charles Masterman cynically observed later in the decade. 'He is full of the poor whom he has just discovered,' Masterman wrote to his wife. 'He thinks he is called by Providence to do something for them.' Churchill was a man of action and could excite himself with the war on poverty as with any other conflict. Also, many of the arguments for reform were practical or prudent – producing healthier soldiers, avoiding social revolution. But Churchill

Yet Churchill was bound to run into conflict with the party leaders, whatever effect this might have on his ambitions. Even had there not been a debt of filial piety to pay – for these were the 'old guard,' the men he believed had ruined his father's career – he would still have been incapable of following the party line and bending his will to discipline. He was too restless and self-willed to hide his personal sentiments and attitudes when they conflicted with his party's view.

Churchill's first chance to take up his father's cause directly came in May 1901, when the Secretary of State for War proposed a reorganization of the Army that would involve a substantial increase in military spending. This was, of course, the issue on which Lord Randolph had ill-fatedly resigned 15 years before. No better occasion for a demonstra-

forth in company, and had a noted penchant for monologue rather than conversation. His self-obsession could make him a bore, but was happily relieved by a genuine gift for humour.

The liveliest thumbnail sketch of Churchill at this time is the rather unkind description jotted down by Beatrice Webb after their first meeting: 'Restless . . . egotistical, bumptious, shallow-minded and reactionary, but with a certain personal magnetism. . . . More of the American speculator than the English aristocrat.' This is probably how Churchill appeared to most people who did not know him well; those admitted within the circle of his friendship were more impressed both by his mental ability and by his warmth and charm. Those who had known Lord Randolph were struck by the resemblances between father and son. In 1903 the poet Wilfrid Scawen Blunt wrote: 'In mind and manner he is a strange replica of his father – with all his father's suddenness and assurance and I should say more than his father's ability.' Blunt particularly recognized in Churchill his father's 'gaminerie and contempt for the conventional' (qualities that especially disturbed the more staid Tory leaders).

In Parliament, Churchill was admitted to be a formidable orator, if excessively given to wounding personal jibes that many found in bad taste. His speeches were always carefully prepared and learnt by heart. He was by contrast a poor debater, unhappy thinking on his feet and disturbed if any interruption broke the flow of his rhetoric. He was not physically an impressive figure – 'a medium-sized, undistinguished-looking young man, with an unfortunate lisp in his voice,' as a hostile newspaper described him after his maiden speech. Nevertheless, his unpredictable attitudes and quotable phrases captured plenty of attention for his parliamentary performances.

As early as the end of 1901, Churchill was already toying with the idea of leaving the Tory party. He was out of tune both with its jingoism and its resistance to social reform. His father had at one time briefly sought to establish a centre party and this was the direction in which his own thoughts first tended. The search for a centre party or coalition to represent the national interest was to be a recurrent theme in his long political life; but there was no serious chance of it becoming a reality at this time or for many years to come. If he was going to desert the Tories, he would have to join the Liberals.

In May 1903 the complacent Tory majority was thrown into utter disarray when Colonial Secretary Joseph Chamberlain, the most prominent politician in the country, declared himself against Free Trade and in favour of tariffs that would create a closer economic union with the Empire. Most countries had abandoned Free Trade as international competition sharpened in the late nineteenth century, but in Britain it still had the status of a natural law; the Liberal leader, Sir Henry Campbell-Bannerman, described opposing Free Trade as 'like disputing the law of gravitation.' The Tory party was split down the middle between Free Traders and supporters of Chamberlain.

was certainly moved by genuine humanitarian sentiments as well. Touring one of the poorest districts of Manchester during the 1906 election, he was appalled by the slum conditions: 'Fancy living in one of these streets, never seeing anything beautiful, never eating anything savoury, never saying anything clever!' Evidently his imagination was impotent to leap over the vast gulf that separated his life from that of the poor; yet his compassion was real.

Mental adjustment to the spirit of social reform did not inhibit Churchill's expensive lifestyle. Although his immense capacity for hard work and his sexual continence suggest a Puritan streak in his character, he could be self-indulgent and unashamedly hedonistic. He regarded good food and drink as the indispensable basis of a civilized existence – 'there has never been a day in my life when I could not order a bottle of champagne for myself and offer another to a friend.' He pampered his chubby body, frequenting Turkish baths and wearing silk underwear for its exquisite comfort on his delicate skin. He spent a small fortune on fox-hunting and enjoyed gambling for high stakes. He was also a frequent guest at the most fashionable dinner tables and country houses, although his manner sometimes left much to be desired: he enjoyed holding

LEFT: *The contrasts of wealth and poverty in Edwardian society were blatant and extreme. The lives of slum-dwellers, like these inhabitants of Whitechapel, were almost unimaginable to a man of Churchill's privileged class.*

BELOW: *Wealth was displayed with an ostentation never equalled in British society before or since. Churchill sympathized with the poor, but he would also later regret the passing of the glittering high society of the Edwardian era.*

It might have been logical for Churchill to follow Chamberlain: strengthening the Empire was a cause which in general appealed to his strongest political emotions. But his father, after toying with 'Fair Trade,' had in the end come down in favour of Free Trade; he would do likewise. In any case, it was an excellent pretext for an open breach with the Tory leadership. Churchill became a leading spokesman

for Free Trade in the Tory ranks, establishing the Free Food League which had the support of about 60 Tory MPs. Prime Minister Arthur Balfour hedged desperately in an attempt to hold the party together, but many Conservative associations in the country backed Chamberlain. By the autumn, Churchill no longer had the support of his Oldham constituency party.

He was now free to give vent to that deep-seated hostility toward the Tory establishment which he had stored up ever since his father's downfall. In October 1903, in an extraordinary letter to Lord Hugh Cecil, he wrote: 'I am an English Liberal. I hate the Tory party, their men, their words and their methods.' The following December he addressed a Free Trade meeting with the ringing declaration: 'Thank God we have a Liberal Party!' Only the formality of changing sides remained to be accomplished.

By March 1904 the rift between Churchill and the Tories was almost complete. When he rose to speak in a debate on 29 March, first the front bench and then all but a handful of the Tory backbenchers walked out of the chamber in a calculated gesture of contempt. The strain and isolation weighed heavily on him. On 22 April he was unable to complete a speech, stumbling to a halt in a manner chillingly reminiscent of his father's declining years. Churchill's doctor diagnosed 'overstrain.' The only real remedy was to resolve the political dilemma. On 31 May, when Parliament reassembled after the Whitsun recess, Churchill took a seat on the Liberal benches.

The act of 'crossing the floor' was politically perilous. Churchill became a natural target for the sneers and jibes of Tory MPs and the Tory press. They nicknamed him 'the Blenheim rat,' reviled him as 'a violent and reckless political adventurer.' Many in the Liberal Party also regarded him with suspicion. Despite his impeccable views on social reform and Free Trade, his manner and background were so strikingly Tory that he would never blend easily into the Liberal ranks. He was also open to the charge of opportunism, having deserted the Tories in their disarray to hitch his wagon to the rising star of Liberalism. But the violence of his attacks on the Tory leadership, and especially on Balfour, did much to recommend him to his new party. He was not popular in the House of Commons – his use of personal invective was considered vulgar and earnt him some stinging rebukes – but no one could deny his force and vigour. Still a very junior MP, he was already one of the most notorious political personalities in the country.

Outside Parliament, Churchill devoted much of his time during 1904 and 1905 to compiling a biography of Lord Randolph. He was motivated in part by a desire for an intimate knowledge of his father that had been denied him during Lord Randolph's lifetime. He also needed the money that the biography would bring in. But above all he wanted to justify his decision to join the Liberals, both to himself and to the public, in terms of his father's career. His account presented Lord Randolph as a creative innovatory force hopelessly wasted in the hidebound Tory party, driven into a position where the only logical act was to cross the floor of the House, but tragically held back by a sense of honour. Thus Churchill's own desertion of the Tories could be presented as a continuation of his father's career along a pathway it should have taken, but never did.

When the book emerged in 1906, it was widely hailed as one of the best political biographies in English and its prose style is still greatly admired today. There is no doubt that Churchill presented his father in a more favourable light than was strictly just, understating his inconsistency, cynicism and opportunism, and ignoring the discreditable aspects of his private life. But contemporary readers were more struck by the frankness and openness of the account, contrasting favourably with the pious acts of homage served up as biography by other sons of famous fathers. It was, after all, a study in failure rather than success. The writing of the biography marked the point at which Churchill at last outgrew his father's memory. In so much he had imitated his father, but his failure he did not intend to follow.

By the time the biography of Lord Randolph was published, Churchill had achieved his first government appointment. The Tory government resigned in December 1905 and a minority Liberal administration took its place under Sir Henry Campbell-Bannerman. Churchill was offered the post of Financial Secretary to the Treasury, but turned it down in favour of the Colonial Office. The Colonial Secretary was a peer, Lord Elgin, so as Parliamentary Under-Secretary Churchill would have full responsibility for presenting and defending colonial policy in the House of Commons. He was also much more familiar with questions of Empire, particularly South Africa, than with financial affairs. To help cope with his new responsibilities, Churchill took on a private secretary, the epicene Eddie Marsh, who was to remain with him for the next 20 years, a willing slave to a demanding and unpredictable master.

Needing a parliamentary majority to govern effectively, the Liberals immediately called a general

election for January 1906. Churchill stood in the North-West Manchester constituency, traditionally a safe Tory seat but a stronghold of Free Trade sentiment. His flamboyant electioneering attracted a good deal of attention nationwide. The main disruption to his campaign came from suffragettes. As part of his new-found radicalism, Churchill had voted for female suffrage in the House of Commons in 1904. Now, irritated at the interruption of his speeches, he turned against it – 'I am not going to be henpecked on a subject of such grave importance,' he declared, to the great satisfaction of the male voters of Manchester. Naturally, the Tories brought up the uncomfortable subject of Churchill's rapid shift from conservatism to radicalism. Confronted by his own past statements totally contradicting his present political position, Churchill bluntly disowned his younger self: 'I said a lot of stupid things when I was in the Conservative Party, and I left them because I did not want to go on saying stupid things.' On 13 January he was returned to

ABOVE: *Churchill the young politician, as caricatured in* Vanity Fair. *His appearance was generally considered undistinguished and his abrasive manner frequently offended House of Commons etiquette.*

CRITICIZING OLD FRIENDS: MR. WINSTON CHURCHILL HECKLING THE GOVERNMENT

A SKETCH IN THE HOUSE OF COMMONS BY SYDNEY P. HALL, M.V.O.

Parliament with a comfortable majority, one of many successes in a Liberal landslide. Operating an electoral alliance with the new Labour Party, the Liberals won 377 seats to the Tories' 157; Labour took 53 and there was the usual block of 83 Irish MPs. It was a political earthquake, raising widespread hopes (and fears) of a new era of social reform.

Back at the Colonial Office, Churchill was immediately in the thick of the political action. Second only to Free Trade as an issue in the general election had been the question of the importation of some 50,000 Chinese as indentured labour to work the South African gold mines. The Liberals had denounced this use of Chinese coolies as slavery and made much of the dreadful conditions under which the labourers were kept. Now the Colonial Office was charged with fulfilling the election promise to release the Chinese from their bondage. Unfortunately, this proved impossible to accomplish swiftly without riding roughshod over the sacrosanct law of contract. Defending the government's failure to act decisively, Churchill produced the most unfortunate of his many famous phrases: he told the House of Commons that the use of coolie labour could not be described as slavery 'without some risk of terminological inexactitude.' Although not so intended, 'terminological inexactitude' was taken to be a sesquipedalian euphemism for 'a lie' and as such passed into the language. This was an unpromising start to a career in government.

Yet Churchill's outstanding ability was soon in evidence. The question of the future of the Transvaal had remained unsettled since the end of the Boer War. The Tories were content to keep the Boers in permanent military subjection. Churchill had always been an advocate of a magnanimous peace; he admired the Boers, who had been courageous and chivalrous adversaries, and wished to rally them to the British Empire. After such a bitter war, this was an ambitious project. But the Liberals were convinced the Boers would respond favourably to generous treatment. Churchill was entrusted with the task of drawing up a grant of self-government for the Transvaal within the British Empire. His speech proposing this measure to the House of Commons was the first to bear the mark of a statesman, rather than a politician. Aware of the need to effect a genuine reconciliation with the erstwhile enemy, he appealed for the Conservatives to support the measure and make the grant of self-government 'the gift of England' rather than of a single political party. It was an impressive performance, even if it fell on deaf ears. Against Tory opposition, the Liberal majority ensured that the Transvaal received self-government in 1907.

This South Africa policy was once viewed as the most notable triumph of Campbell-Bannerman's government. It led directly to the formation of the Union of South Africa in 1910 and ensured that South African troops would fight alongside the British as part of the imperial forces in two world wars. But the 'men of colour' who made up 90 percent of the population were explicitly excluded from the rights accorded to the White Man. The Liberals, and Churchill most prominent amongst them, had contributed to the foundation of the most enduringly racist state in the world.

Churchill's attitudes toward relations between white and black in Africa were those of a typical

LEFT: *Churchill campaigning during the general election of January 1906. The election was a triumph for the Liberal Party and a personal success for Churchill, who won his Manchester constituency by a comfortable majority.*

ABOVE: *Sir Henry Campbell-Bannerman, Liberal Prime Minister from 1905 to 1908.*

RIGHT: *A newspaper advertisement for Churchill's account of his journey through East Africa in 1907. Despite his salaried position as colonial under-secretary, writing remained an essential source of income.*

chief.' Others got on less well with Churchill, put off by his pushy manner and insatiable demand for action: a leading civil servant, Sir Francis Hopwood, described him as 'most tiresome to deal with' and likely to 'give trouble – as his Father did – in any position to which he may be called.' But the King was impressed by his new air of responsibility and elevated him to the Privy Council.

In October 1907, Churchill set out to see more of the Empire for himself, embarking on an extensive tour of East Africa. This was ostensibly a private trip but soon turned into an official progress replete with speeches and formal receptions. Memos flowed back to London recommending a whole variety of improvements in the running and exploitation of Britain's East African possessions, seriously offending Lord Elgin who had in no way authorized Churchill to carry out a personal inspection of the colonies. He was also not overpleased to discover that Churchill had a contract to write articles on the trip for the *Strand* magazine (later published as a book, *My African Journey*), an unprecedented combination of the functions of journalist and member of government. Churchill's income as a parliamentary under-secretary was quite inadequate to finance his extravagant lifestyle and journalism was still an essential source of funds.

Churchill certainly did Africa in style: on his 20-day safari from Uganda north into the Sudan he

Liberal of his day. He was outraged at any ill-treatment of the native population and rejected an imperialism based on naked force. British domination must be justified by the spread of peace, material progress and the rule of law. But although he regarded the Africans as in theory 'capable of being instructed and raised from their present degradation,' he could not envisage an equal relationship between the white representatives of Western civilization and black 'savages.' In any case, he knew that in South Africa the white population, Boer and British alike, simply would not stand for 'native rights.' He had been so outraged by the behaviour of the white government of Natal toward its Zulu population in 1906 that he described the colony as 'the Hooligans of the British Empire.' Yet acquiescence in such injustice was the price that had to be paid for white South African allegiance to the Crown.

Churchill's relentless ambition made him an uncomfortable subordinate, always ready to overstep the limits of his office, and relations with Lord Elgin were never smooth. Yet the elderly unassertive Colonial Secretary managed the considerable feat of both keeping Churchill under control and getting the best use out of his energy and drive. By January 1907, Lord Elgin was expressing his gratitude for Churchill's 'courage and ability' and Churchill was referring to Lord Elgin as a 'trustful and indulgent

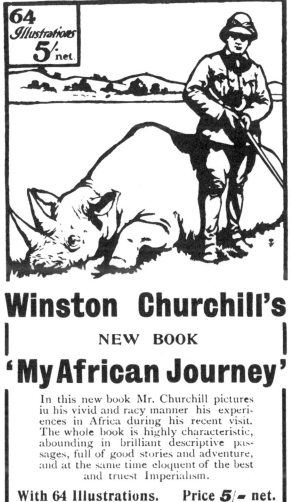

employed 350 porters. He was very proud of the dreadful pun 'sofari sogoody' which he repeated at every opportunity. His chief recreation in Africa was big-game hunting, a relatively new pastime for adventurous men eager to prove their machismo. The white rhino was his most prized target, but almost anything that moved was worth killing. In a letter to an acquaintance in England, he wrote:

We have shot lion, rhinoceros, elephant, buffalo, hippopotamus, hartebeest, wildebeest, roan antelope, gazelle of many kinds, crocodile, zebra etc. 23 species in 10 days shooting.

Yet amid this jovial slaughter, Churchill's thoughts turned to politics at home. In the same letter, he expressed his conviction of the need to adopt radical policies to combat social injustice:

The people will not tolerate the existing system by which wealth is acquired, shared, and employed. . . . Minimum standards of wage and comfort, insurance against sickness, old age, these are the only questions by which parties are going to live in the future.

By the time he arrived back in London in January 1908, changes were afoot. Campbell-Bannerman was mortally ill. His successor designate, Herbert Asquith, would choose a new government team and Churchill had every expectation of promotion to cabinet rank. Also, fate held in store a meeting with Clementine Hozier that was to transform his private life. Right through his early political career, Churchill had been an ambitious adventurer. Now he was to take on the mature burdens, and enjoy the delights, of power and domesticity.

CHAPTER FOUR

The Radical Warrior

LEFT: *Churchill out riding with his wife in Hyde Park in 1908. As a pugnacious Liberal minister, he became one of the most controversial figures in British political life.*

WHEN he fell in love with Clementine Hozier in March 1908, Churchill was 33 years old. He had lived most of his life in an exclusively male environment – Harrow, Sandhurst, the Army, London clubs, the Houses of Parliament. His view of women was romantic but patronizing, and in his dealings with them he was uncharacteristically gauche. His social behaviour toward the opposite sex then was much the same as when his daughter Mary observed it many years later:

... athough he greatly liked the company of beautiful, lively women he quickly tired of their conversation, and would always prefer to talk (or even shout!) 'across' them to some man, if one happened to be present. If he was trapped with no relief in sight, he tended to sink into a total and daunting silence.

He had made one early, rather foolish attempt to marry, proposing to an heiress, Muriel Wilson, who very sensibly turned him down. He concluded that marrying for money was not a wise course to follow. Later, in India, there was an emotional involvement with the vivacious daughter of the Resident at Hyderabad, Pamela Plowdon; she subsequently married Lord Lytton but always remained on friendly terms with Churchill. More recently, he had courted the American actress Ethel Barrymore. None of this amounted to anything very serious. Churchill had once jokingly told Pamela Plowdon that he loved 'one above all others' – himself! There was a lot of truth to this pleasantry. Although gregarious and warm-heartedly loyal to his family and friends, he had shown no gift for intimacy.

The 23-year-old Clementine had survived a difficult upbringing. The marriage between her mother Blanche, the eldest daughter of the Earl of Airlie, and Colonel Henry Hozier, a distinguished officer, war correspondent and later Secretary of Lloyds, was a disastrous failure, ending in a hostile separation. Clementine may well have been the daughter of one of her mother's extramarital lovers. She was brought up outside the mainstream of polite society, as her mother pursued her independent and sometimes erratic course through life hampered by constant lack of money and the stigma of separation from her husband. Yet Clementine was blessed with both beauty and intelligence. Because her mother could not afford a governess, she was sent to a grammar school where she received a much better education than most of her upper-class contemporaries and imbibed the liberal feminist principles of the day. Her mother still had good enough social connections to launch Clementine into the best society when the time came, and once she went out into the world she was pursued by admiring men of wealth and standing. Before meeting Churchill she had twice been engaged and had each time broken the engagement off, showing both a spirited independence of attitude and an underlying emotional uncertainty.

After their first meeting at a dinner given by a mutual friend, Churchill's insistent attentions quickly overwhelmed her defences: 'I feel no one can know him, even as little as I do,' she wrote in April 1908, 'without being dominated by his charm and brilliancy.' His rapid courtship was a strange

BELOW: *A photograph of Churchill and Clementine Hozier taken at the time of their engagement in the summer of 1908.*

ABOVE RIGHT: *The news of Churchill's election victory at Dundee made the front page – although it was a safe Liberal seat set up for him to win.*

LLOYD'S WEEKLY NEWS

SPECIAL SUNDAY EDITION. CIRCULATION OVER A MILLION AND A QUARTER.

No. 3,416. REGISTERED AT THE G.P.O. AS A NEWSPAPER. LONDON: SUNDAY, MAY 10, 1908. *Entered as Second-Class Matter at the New York, N.Y., Post Office, 1903.* ONE PENNY.

CRUISER'S FIGHT IN THE PERSIAN GULF.

Exciting Encounter with Afghan Gun Runners.

BRITISH SAILOR KILLED.

Mail advices received in Portsmouth yesterday from H.M.S. Proserpine give details of an exciting engagement which the vessel had in the Persian Gulf with gun-runners, whom the writer describes as Afghans. During the encounter one bluejacket was mortally and another dangerously wounded, and the officer in charge had a narrow escape.

The letter is dated from Jask, whither the Proserpine proceeded on April 14 from Bushire. It states that on the 18th the warship captured a dhow containing 1,650 rifles and about a million rounds of ammunition, most of the weapons being of French manufacture. The dhow's crew were armed and had ammunition on them, but they were evidently surprised and overawed.

On the following day the Proserpine was joined by the cruiser Hyacinth, the flagship of the East Indies Squadron, and the Hyacinth remained, in consequence of Afghan threats to wipe out the English reservation at Jask.

Further dhows being expected to land at Bunji with guns and ammunition, and two suspicious craft being sighted, the Proserpine despatched a steamboat, cutter, and whaler, under First Lieut. Baillie Hamilton, to examine them.

The water was very shallow, and two of the boats grounded, and as the crew began to wade ashore a perfect hail of bullets was rained upon them from under the shel-

ADVANCE IN FORCE ON AFGHAN FRONTIER.

Hostile Mohmands Refuse to Discuss British Terms.

TWO BRIGADES TO ACT.

SHANKARGARH, Saturday.

The hostile sections of the Mohmands have defiantly refused to come in to discuss the British terms.—Reuter.

PESHAWAR, Saturday night.

General Willcocks has been definitely ordered to proceed against the Mohmands on account of their failure to comply with the summons to attend a jirgah for the discussion of terms. Although the precise date of his march is as yet uncertain, it is understood that it will be started with the utmost promptitude.

Sir James Willcocks will have two brigades under Generals Anderson and Barrett with him.—Reuter.

The above telegrams evidence that the situation on the Afghan frontier has once again assumed a serious aspect. It was hoped that the prompt advance of Sir James Willcocks against the Afghan force of some 20,000 tribesmen that at the end of last week invaded the Khyber region, and the retreat and dispersal of the enemy after some sharp fighting on Wednesday, had ended the trouble more especially as it was understood that the hostile Mohmands were coming in for a discussion of terms.

THE WOMAN BLUEBEARD.

TOTAL OF VICTIMS NOW PUT AT TWENTY-ONE.

FURTHER DISCOVERIES.

MOST AMAZING CRIMINAL OF MODERN TIMES.

It is now known that the victims murdered by Mrs. Gunness, the handsome woman "Bluebeard" of Indianapolis, U.S., number at least twenty-one.

How she advertised for a husband with money, lured her suitors down to her farm, and then chloroformed and slew them in a padded room is described on Page Five.

Sixty letters from the woman to her farm hand, Lamphere (the man who has been arrested as an accomplice), were seized yesterday.

Search is still being made for bodies Inveterate sensation seekers have stolen portions of bodies recovered as mementoes.

The murderess is believed to have escaped from the country after setting fire to the farm to destroy the evidences of her crimes.

FIFTEEN-MILE FLIGHT.

Brothers Wright Achieve Great Aeroplane Feat.

OVER-SEA JOURNEY.

Return Trip of 150 Miles in Prospect.

MANTEO (N. Carolina), Saturday.

The Wright Brothers' airship yesterday performed a flight of fifteen miles out to sea at a height of 1,000 feet.

After circling, it returned to the starting point.

The wind velocity during the trial was ten miles an hour, but this in no way hampered the movements of the airship, which was under absolute control.—Reuter.

The performance, says the Central News, was regarded as so satisfactory by the Brothers Wright that on Monday an attempt will be made to take the airship over the seventy-five miles to Cape Henry and back.

ROMANCE OF INVENTION.

There is every element of romance in the conquest of the air by the Wright Brothers, once simple cycle makers of Dayton, Ohio.

From their early years they experimented with models in mechanical flight, later devoting their vacations to soaring experiments on the Carolina shores with wings of

CHURCHILL WINS.

SPLENDID LIBERAL VICTORY AT DUNDEE.

FREE TRADE TRIUMPHS.

SCENES OF WILD ENTHUSIASM IN THE STREETS.

The result of the poll at Dundee was declared last night as follows:—

Mr. Winston Churchill (L)	7079
Sir Geo. Baxter (C)	4370
Mr. Stuart (Lab.)	4014
Mr. Scrymgeour (Prohib.)	655

Liberal Majority over Conservative	2709
Liberal Majority over Labour	3065

INTENSE EXCITEMENT.

(From Our Special Correspondent.)

DUNDEE, Sunday Morning.

The poll was declared at midnight at the Sheriff's Court in Bell-street. The first candidate to arrive at the court was Mr. Scrymgeour. The second was Mr. Stuart, then Sir Geo. Baxter, and, last of all, Mr. Winston Churchill, who drove up in his motor-car at

---

mixture of hot pursuit and absent-mindedness. He proposed on 11 August in the gardens of Blenheim Palace – but only after being almost unforgivably late for the assignation. She accepted, then seriously considered breaking off her third engagement as she had the first two; the prospect of marriage to such a notorious political personality as Churchill might well have seemed daunting to the most resolute of women. But this time she stood the course, perhaps because Churchill typically insisted on such haste. The engagement lasted just one month. The couple were married on 12 September 1908 in London, at St Margaret's, Westminster.

It was a genuine love-match. Neither party was exactly a desirable catch in social terms. Churchill had no fortune and was widely considered insufferable for his pushiness and brashness. Clementine was impecunious and from a dubious background. But the marriage brought great happiness. The tough politician and man of action melted into sentimental baby-talk with his wife: she was 'Kat' or 'Catkin,' he was 'Pug' or 'Pig.' They decorated their letters with drawings of animals and were even given to exchanging playful woofs and miaouws. Churchill's assertiveness would have reduced most women to a shadow, but Clementine had the self-possession to stand up to him and the serious intelligence to participate fully in his political struggles. She was appalled by some of her husband's habits: his extravagance, his drinking and gambling. Far more perceptive than her husband, she disliked many of his friends, whose glaring faults she saw all too clearly. A true Liberal, she opposed his enduring Tory tendencies, his occasional rashness and arrogance. Many of Churchill's admiring acquaintances

found Clementine dull and priggish, a drag on a brilliant man. Yet this yoking together of very different, strongly defined characters was an improbable but indisputable success.

BELOW: Churchill at the opening of one of the first Labour Exchanges, which he had been responsible for establishing.

Churchill's courtship and marriage coincided with a period of frantic political activity. Asquith succeeded Campbell-Bannerman as prime minister in April 1908 and invited Churchill into the cabinet. He turned down the Admiralty in favour of the post of President of the Board of Trade, where he could find an outlet for his enthusiasm for social reform. At that time, any MP newly elevated to cabinet rank

had to resign his seat and face a by-election before taking up office. This was unfortunate for Churchill, since the government's popularity was on the wane and his Manchester constituency would be difficult to hold. After a two-week campaign, marked by especially bitter Tory attacks on the hated renegade and the disruption of his meetings by suffragettes, Churchill was defeated by 429 votes. This was only a temporary setback. He was offered his pick of safe Liberal seats, chose Dundee, and set off to campaign there the day after his Manchester defeat. On 9 May he was voted back into Parliament and took up his post at the Board of Trade.

Asquith's cabinet, a galaxy of exceptional individual talents, was run on very loose lines, with little central direction. Ministers were to a great extent left to exercise their own initiative and their levels of activity varied wildly. Churchill brought to the Board of Trade his habitual enthusiasm, a great capacity for hard work and an overwhelming determination to make things happen. In his hands, the department proved a most effective instrument for social reform. He pushed through the Coal Mines Bill which limited the time a man could work underground to eight hours a day – 'The general march of industrial democracy,' he told the House of Commons, 'is . . . towards sufficient hours of leisure.' His Trade Boards Act of 1909 offered some protection to workers in the worst-paid 'sweated' trades. Most significantly, he created the first Labour Exchanges to help the unemployed find work (entrusting a young Oxford don, William Beveridge, with the practical implementation of the scheme). This was the essential first step toward the introduction of unemployment insurance three years later.

Churchill's energy and enthusiasm were not universally welcomed by his cabinet colleagues. As an MP and a Colonial Under-Secretary, he had gained the reputation of being a disruptive influence, at times rude, interfering and overambitious. This reputation was fully confirmed by his behaviour as a minister. He had no hesitation in advising his more experienced colleagues on the business of their departments and his aggression introduced a new note of personal animosity into cabinet meetings. His hectoring radicalism disturbed the more conservative Liberal ministers and pushed him into close alliance with David Lloyd George, his predecessor at the Board of Trade and now Chancellor of the Exchequer.

Lloyd George and Churchill were on the face of it unlikely allies. But the son of a Welsh schoolmaster who had made his reputation opposing the Boer War, had more in common with Churchill, the war hero and grandson of a duke, than immediately met the eye. Both were self-made men who had forced their way to the top of the political ladder through a gift for flamboyant rhetoric and dramatic public gestures. And both were essentially outsiders in the polite political game, regarded with suspicion by their colleagues who recognized their brilliance but feared their ambition, their unpredictability and their disregard for convention. The fundamental difference between the two men was one of character.

Lloyd George was the supreme political opportunist, a calculating demagogue loyal to no one but himself. Churchill was in essence a conviction politician – even if his convictions sometimes changed with great rapidity – almost naively incapable of deviousness or intrigue. He was also intensely loyal to his friends. As the older and more experienced of the two, Lloyd George became for a time Churchill's mentor.

From 1908 to 1910 the two men led a faction within the government known as the 'economists,' keen to improve the living standards of the poorer strata of the population and generally pro-German. These two apparently unconnected attitudes were in fact tightly linked. Tory politicians and the Tory press had whipped up a public clamour for more spending on armaments to counter the growing might of Germany. The Liberal Party had a long tradition of dedication to peace – this was one of the main points which distinguished it from the Conservatives – but some prominent members of the government, notably Foreign Secretary Sir Edward Grey and Secretary for War R. B. Haldane, had also become concerned at the German threat and wanted to strengthen Britain's defences. Both Lloyd George and Churchill believed that an arms race would soak up the money needed for social reform. They campaigned against war-hysteria and Germanophobia,

dismissing the possibility of war as ridiculous. A speech by Churchill in August 1908, in which he publicly declared his pro-German sentiments, caused great resentment amongst his opponents in the Cabinet. What business had the President of the Board of Trade expressing opinions on foreign affairs and defence? A serious Cabinet split loomed.

The storm broke in December 1908, when the Admiralty demanded a stepped-up naval building programme to counter the expansion of the German fleet. They wanted six new dreadnoughts instead of the previously planned four. Lloyd George, Churchill and two other members of the cabinet dug in their heels, threatening to resign if the Admiralty got its way. The inspired but eccentric First Sea Lord, Admiral Sir John Fisher, promptly upped the demand to eight dreadnoughts and the Tory press manufactured the slogan: 'We Want Eight and We Won't Wait.' By February 1909 the government was in serious danger of collapse. Either Lloyd George and Churchill or their opponents would resign, depending which way the decision went. At the last moment, Asquith produced a compromise: four dreadnoughts to be built for certain, four more if the necessity was proven. The extra four were eventually built, so as Churchill later put it, 'a curious and characteristic solution was reached. The Admiralty had demanded six ships; the economists offered four; and we finally compromised on eight.'

This decision led directly to the 'People's Budget' and the conflict with the House of Lords which were to occupy so much of Churchill's time and energy over the next two years and confirm his reputation as a fearsome radical reformer. In 1909, needing to finance naval expansion and old age pensions for the

ABOVE: *Asquith puzzles over how to fit the varied talents of the Liberal Party into a coherent government. His cabinet was always to remain a collection of exceptionally gifted individuals with little common purpose.*

RIGHT: *The 12-inch guns of a Dreadnought-class battleship, the subject of a major cabinet split in 1908-09.*

OPPOSITE: *Churchill with his radical mentor, Chancellor of the Exchequer David Lloyd George, on budget day 1910.*

II.

—HIS PROFESSIONAL
MAKE-UP AS —

WHAT INDEED !?

"WHAT ARE WE TO THINK OF A LEGISLATOR
WHO FOUNDS THE WHOLE OF HIS
ARGUMENT UPON A TOTAL AND
ABSOLUTE MISSTATEMENT AND
PERVERSION OF SIMPLE AND
NOTORIOUS FACTS ? "
WINSTON CHURCHILL.
SOUTHPORT
DEC. 4th 1909.

WHAT INDEED !?

ABOVE: Churchill's advocacy of radical reforms, and especially his involvement in the campaign against the House of Lords, exposed him to bitterly hostile criticism in the Tory press. This vituperative cartoon was published in 1909.

Churchill became President of the Budget League and stumped the country making aggressive speeches denouncing the privileged class of his birth. Even more than Lloyd George, he was the focus of Tory outrage and anger. They hated the 'cant' of a man who dined off gold plate on visits to his cousin Sunny at Blenheim, yet preached against wealth and luxury. The Duke of Beaufort declared he would be glad to see both Lloyd George and Churchill 'in the middle of 20 couple of dog-hounds.'

In November 1909 the House of Lords took the momentous step of rejecting the budget. The government had no choice but to call an election on the issue of 'the peers against the people.' Churchill cherished a romantic view of the British aristocracy and the traditions it embodied, but his lifelong dedication to the House of Commons was unswerving. As early as June 1907 he had urged the Liberals to 'wrest from the hands of privilege and wealth the evil, ugly and sinister weapon of the Peers' veto, which they have used so ill for so long.' Now he threw himself into the fray. The issue was not just the People's Budget but the powers, and the very existence, of the House of Lords – dismissed by Lloyd George as '500 men . . . chosen accidentally from among the unemployed.'

The result of the election in January 1910 was a severe disappointment for the Liberals. Churchill was returned comfortably at Dundee but the absolute Liberal majority in the House of Commons was lost. Yet with the support of the Labour and Irish MPs the government majority was still substantial. When Parliament reassembled, the House of Lords bowed to the popular will and passed the People's Budget without a vote, but the peers were then confronted by a Parliament Bill designed to remove their veto on legislation and replace it by a delaying power of two years. Since the Upper House would inevitably veto the abolition of its veto, there was once more a deadlock.

The constitutional crisis raged for another 18 months. Churchill was ever in the forefront, prominent in the search for a compromise in the summer of 1910, eloquent in denouncing the House of Lords' veto when compromise failed, aggressive in pressing Asquith to resort to a massive creation of Liberal peers to swamp the Tory majority in the Upper House. It was the threat of this measure of last resort that finally overcame Tory resistance in August 1911. The House of Lords veto was abolished and the path to further Liberal reforming legislation was wide open.

The constitutional conflict left a heavy legacy of bitterness. Churchill himself always tried to maintain good relations with individuals on both sides of the House of Commons. Among his closest friends during this period and for many years afterwards was F. E. Smith, one of the most reactionary Tory MPs. The two men organized 'the Other Club,' an informal gathering of selected individuals of all shades of opinion who met regularly to discuss the affairs of the day without animosity. But a large number of Conservatives nursed a fanatical hatred of Churchill.

poor, Lloyd George drafted a budget that was to soak the rich, and above all the landed aristocracy: there were to be death duties, super-tax and a land tax. To the Tories this was red revolution. Given the size of the Liberal majority in the House of Commons, the only chance of stopping the budget lay with the Conservative-dominated House of Lords, which had used its powers unscrupulously over the previous three years to block reforming legislation. But traditionally the Lords could not interfere with a Money Bill. If they rejected the budget, there would be a constitutional crisis.

Churchill had private qualms about taxation which he thought might impoverish his own ducal relatives, but publicly he sprang to Lloyd George's aid. The campaign for the 'People's Budget' was one of the most acrimonious ever fought in British politics.

LEFT AND FAR LEFT: *Two propaganda posters issued by the Conservative Party's Budget Protest League, attacking Lloyd George's 'People's Budget' of 1909: John Bull, rendered defenceless by Free Trade, sinks beneath the waves, and Lloyd George's boulder, aimed to hit the plutocrat, in reality strikes the honest labourer.*

BELOW: *Churchill with F. E. Smith (seated) and Lord Dudley, in a splendid Napier car. Throughout his most radical period, Churchill remained a close friend of Smith, a right-wing Tory and dedicated opponent of Liberal reforms.*

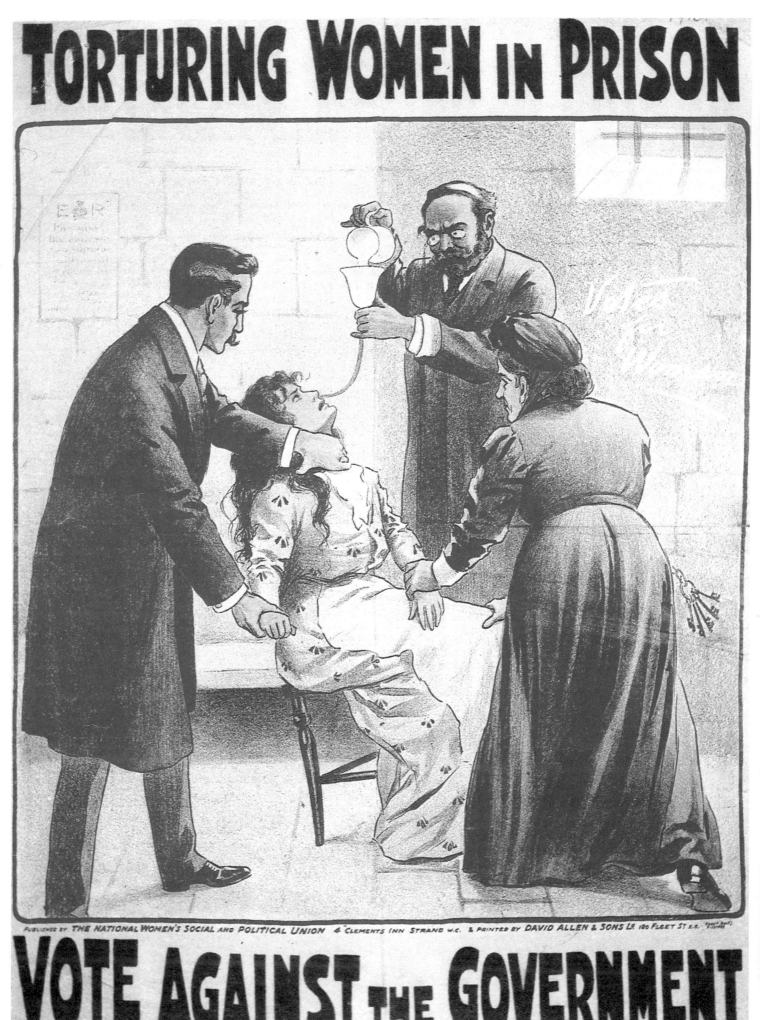

Meanwhile Churchill had won further promotion in the government ranks. His efforts in support of the budget, as well as his reforming measures at the Board of Trade, had greatly enhanced his reputation, at least among Liberals. Even those who were critical of him could not deny his outstanding qualities. Asquith distrusted Churchill's tendency to get carried away by his own rhetoric – 'he thought with his mouth' – yet acknowledged he was an exceptionally able minister. When Asquith formed his new government in February 1910, Churchill was appointed to the Home Office. At the age of 35, he was the second youngest Home Secretary in history (after Sir Robert Peel).

Churchill went to the Home Office at a most unenviable time. As the minister responsible for law and order, he had to face both suffragette agitation and large-scale industrial unrest. There was violence on both sides and Churchill's reputation was to suffer for his part in the repression of disorder. This was not the only drawback of the job. A particularly unpleasant duty of the Home Secretary was exercising the power of life or death over convicted murderers, on average one every fortnight. Although a believer in capital punishment, Churchill described signing death warrants as a 'nightmare' and exercised clemency whenever he felt it justified.

In general the Home Office was not a place where a minister could expect to pursue a career as a social reformer. Yet in one area at least Churchill did initiate notable reforms. He always claimed to have been the only Home Secretary who had experience of prison from the inside. This was an absurd inflation of his brief experience as a cossetted prisoner of war in Pretoria, but the myth inspired him to prison reform – he took it personally. His attitude to prisoners showed his usual inability to understand the lives of the common people: he once suggested lightening the burden of their imprisonment by giving them Gibbon and Macaulay to read. But he did introduce books and entertainments into prisons and set in motion a drastic reduction in the number of people imprisoned for debt and other minor offences. He also established as accepted policy that young offenders should if possible be kept out of jail altogether. 'The first real principle which should guide anyone trying to establish a good system of prisons,' he stated, 'should be to prevent as many people as possible getting there at all.'

The treatment of suffragettes in jail was an especially contentious issue. Churchill introduced measures to mitigate their punishment – and thus reduce the propaganda effect of martyrdom – but maintained force-feeding of hunger strikers. He was held responsible for the brutal handling of suffragette demonstrators by police on 'Black Friday,' 18 November 1910. Like other leading members of government, he was physically attacked. Theresa

ABOVE: *Suffragette demonstrators arrested by police outside Buckingham Palace.*

OPPOSITE: *A suffragette election poster of 1909 shows a hunger striker being force-fed in prison. While Home Secretary, Churchill mitigated the harsh treatment of suffragette prisoners, but retained force-feeding.*

The Daily Mirror

THE MORNING JOURNAL WITH THE SECOND LARGEST NET SALE

No. 2,244.   Registered at the G. P. O. as a Newspaper.   WEDNESDAY, JANUARY 4, 1911   One Halfpenny.

TWO HOUNDSDITCH MURDERERS COMMIT SUICIDE IN A BURNING HOUSE IN MILE END AFTER FIGHTING WITH ARMED POLICE AND GUARDSMEN FOR OVER EIGHT HOURS.

Not even the murder of three policemen by armed burglars in Houndsditch was half as extraordinary as its sequel, which took place yesterday. When the police attempted yesterday morning to enter a house in Sidney-street, Mile End, where they believed the two wanted men, "Fritz" and "Peter the Painter," were hiding, they were fired upon with revolvers. As a consequence, Scots Guards, armed with rifles, were called out to assist in the capture, and for eight hours Guardsmen and policemen armed with shot-guns and revolvers took part in a pitched battle, during which several were wounded. Then the house caught fire, and, when the firemen entered to quench the flames, the two "wanted" men were found dead, they having committed suicide. Above is a photograph-diagram, which shows Sidney-street, with two Guardsmen waiting to fire in the foreground, and which also explains how the battle was fought.—(*Daily Mirror* photograph.)

Garnett had threatened him with a whip on Bristol railway station in 1909 and a male suffragette sympathizer, Hugh Franklin, tried to assault him on a train after 'Black Friday.' This behaviour brought out all Churchill's pugnacity and he stubbornly opposed an attempted compromise measure offering votes to women of property. His wife was a suffragette sympathizer; this was the first of many issues on which their views would clash, although it did not cloud their mutual respect and affection.

Some of Churchill's inspirations at the Home Office were of dubious quality. He suggested setting up labour camps for those unwilling to work – although he mitigated the reactionary flavour of the proposal by pointing out that there were idle rich as well as idle poor. He was also momentarily captivated by the contemporary enthusiasm for eugenics and suggested to Asquith that the mentally retarded should be prevented from breeding by being locked up and sterilized, thus preserving Britain's sturdy stock from taint. Fortunately the bill in which he intended to embody this proposal never saw the light of day.

It was at this time that there occurred the strange affair of the Sidney Street siege, which showed how easily Churchill's reckless love of action could stir up controversy. A gang of Latvian anarchists, refugees from Tsarist Russia, had been carrying out armed robberies in London and in the process had killed three unarmed policemen. On 3 January 1911 a part of the gang was cornered in a house in Sidney Street, Stepney. Churchill not only authorized the use of the Scots Guards and the Horse Artillery in support of the police, but insisted on visiting the scene himself. When the building caught fire, incinerating the anarchists, he ordered the fire brigade to hold off. He wrote immediately afterwards: 'I thought it better to let the house burn down rather than spend good British lives in rescuing these ferocious rascals.' Public opinion was outraged not only by the overkill involved in the use of guardsmen and artillery against a small band of criminals, but also by Churchill's decision to witness the action in person. The impression was created that the whole event had been an exercise in Napoleonic megalomania, an indulgence of Churchill's personal fantasies of military leadership on the streets of London. It was specially unpopular among Liberals, who always favoured negotiated solutions and peaceful methods.

But it was Churchill's handling of strikes that brought the most severe criticism from his own party and earnt him the lasting hatred of the Labour movement. Biographers well-disposed to Churchill always delight in pointing out that the story of his sending troops against striking Welsh miners at Tonypandy in November 1910 is a popular myth. In fact, he countermanded an order for the dispatch of troops made by the local army commander and instead sent extra police to control the rioting. Indeed, he was roundly condemned for his weakness by the Tory press. Defending himself in the House of Commons the following February, Churchill stated: 'For soldiers to fire on the people would be a catastrophe in our national life.'

Yet his behaviour during the torrid strike-torn month of August 1911 did not live up to this fine Liberal principle. In a number of separate incidents

RIGHT: *Churchill gives evidence at the Sidney Street inquest a fortnight after the event.*

BELOW: *Winston and Clementine with their first baby, Diana, in 1909. Unlike his own father, Churchill took a close interest in events in the nursery.*

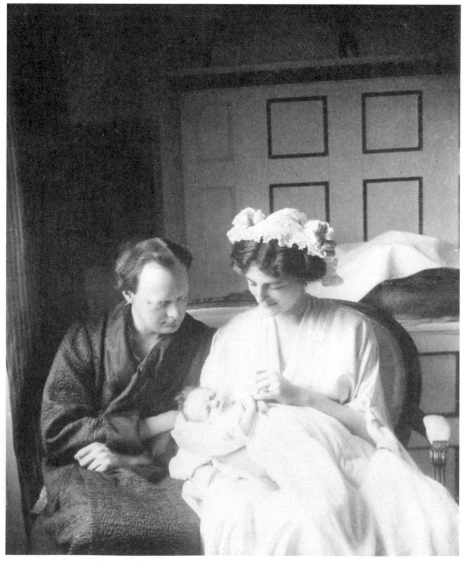

troops were deployed against rioters and even opened fire. The climax came when the railway workers struck on 18 August. There was more than a whiff of hysteria to Churchill's response. He described the strike as 'an abyss of horror which no man dared to contemplate.' He was sure it would ruin British industry and reduce the people to starvation. Without any attempt to negotiate a return to work, he instituted virtual martial law across much of the country, deploying 50,000 troops in defence of railway installations. Surrounding himself with maps, he directed the confrontation with the strikers like a military campaign. Fortunately, Lloyd George intervened and, employing all his powers of persuasion, arranged a settlement of the dispute in two days. Churchill was sorry to see an agreement reached so soon. He told Lloyd George: 'It would have been better to have gone on and given these men a good thrashing.' In all, six civilians were shot by troops in the various disturbances. The Labour leader, Kier Hardie, denounced Churchill in the House of Commons – strikers had been 'murdered by the government in the interest of the capitalist system.' Henceforth Churchill was a fixed target of Labour hostility, being cursed as a blood-stained reactionary.

In defence of Churchill's actions, it needs to be said that the summer of 1911 was a time of quite exceptional political crisis. The confrontation with the House of Lords was at its climax and, simultaneously, a piece of ill-considered German gunboat diplomacy at Agadir in Morocco had for the first time brought Britain and Germany to the brink of war. The railways were, of course, essential to military organization. One reason for Churchill's extreme

response was his totally erroneous conviction that the strikers were financed by 'German gold.'

It seems extraordinary that during these years of intense political activity, Churchill found any time for other aspects of life at all. Yet he was simultaneously starting a family. He had moved from his bachelor flat into a house in Eccleston Square, ready for the birth of his first child, Diana, in July 1909. (When he pronounced his daughter 'the prettiest child ever seen,' Lloyd George assumed she must take after her mother; 'No' said Churchill, 'she is exactly like me.') The daughter was followed in May 1911 by a son, Randolph. Churchill doted on his children and on their mother. Determined not to repeat his father's mistake, he took a constant interest in the infants' domestic routines and when they were slightly older played games with them and bought them toys. But he did not always see much of them, or their mother, because of the sheer business of his life. As well as fulfiling his onerous ministerial duties, he found time to attend military manoeuvres on the Continent every year as an observer and to take part in regular training with the Oxford Yeomanry – an occasion for much gambling and heavy drinking.

As a convinced Liberal, Clementine identified fully with the reforming drive of Churchill's policies between 1908 and 1911. She would never so approve of his politics again. Churchill did not turn against social reform; he simply moved on to other concerns. By the summer of 1911 he had discovered the issue that was to be the focus of his life's work: the threat of German military expansionism. Gone were the days when he and Lloyd George had ridiculed the German menace. Both men succumbed to the mood of the times.

The Agadir scare had revealed hopeless disarray in Britain's war plans. The Army intended to move 160,000 men across the Channel to join forces with the French. But the Navy had no plans to transport these troops and indeed flatly refused to do so. Haldane, the Secretary for War, was appalled and threatened to resign unless Asquith instituted a shake-up at the Admiralty. Churchill now desperately wanted a defence appointment. Perhaps recognizing that Churchill was too bellicose to continue fighting on the home front, Asquith duly appointed him First Lord of the Admiralty in October 1911, rejecting Haldane's bid for the post. He had been Home Secretary for just 20 months.

Churchill once described his time at the Admiralty as the most memorable years of his life (although this was before the heady excitements of World War II). His imagination thrived on the past glories of the Royal Navy and the high responsibilities which the post of First Lord entailed. It was almost universally accepted that the defence of Britain and its Empire depended on the Navy, not the Army. Churchill saw himself as holding the fate of the Empire in his hands and revelled in a sense of historic duty. He consciously and deliberately dramatized the situation, as a spur to effort. He kept a chart on the wall of his office, for instance, where the position of the German fleet was marked every day. 'I did this less to keep myself informed,' he wrote, '. . . than in order to inculcate in myself and those working with me a sense of ever-present danger.'

His immediate task was to shake up the structure of the Admiralty and its war plans against the fixed opposition of the incumbent Sea Lords. He also had to decide the course and scope of Britain's naval building programme to maintain a decisive technological and numerical superiority over any potential enemies. In both these tasks he was hampered by his lack of expert knowledge of naval matters. He needed a more experienced ally, and found him in the recently retired First Sea Lord Sir John Fisher, now Baron Fisher of Kilverstone. Fisher was a great innovator who had transformed the Victorian Navy into a modern fighting force. But he was also intolerant, vindictive, domineering and madly eccentric – he ended his rambling letters to Churchill with flourishes such as 'Yours to a cinder' or 'Yours till Hell freezes.' Churchill and Fisher had crossed swords during the 1908 crisis over the naval building programme, but once Fisher realized the new First Lord had recanted and was now dedicated to expansion of the fleet, he offered his whole-hearted assistance – or in Churchill's phrase,

BELOW: *In 1909 Churchill was invited to attend military manoeuvres in Germany as a guest of Wilhelm II. At this time Churchill was still one of the pro-German faction in the British government.*

'passed into a state of vehement eruption.' As an unofficial adviser, Fisher for a time virtually dictated policy, from the selection of admirals for important posts to decisions on gun sizes and battleship design, inundating Churchill with an unstaunchable flood of suggestions and recommendations.

The changes Churchill pushed through under Fisher's influence were almost wholly beneficial. He made a clean sweep of the Sea Lords, including among his new appointees Prince Louis of Battenburg, a choice much resented in some circles because of Prince Louis' German connections. Churchill also promoted Admiral John Jellicoe over the heads of longer-serving officers; Fisher was determined Jellicoe should be in command of the Home Fleet by the time war broke out, which Fisher was sure would happen in October 1914. The hardest struggle was to create an efficient Naval War Staff. Although a war staff was established, naval staff work remained inadequate and was a weakness throughout World War I. Still, cooperation with the Army much improved and a substantial degree of joint war planning was achieved.

Some of Churchill's boldest decisions concerned warship construction. Fisher was keen on 15-inch guns, larger than any naval guns in existence at the time, and on oil-fired ships instead of coal-fired – oil-firing would increase speed and reduce the size of the crew. With these improvements he believed the Royal Navy could outgun and outrun any German vessel. But innovations involve risks. The proper development of new guns would take time for tests and trials. Churchill thought it would take too long and decided to put untested 15-inch guns in the new generation of dreadnoughts. He knew that if they did not work he would have no choice but to resign. Fortunately, they did.

Oil-firing posed other serious problems. Britain had a plentiful domestic supply of coal, but where

RIGHT: *Admiral John Jellicoe, promoted over the heads of more senior officers by Churchill, on Fisher's advice. Fisher was determined that, when war broke out, Jellicoe should be in command of the Home Fleet.*

BELOW: *Royal Navy battleships* Royal Sovereign, Revenge *and* Resolution. *Churchill helped maintain Britain's lead in naval technology by introducing oil-fired superdreadnoughts with 15-inch guns.*

were the oil stocks to be found? In one of his most successful coups, Churchill arranged a deal with the Anglo-Persian Oil Company to provide a guaranteed supply of fuel. The government invested £2 million in the development of new oilfields in Persia, taking a majority shareholding in the company which was to grow in value by about 1000 percent over the next 20 years. Churchill was proud to claim that this was the only occasion upon which expenditure on armaments had made the government a profit. It also involved a rapid expansion of British influence in the Middle East oil zone.

The 15-inch-gun oil-fired Fast Division battleships were not Churchill's only technical innovation. Impressed by the potential of airpower, he created the Royal Naval Air Service in 1912 and anticipated the future role of the aircraft carrier. Always fascinated by new inventions and new adventures, he insisted on flying himself, despite the extreme danger this involved in the rudimentary machines of the day. It was, he claimed, the best fun he had had since the South African war. He did not fly alone – he never adequately mastered take-off and landing – but he clocked up a respectable time at the controls with an instructor and would eventually have qualified as a pilot if Clementine had not persuaded him, for her sake, to desist. It was probably the greatest sacrifice he ever made for his marriage.

Royal Navy – for example, its defences against submarines and mines were totally inadequate and

LEFT: *Churchill the aviator. He thought his experience as a trainee pilot the best fun he had had since the Boer War – the danger was a perfect distraction from the complications of 'tiresome party politics.'*

BELOW: *Churchill engaged in one of his many tours of inspection of Royal Naval installations, on this occasion in Scotland.*

submarines and mines were totally inadequate and standards of gunnery were poor – but without Churchill's pre-war efforts things would have been far worse. His work rate was phenomenal. He insisted on visiting naval forces, dockyards and shipyards all around Britain and in the Mediterranean, observing every aspect of operations and interrogating officers and men on the exact details of their particular duties. In the process he risked making himself thoroughly unpopular. As one officer later expressed it, the Royal Navy 'was at heart a conservative service, accustomed to a First Lord who . . . abided by the advice of his professional colleagues on all technical matters, on strategy and on training.' Churchill was an opinionated civilian intruding upon naval matters, and a person who showed no respect for the niceties of rank and tradition. His habit of eliciting information and ideas from junior officers, who often contradicted the statements of their hierarchical superiors, caused uproar, on one occasion almost leading to the resignation of the entire Admiralty Board. As for naval tradition, Churchill memorably dismissed it as 'rum, sodomy and the lash.' Still, the German naval attaché could accurately conclude in June 1914 that although there had been friction caused by Churchill's 'stubborn and tyrannical character,' the Navy was on the whole satisfied because he had 'accomplished more for them than the majority of his predecessors in office.'

Churchill's visits of inspection were made on board the *Enchantress*, a luxurious steam yacht with a crew of about a hundred that was one of the perks of the First Lord's office. Although a poor sailor prone to sea-sickness, Churchill loved this nautical extravagance and spent on average about three months of each year afloat during his peacetime service at the Admiralty. Questions were asked in the House of Commons about this misuse of taxpayer's money, one member having the temerity to suggest that the First Lord could visit naval bases in Scotland more quickly and more cheaply by rail.

The spacious appartments on the yacht provided plenty of room for Churchill to invite guests aboard, and tours of inspection frequently doubled as luxury pleasure cruises for his colleagues, relatives and friends. The prime minister's daughter, Churchill's close friend Violet Asquith (later Violet Bonham-Carter), has written a glittering account of cruises in the Mediterranean in 1912 and 1913, when the inspection of ports and the witnessing of naval exercises were interspersed with visits to classical sites, leisurely plunges into the clear warm waters, endless conversation and games of bridge. On board at various times, along with a smattering of admirals and private secretaries, were the prime minister himself and his wife Margot, Clementine and her sister Nellie, Churchill's mother and his sister-in-law Gwendeline ('Goonie'). This was typical of the company the Churchills now kept. As a result of the

BELOW: *The luxurious Admiralty yacht* Enchantress, *one of the perks of the First Lord's post. Churchill spent so much time on board the* Enchantress *in the pre-war years that it became, in his own words, 'largely my office, almost my home. . .'*

bitter political disputes of the past few years they had been ostracized by the aristocracy. In any case, Churchill's serious dedication to his work and his obsession with politics cut him off from the frivolous world he had once much frequented. Political colleagues and close relatives formed the small circle in which he mostly lived.

Despite the sumptuous trappings of a First Lord's office, shortage of money was a constant problem.

Churchill's pay was inadequate to support his family and his journalism was now restricted since all his time and energy were devoted to his Admiralty work. Clementine, who bore the burden of their domestic economy, at first resisted moving into the magnificent Admiralty House in Whitehall because they could not afford the domestic staff it would require. In 1913 Churchill finally persuaded her to leave Eccleston Square, but she kept part of her

UNDER HIS MASTER'S EYE.

Scene—*Mediterranean, on board the Admiralty yacht "Enchantress."*

Mr. Winston Churchill. "ANY HOME NEWS?"

Mr. Asquith. "HOW CAN THERE BE WITH YOU HERE?"

LEFT: *A famous* Punch *cartoon of May 1913 shows Churchill and Asquith enjoying a lazy Mediterranean cruise on the* Enchantress. *The caption is a tribute to Churchill's reputation for stirring up political storms. His egotism is subtly suggested by the book he has supposedly chosen for holiday reading – his own account of his African travels!*

ABOVE: *Churchill in a humorous mood, posing for the camera during a round of golf in 1913.*

OPPOSITE: *Cartoonist David Wilson has presented the First Sea Lord very much as he would wish to be seen – a vigilant defender of Britain and its Empire in the tradition of Horatio Nelson.*

extensive new home closed up so the number of servants could be restricted to nine. The financial crisis was so acute in 1914 that Clementine sold a diamond-and-ruby necklace she had received as a wedding present to pay some domestic bills. Churchill was distressed when he discovered what she had done, but his extravagance with money continued.

This was true in his public life also. The dreadnought programme was extremely expensive. The man who had twice stood out against increased military expenditure now fought for every penny both in the cabinet and the House of Commons. Opposition was muted in 1912 and 1913, when a large measure of agreement existed on the reality of the German threat, but by 1914 international tension had relaxed and the Liberal Party's traditional hostility to excessive armaments found a freer expression. Churchill's naval estimates for that year ran into serious difficulties as a substantial number of ministers, including Lloyd George, ranged themselves against further increases in spending. It was a repeat of the 1908-09 crisis all over again, but with Churchill on the other side. At the end of January 1914 it seemed that either the First Lord or his cabinet opponents would have to resign. But Churchill enjoyed Asquith's confidence and with his usual stubbornness ultimately carried the day. Lloyd

George claimed to have given in at the last moment on the advice of his wife, who did not like him 'having an argument with that nice Mr Churchill about dreadnoughts' and suggested 'it would be better to have too many than too few.'

Churchill was not a warmonger. He actively supported attempts to end the naval arms race by agreement with Germany (although he inadvertently sabotaged one round of negotiations by publicly referring to the German Navy as a 'luxury,' a remark which caused much offence in Berlin). He conscientiously sought to avoid provoking Germany into conflict. He associated himself publicly with the argument of his cabinet colleagues Asquith, Grey and Haldane, that strong armaments were needed not to make war, but to preserve peace. Yet his emotional attitude was very different from theirs. The idea of war excited and fascinated him. As Violet Bonham-Carter wrote: 'He never shared the reluctance which inhibits Liberals from invoking force to solve a problem.' His dedication to expanding armaments further harmed his reputation within the Liberal Party.

It was partly in an attempt to restore his popularity with the Liberal rank-and-file that Churchill became so actively involved in the crisis over Ireland which dominated British politics in the

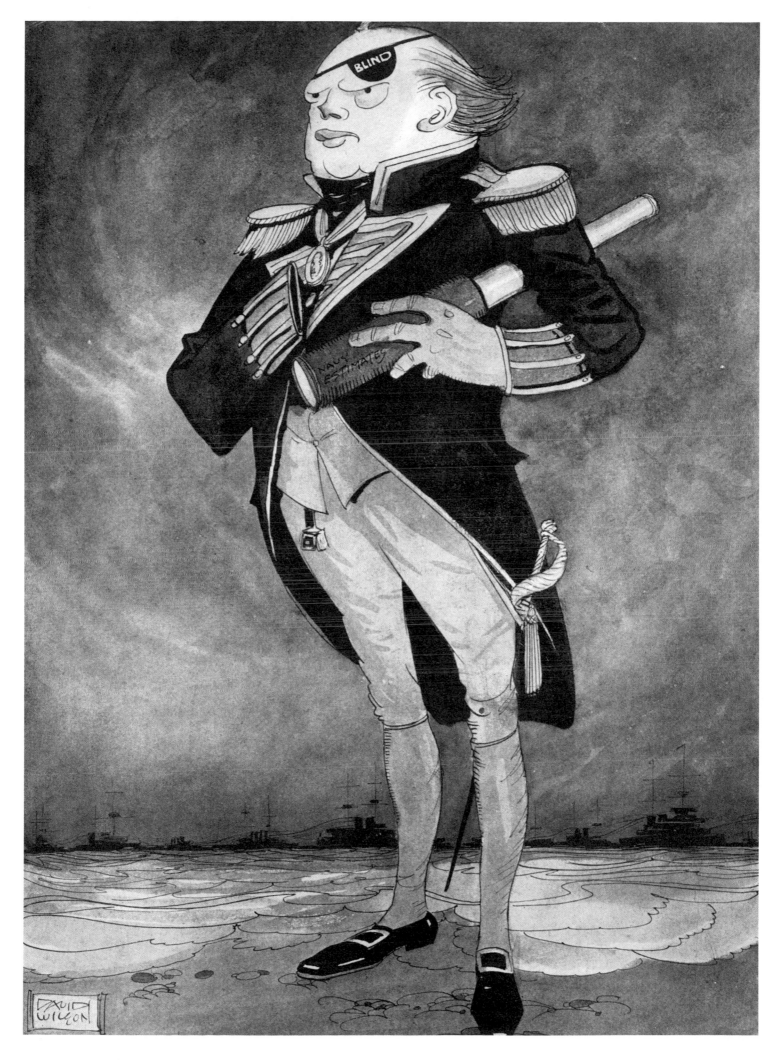

immediate pre-war period. A Liberal bill to grant Home Rule to Ireland had been passed by the House of Commons in 1893, but had then been thrown out by the House of Lords. Now with the peers' veto removed, the road to Home Rule was at last open. The Liberals had no choice but to take that path, because they were dependent on the votes of Irish MPs for their parliamentary majority. In April 1912 Asquith introduced a bill to create a Dublin parliament with strictly limited powers – control of defence, foreign affairs and taxation would remain with the British government. Even this moderate measure, however, outraged the Tories and the Protestants of Ulster. Knowing that the House of Lords could only delay the bill for three years, they began to plot armed rebellion.

Churchill had before him the example of his father, who had backed Ulster resistance to Home Rule in 1886, but he shrugged off his ancestry and threw himself heart and soul into the government's struggle. From the start, in February 1912, he put himself into the front line by accepting an invitation to address a meeting in Belfast, against the advice of the military authorities. Clementine went with him on the ferry, where they were kept awake all night by suffragettes chanting outside their cabin. On arrival in Belfast, they were mobbed by hostile fist-waving Protestant crowds who at one point almost succeeded in overturning their car before being beaten off by police. The reception in Catholic areas

of the city was very different, and Churchill succeeded in delivering a ringing speech in which he faced up to his legacy from his father:

It is in a different sense that I adopt and repeat Lord Randolph's words, 'Ulster will fight and Ulster will be right.' Let Ulster fight for the dignity and honour of Ireland; let her fight for the reconciliation of races and for the forgiveness of ancient wrongs. . . . Then indeed Ulster will fight and Ulster will be right.

Churchill regarded some compromise on the Irish question as essential. He insisted that the government would not coerce the Ulster Protestants into acceptance of Home Rule and backed the temporary exclusion of Ulster from the provisions of the bill. This was a solution acceptable neither to Irish Catholics nor to Ulster Protestants, however, and all attempts at a negotiated settlement failed. Weapons were shipped into northern Ireland to equip the Ulster Volunteers, who stage-managed demonstrations of strength to intimidate the British government. Astonishingly, the Tory leader Bonar Law backed the principle of armed revolt, identifying his party with the threat of a violent uprising against the constitutionally elected government. Prominent Army officers, including General Sir Henry Wilson, the Director of Military Operations, were conspiring with Ulster leaders against the government and there were strong indications that the Army would not obey orders to enforce Home Rule.

BELOW: *Ulster Protestants demonstrate their opposition to Home Rule in September 1912. Supported by the Conservative Party and some senior British Army officers, the Protestants were prepared to use force in their resistance to the British government's Irish policy.*

By March 1914 the country was on the brink of civil war. Churchill denounced the Conservatives' endorsement of violent and illegal methods as a doctrine 'from which every street bully with a brick-bat and every crazy fanatic who is fumbling with a toy pistol may derive inspiration.' Authorized by Asquith to make a strong speech insisting on the maintenance of the rule of law, he delivered a memorable oration, concluding: 'I can only say to you, "Let us go forward and put these grave matters to the proof."' It was taken by the Tories and their Ulster allies as a virtual declaration of war. On 19 March, without informing Asquith, Churchill moved eight battleships to the Isle of Arran, 70 miles from Belfast. Once the prime minister learnt of this provocative order he countermanded it, but too late. The Tories got wind of the fleet movement and denounced a Churchillian plot to carry out an 'Ulster pogrom.' He was reviled as a 'Lilliput Napoleon.' When the opposition attacked the government in parliament for planning to use the armed forces against Ulstermen, Churchill responded with devastating wit: 'What we are now witnessing in the House is uncommonly like a vote of censure by the criminal classes on the police.'

These events none the less further harmed Churchill's reputation. The Tories already disliked him for his support of the People's Budget and his attacks on the House of Lords. The 'Ulster pogrom' confirmed him as their most hated opponent. Liberals once more saw evidence of Churchill's rashness and his taste for the use of military force, contrary to the whole spirit of Liberalism. Paradoxically, they also distrusted his efforts to achieve a compromise on Ulster, in which they detected a hidden Toryism.

The Irish crisis dragged on through the summer of 1914. On 24 July a conference called by the King at Buckingham Palace to search for a compromise solution broke up without agreement. In the afternoon, the cabinet met to discuss this impasse. So preoccupied were they by Ireland that when Foreign Secretary Sir Edward Grey began to read out details of an Austrian ultimatum to Serbia, it was some time before ministers paid full attention. Gradually the implications sank in: Europe might be heading for war. Churchill wrote later in *The World Crisis*:

The parishes of Fermanagh and Tyrone faded back into the mists and squalls of Ireland, and a strange light began immediately, but by perceptible gradations, to fall and grow upon the map of Europe.

The following day, Churchill left London for Pear Tree Cottage, near Cromer on the east coast, where Clementine, seven months pregnant, was spending the summer. He played with the children on the beach, digging channels and fortifications in the sand under a cloudless sky. It was the last innocence before Armageddon. By the afternoon of Sunday 26 July, the situation had further deteriorated and he was needed back at the Admiralty. By good fortune, the Navy had carried out a test mobilization that month, culminating in a Grand Review at

ABOVE: *Bonar Law, the dour Conservative leader, who headed the opposition to Home Rule in parliament. The commitment of the Conservatives to the continuation of the union with Ireland was symbolized by the name of their party: they had officially been known as the Unionists since 1886.*

Spithead. The first and second fleets were still fully manned and ready for action. On his arrival in London, Churchill announced they would not disperse to their peacetime stations.

The majority of the cabinet was opposed to any British involvement in a European war. Britain had no formal alliance with any European power, although she was a guarantor of Belgian neutrality. The Liberal Party had traditionally opposed war and some ministers were dedicated pacifists. However, a powerful core of experienced ministers – Asquith, Haldane, Grey and Churchill – were determined that if Germany attacked France, Britain must intervene. Between them they pushed through war preparations over the following week as the cabinet vacillated. Churchill was by far the most enthusiastic. He recognized that war would destroy the humane and civilized values to which he normally subscribed and that peace must be preserved if at all honourably possible. Yet his nature thrilled at the prospect of armed conflict. On 28 July he wrote to Clementine:

Everything tends towards catastrophe and collapse. I am interested, geared up and happy. Is it not horrible to be built like that? The preparations have a hideous fascination for me. I pray to God to forgive me for such fearful moods of levity. Yet I would do my best for peace.

Ever since his childhood manoeuvres with toy soldiers, he had wanted to command large forces in battle. Now he felt the call of destiny.

The cabinet met every day for acrimonious discussion of the evolving situation. On 1 August Asquith noted: 'Winston very bellicose and demanding instant mobilization.' But the anti-war element held its ground. The Conservatives had agreed a truce on Home Rule and were prepared to support the government, but it looked as if the cabinet would simply fall apart. For Asquith, the German invasion of Belgium saved the day. Confronted with an appeal from the King of Belgium for Britain to honour its commitments, Lloyd George and several other former pacifists changed sides. The government was able to lead the country into war almost united; there were only two resignations.

At 11pm on 4 August Britain's ultimatum to Germany expired. Churchill issued the order to all ships and naval establishments: 'Commence hostilities against Germany.' The cabinet sat in gloom and silence. Churchill alone radiated a buoyant optimism that matched the mood of the flag-waving crowds in the streets outside. He would have echoed the sentiment of the poet Rupert Brooke: 'Now, God be thanked Who has matched us with His hour.' He could not have imagined that this war, far from fulfilling his destiny, would hurl him into political disaster, breaking the bright upward trajectory of his meteoric career.

SIR EDWARD GREY.
Ministre des Affaires Etrangères

OPPOSITE: *Flanked by his wife and General Bruce Hamilton, Churchill observes military manoeuvres in 1912.*

LEFT: *Foreign Secretary Sir Edward Grey, the chief architect of Britain's entente with France.*

BELOW: *Fortuitously, in July 1914 the Navy was mobilized for a royal review at Spithead – an economy measure in place of the usual annual manoeuvres.*

CHAPTER FIVE

To Gallipoli and Back

LEFT: *Churchill walks through
Whitehall with Arthur Balfour, his
replacement as First Lord of the
Admiralty, in May 1915. The
disaster of Gallipoli forced Churchill
out of the government and almost
ruined his career.*

I N the first days of the war, the careful planning Churchill had imposed on a reluctant Navy proved its value. The movement of the British Expeditionary Force (BEF) to France was accomplished smoothly without interference from the German Navy. But the Admiralty and its First Lord received little or no credit for this achievement. The universal expectation of a great sea battle between the British and German fleets was not met, and the absence of any decisive naval victory created a sense of anticlimax. As the French and British Armies fought to resist the German onslaught through the desperate months of August and September 1914, it appeared that the Navy stood idly by.

Churchill was more disappointed than anyone when the German fleet failed to come out and fight at the start of the war. He needed to be at the centre of the action. Although he worked tirelessly at the Admiralty, constantly intruding on the conduct of operations by the First Sea Lord and the naval staff, he was drawn irresistibly to the European land war where the decisive fighting was taking place. Toward the end of the second month of the war, Clementine Churchill wrote to her husband:

It makes me grieve to see you gloomy and dissatisfied with the unique position you have reached through years of ceaseless industry and foresight. . . . You are the only young vital person in the cabinet. It is really wicked of you not to be swelling with pride at being First Lord of the Admiralty during the greatest War since the beginning of the World.

This chiding was well justified. Churchill was not content with his place. He wanted to be involved in every aspect of the war, not just at sea but also in the air and on land. This restless quest for action very quickly got him into trouble, as Clementine feared it would.

Churchill's colleagues in the War Council, particularly Asquith and the new Secretary for War, Lord Kitchener, were quite happy to help him diversify his interests. Any inconvenient task could be unloaded on to the most eager workhorse. Kitchener objected to Churchill flitting across the Channel for consultations with Sir John French, commander of the BEF, since this infringed War Office prerogatives. But he was only too glad to hand over responsibility for Britain's air defences to Churchill, on the grounds that the War Office was overburdened with work. Since there were no air defences as such – no anti-aircraft guns or searchlights – Churchill interpreted his new responsibility in an offensive spirit. He based contingents of the Royal Naval Air Service at Dunkirk, with orders to intercept Zeppelins on their way to England and to bomb Zeppelin sheds in Germany.

As well as an air force, Churchill had land forces at his disposal. The Marines were one of the longest-

BELOW: *Volunteers queuing to sign up at the Whitehall recruiting office in 1914. Young men feared they might miss the fighting, which was expected to be brief.*

standing elements of the British armed forces. In 1913 Churchill had decided to supplement these established fighters with elements of the Naval Volunteer Reserve and the Fleet Reserve for whom there was no place to be found at sea. These men were hastily transformed into two ill-trained, ill-equipped brigades of soldier-sailors who, with the Marine brigade, formed the Royal Naval Division.

With the full approval of Kitchener and Asquith, Churchill first sent the Marines to Ostend for a week in mid-September and then moved them to Dunkirk, where they were joined by a detachment of the Oxfordshire Hussars. These moves were made with the maximum of publicity – London double-decker buses were used as an eye-catching means of transport – the idea being to divert German attention from the serious fighting further south. All this razzmatazz was obviously open to misinterpretation at home, however. Churchill's 'Dunkirk circus' of land and air forces looked very like a private army pursuing its own erratic war. This impression was confirmed by the number of Churchill's relatives or acquaintances either at Dunkirk or in the Naval Volunteer Reserve – they included his brother Jack and his cousin Sunny with the Oxfordshire Hussars; and his mother's second husband, George Cornwallis-West, in the Reserve force.

On the evening of 2 October Churchill was on his way to visit his 'circus' at Dunkirk when he was called back by an urgent message from Kitchener. The Belgian King and government had decided to withdraw from Antwerp, which was under bombardment from German artillery. Because of the strict neutrality being observed by Belgium's neighbour, Holland (a neutrality Churchill would have preferred to violate), Antwerp was unusable as a port. But the British cabinet was agreed the city should not be abandoned without a fight. At Kitchener's request, Churchill set off immediately for Antwerp to

RIGHT: *Belgian troops retreat in the face of superior German numbers. The Royal Naval Division, it was hoped, would shore-up the Belgian defences around Antwerp.*

BELOW: *Members of the Royal Naval Division on their way to Antwerp. When the city fell on 8 October, two whole battalions were interned in neutral Holland and 1000 men were taken prisoner by the Germans.*

report on the situation and to stiffen Belgian resolve. The Marines were dispatched from Dunkirk to reinforce the city's defences and the two Naval Brigades were ordered over from their training camps in England. Weightier forces were to follow this initial advance.

Churchill's impact on the situation in Antwerp was electrifying. He was in his element. He reinvigorated the Belgian authorities, stormed about reorganizing the city defences, and with gloriously self-indulgent bravado posed for the cameras smoking a cigar while shrapnel shells burst around him. Beside himself with excitement, on 5 October he telegraphed Asquith requesting to be relieved of his post at the Admiralty and put in command of the defence of Antwerp. In the words of Violet Asquith, it was 'the choice of a romantic child.' The cabinet greeted the proposal with unrestrained laughter – only Kitchener took it seriously and offered to make Churchill a lieutenant-general. Asquith rejected the resignation and told Churchill he was needed back at the Admiralty. A senior army officer was sent to take over command and Churchill returned to London on 7 October, by which time the situation in Antwerp was already beyond saving. The Naval Division evacuated the city the following day. Most escaped, but about 1000 men were captured by the Germans and two battalions marched across the border into Holland where they were interned for the rest of the war.

ABOVE: The Royal Navy
battlecruiser Invincible steaming at
full speed during the battle of the
Falklands in December 1914. This
notable victory was not sufficient to
stem criticism of the Admiralty in the
first six months of the war.

The Antwerp episode did Churchill immense harm. Even his friends thought his behaviour irresponsible. Clementine, who gave birth to a daughter, Sarah, on 7 October, felt he had unnecessarily deserted both her and his post. Asquith in general defended Churchill's conduct, but thought it inexcusable of him to have sent the raw untrained Naval Brigades straight into action (one of Asquith's sons was part of this force). Churchill's enemies had a field day. He was denounced by the press for his prominent role in this 'eccentric expedition' and repeatedly reminded that the proper place of a First Lord was at the Admiralty. Bonar Law put it about as his private opinion that Churchill had 'an entirely unbalanced mind.' The verdict of history has been somewhat more favourable. The defence of Antwerp delayed the German advance toward the Channel coast of France and therefore may have helped save Dunkirk and Calais. It was probably not an effort wasted.

Churchill also found himself on the defensive about the conduct of the Admiralty. In truth, the overwhelming naval superiority he had striven so hard to maintain was secure. Troops were brought safely to Europe from the far-flung corners of the Empire. German seaborne trade ceased under a naval blockade enforced worldwide. The bulk of the German fleet was cooped up in port. But in the absence of any decisive action, the Germans were able to inflict a series of minor humiliations that undermined confidence in the Royal Navy. On 22 September three ageing cruisers patrolling the narrow seas were sunk by a German submarine with great loss of life. A story was put about that Churchill, as usual interfering improperly with the conduct of operations, had ordered the cruisers to stay on patrol against the advice of his admirals. In fact the reverse was true: Churchill had ordered the ships moved as soon as he learnt of the foolish deployment of this 'live-bait squadron' – but unfortunately his intervention had been too late. The false rumour was, however, widely believed. Other setbacks followed in October. The dreadnought *Audacious* hit a German mine and sank, the German cruiser *Emden* wreaked havoc on merchant shipping in the Indian Ocean, and the seaplane carrier *Hermes* was sunk off Calais. This was not at all what the British public had expected.

Criticism was directed not only at Churchill but at the First Sea Lord, Prince Louis of Battenburg. His German origins made him an easy target and by the end of October the ignorant outcry against him was so loud he had no choice but to resign. Although lamenting the way Prince Louis had been hounded out of office, Churchill seized on his resignation as a chance to install the First Sea Lord of his choice: the

BRITONS

"WANTS YOU"

JOIN YOUR COUNTRY'S ARMY!

ABOVE: *Lord Kitchener, Secretary for War, was used as the symbol of stern patriotism in the most famous poster of World War I. It is ironic that Churchill should have found himself in the War Cabinet with the man who, 15 years earlier, had tried to keep him out of the Sudan.*

In the North Sea, however, the Royal Navy had less success. Despite the fact that the cryptographers in Room 40 of the Admiralty were reading intercepted German radio messages and thus had advance warning of enemy fleet movements, the Navy twice missed chances to inflict decisive losses, in December when German ships bombarded English east coast towns, and in January 1915 at the battle of Dogger Bank. Criticisms were not stilled.

As the war dragged on, dissensions within the War Council (a body comprised of the top military and civilian leaders) became acute. Churchill and Kitchener had got on well together in the first months of the war, but now returned to their old hostility of the Sudan period. Kitchener resented Churchill's influence over Sir John French and disliked his 'Dunkirk circus,' still in place with a force of armoured motorcars defending the Navy airfield. In December, Kitchener forced Churchill to hand over his circus to the Army and insisted he limit his visits to the BEF headquarters in France. Churchill could not be entirely deterred from taking an interest in land warfare, however, and under the direction of the Admiralty Landships Committee work continued on the development of a new type of armoured vehicle, the tank (dismissed by Kitchener as 'a pretty mechanical toy'). Churchill was also still responsible for Britain's air defences. On Christmas Eve, a Zeppelin dropped a bomb on Dover. Fisher went into a paroxysm of self-righteous anger and threatened to resign unless German prisoners were shot in retaliation for air attacks. Churchill calmed him down, but was for the first time worried by this outward sign of his worsening mental condition. Asquith lamented the War Council's inclination to fight one another, rather than the enemy.

No one was happy with the bloody stalemate on the Western front. The standard Army opinion was that all available strength should none the less be concentrated there, to engage the enemy's major forces. In the War Council, the predominant view was that some initiative should be taken to open up a new front with better prospects for a swifter and less costly success. Churchill was an enthusiastic supporter of any alternative to sending more and more men to 'chew barbed-wire in Flanders.' His mind was ever fertile with fresh schemes and stratagems; with his romantic image of warfare, he shied away from the unimaginative attrition of great forces. He could not accept war as a slogging match, barbaric butchery. Some inspired example of ingenuity, heroism or daring must be capable of turning the tide to victory. Only this was compatible with his belief in war as a field for the highest human endeavour.

There was an added advantage at a more practical level: a fresh initiative would inevitably involve the use of seapower, bringing the Admiralty back to the centre of the stage. The most promising options from Churchill's point of view were the seizure of the German island of Borkum as a stepping stone to the invasion of Schleswig-Holstein, or an attack on the Dardanelles, forcing a passage to Constantinople, the capital of Germany's ally Turkey. In early

74-year-old Lord Fisher. This was a controversial appointment – George V would have blocked it if he could. Yet Churchill was sure Fisher was the man to reinvigorate the Navy. Everyone knew Fisher would be difficult to work with. He was eccentric, bad-tempered, domineering and unpredictable. But Churchill was convinced he could handle the tempestuous old sailor. It was a decision he would live to regret.

At first cooperation between these two forceful men went well. Churchill's enthusiasm for the Admiralty was reborn. He habitually worked from eight in the morning until two o'clock at night, with an hour's siesta to keep him fresh in the middle of the day. Fisher started work in the early hours of the morning, but faded in the afternoon. Between them, they maintained the watch virtually 24 hours a day.

The first crisis faced by the new Admiralty team displayed Fisher's best qualities. On 3 November, the cruisers *Monmouth* and *Good Hope* were destroyed by Admiral von Spee at the battle of Coronel in the South Pacific. Fisher organized a swift and decisive response and four of von Spee's five ships were sunk off the Falkland Islands on 8 December.

LEFT: *Prince Louis of Battenburg, the First Sea Lord whose German origins made him the obvious scapegoat for naval failures.*

RIGHT: *A zeppelin shot down during a raid on England. Air defences were non-existent at the start of the war, so Churchill interpreted his brief to prevent zeppelin raids in an entirely offensive spirit.*

BELOW: *The four Allied commanders at Gallipoli, from left to right, Admiral Boue de Lapeyrere of the French Navy; General Sir Ian Hamilton, the British commander of ground forces; Admiral Sir John de Robeck of the Royal Navy; and General Bailloud, French Army.*

January 1915 the issue was settled by an urgent request from the Russian commander in chief for an Allied diversionary attack on Turkey to relieve pressure on his southern flank. Churchill induced the naval commander in the eastern Mediterranean, Vice Admiral Carden, reluctantly to agree that it might be possible to force the Dardanelles strait.

The War Council authorized a naval operation to occupy the Gallipoli peninsula and sail on up to Constantinople.

Churchill was not the originator of this plan, but he made it his own. The Dardanelles became his obsession. He was convinced that if Constantinople fell, Russia would be reinforced, the Balkan

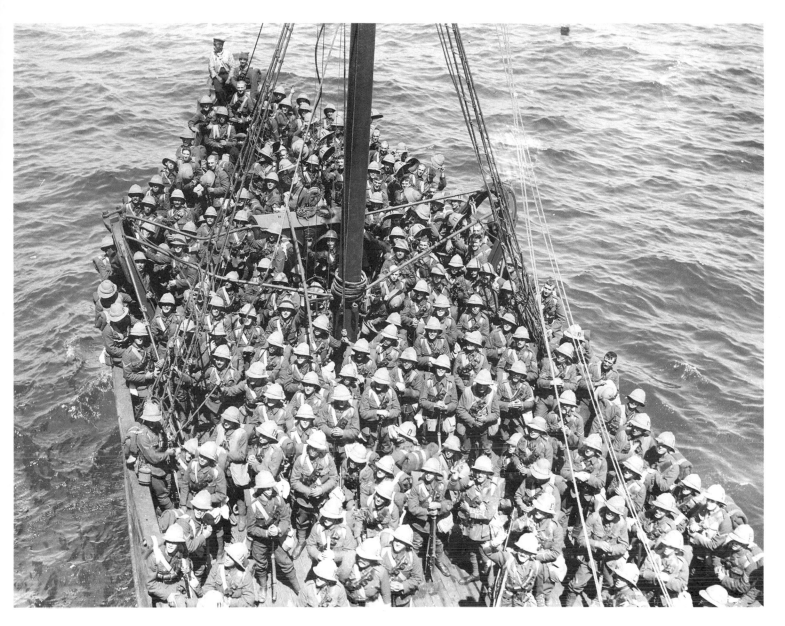

countries would unite behind the Allied cause, and somehow this would lead to the collapse of Austria and Germany. Some of his colleagues were less convinced. Fisher had been an advocate of the Borkum scheme. He privately thought the Dardanelles could only be taken with the support of 150,000 troops, yet acquiesced in the plan for an attack by the Navy alone. Kitchener backed the operation, yet at first refused to provide any troops. During February he changed his mind twice, and finally agreed to send a military force of about 40,000 men, to be commanded by General Ian Hamilton. Through all this prevarication, only Churchill pressed steadfastly and consistently for the urgent deployment of adequate forces, devoting all his formidable powers of oratory to the task of invigorating his lukewarm colleagues. Now he had embarked on a bold enterprise, his joy was unbounded. He told Violet Asquith:

I think a curse should rest on me because I am so happy. I know this war is smashing and shattering the lives of thousands every moment and yet – I cannot help it – I enjoy every second I live.

A curse on him perhaps there was. The operation was plagued by delays, poor organization and by bad luck. The initial naval bombardment of the forts guarding the strait, begun on 19 February, proceeded without a hitch for almost a month until 18 March when, with the Turkish guns almost silenced and victory in sight, the Anglo-French naval force ran into a line of uncleared mines; three battleships were sunk and two others crippled. The commander of the force, Admiral Sir John de Robeck, lost his nerve. Churchill wanted to order him to resume the offensive, but Fisher adamantly refused, substituting a mere recommendation of action which de Robeck chose to ignore. Fisher henceforth obstructed the operation in every way possible; Churchill had to fight for 'every officer, every man, every ship, every round of ammunition required for the Dardanelles.' Hopes of success now lay with the Army. But the landings on Gallipoli were delayed until 25 April, by which time the enemy was fully prepared to resist them. The landing force sustained heavy losses and the operation was immediately bogged down in the same stalemate of trench warfare as on the Western front.

The prospect of failure loomed and the War Council was riven by recriminations. Fisher declared he was opposed to the whole operation and always had been. Kitchener threatened to withdraw the land

ABOVE: *Men of the Lancashire Fusilier Brigade prepare to land at Gallipoli, 5-6 May 1915. Compromise and delay undermined the operation, which resulted in a bloody stalemate rather than the swift victory originally envisaged.*

forces if he could not depend on the support of the Navy. Churchill, still unwavering in his objective, told Asquith he would overrule Fisher if he persisted in blocking a forward policy at Gallipoli. 'I cannot undertake to be paralysed,' he wrote, 'by the veto of a friend who, whatever the result, will certainly say, "I was always against the Dardenelles."'

That Churchill still referred to Fisher as 'a friend' on 14 May 1915 shows how naive he could be about people. Himself lacking in duplicity, he could not

RIGHT: *Churchill in a determined mood, fighting for his political life in the crisis of 1915.*

RIGHT: *Churchill in a determined mood, fighting for his political life in the crisis of 1915.*

BELOW: *Now Chancellor of the Duchy of Lancaster, Churchill addresses munitions workers at Enfield in September 1915. His wife is seated to his right – she was soon to take up voluntary work providing proper canteens in munitions factories.*

recognize it in others. Clementine had long warned him about Fisher's behaviour, which was both increasingly odd and personally vindictive. Once, when Churchill was visiting Army commanders in Paris, the old admiral had told her that her husband was in reality spending his time with a French mistress, a lie apparently made up on the spot out of pure malice. A natural autocrat, Fisher deeply resented Churchill's predominant influence in the Admiralty. He could not resist the force of Churchill's personality or the strength and eloquence of his arguments. Jealous and resentful, he had convinced himself that Churchill was 'a bigger danger than the Germans.'

On 15 May, Fisher resigned. To stop Churchill finding him, he announced he was leaving for Scotland, then went into hiding at the Charing Cross hotel 200 yards from Admiralty House. There he was eventually discovered and ordered by Asquith to resume his post. Churchill offered to discuss any outstanding differences and begged him to return. But reconciliation was impossible. Fisher demanded complete control of the Admiralty as the price for withdrawing his resignation. Asquith dismissed this as megalomania and accepted that Fisher would have to go.

Churchill's position was now precarious. The setbacks at Gallipoli and a separate scandal about shortages of shells on the Western front had raised much criticism of the government's handling of the war to fever pitch. No one was more abused than Churchill, the favourite whipping-boy of the Tory press, now blamed for Gallipoli, as well as for the Antwerp escapade and every misfortune suffered by the Navy

since the war began. Fisher's resignation was the last straw. The Conservatives in Parliament had so far officially supported the Liberal government in its prosecution of the war, but Bonar Law made it clear to Asquith that if Fisher resigned and Churchill remained in place, his party would withdraw its support from the government. Under pressure to maintain national unity at all costs, Asquith entered into negotiations with the Tories for a coalition. This meant sacrificing Churchill.

On 20 May, Asquith wrote to Churchill: 'You must take it as settled you are not to remain at the Admiralty.' Churchill fired back a six-page plea for a reprieve. 'It is not . . . my own interest and advancement which moves me,' he wrote. 'I am clinging to my *task* and to my *duty*.' Clementine also pleaded on his behalf in an eloquent letter to Asquith:

Winston may in your eyes . . . have faults but he has the supreme quality which I venture to say very few of your present or future cabinet possess – the power, the imagination, the deadliness to fight Germany.

It was all in vain. In the new coalition government Churchill was relegated to a virtual sinecure as Chancellor of the Duchy of Lancaster. As a consolation, he retained his seat in the cabinet and on the War Council, which was reconstituted as the Dardanelles Committee. However, this barely softened the blow.

In retrospect, there was nothing surprising in Churchill's downfall. Asquith, very perceptive in such matters, had long felt doubts about Churchill's political future. He was struck by the fact that Churchill had 'no personal following.' This was dangerous for a man who had made many enemies. 'He will never get to the top in English politics,' Asquith wrote, 'with all his wonderful gifts; to speak with the tongues of men and angels, and to spend laborious days and nights in administration, is no good if a man does not inspire trust.' Everyone recognized his drive and his exceptional abilities. Yet he was distrusted by the Liberals and hated by the Tories. For this isolation and unpopularity, Churchill was himself in large part to blame. He had earnt his reputation for rashness and irresponsibility by some very ill-judged gestures – of which Sidney Street and Antwerp were the most unnecessary. He simply did not understand other people enough to calculate their response to his words or deeds. He was constantly surprised by their reactions.

Once Churchill's imagination was fired by a project, he would ride roughshod over all opposition. If he could imagine a thing done, then it must be feasible. The Gallipoli debacle occurred because, instead of listening to contrary opinion, Churchill used his capacity for tireless argument and his limitless enthusiasm to get his way regardless. He did not really win the doubters over to his side, he merely steam-rollered them into acquiescence. He drove them ahead in a project to which they were not really committed – hence the disastrous hesitations and half measures that followed.

For the last 20 years Churchill's life had been a brilliant sequence of victories. Now he felt betrayed and humiliated. He did not lose his self-belief or regret his past actions, every one of which he was prepared to defend. But the change in his life was sudden and extreme. With no department to run, he was flung from frantic activity into virtual unemployment. Churchill found the exact image for his situation: 'Like a sea-beast fished up from the depths,' he wrote, 'or a diver too suddenly hoisted, my veins threatened to burst from the fall in pressure.'

As First Lord, Churchill had lived in regal style with a private train always ready to carry him to Dover, a destroyer on call to take him across the Channel. Now he and his family were put out of the Admiralty and his income was virtually halved. As an economy measure he moved his family in with his brother Jack's household at 41 Cromwell Road. Constant vituperative attacks were made upon him in the press and he was powerless to defend himself, since the details of Gallipoli and the decisions leading up to it were still secret. He suffered deep depression, the 'Black Dog' that he was to fear all his life. His haggard, defeated appearance worried his family and friends. Clementine thought he would simply 'die of grief.'

By good chance, at this darkest hour he discovered a new interest that was a balm to his wounds. At the end of May, staying in a small rented house near Godalming that the Churchills had taken as a holiday retreat, he observed his sister-in-law Goonie painting with watercolours and decided to try his hand. He quickly changed to oils and under the guidance of a London neighbour, the artist John Lavery, developed the beginnings of a passable amateur technique. Violet Asquith, observing Churchill painting for the first time that June, noted that it was the only occupation she had ever seen him practise in silence. It was the silence of pure delight. His enthusiasm for painting was to last the rest of his life, and he hoped it would continue in Heaven also, where orange and vermilion would be 'the dullest, darkest colours.'

His real consolation should have been his power still to pursue the Gallipoli operation. But here all was disaster. In July, last-minute opposition from Tories in the cabinet stopped him making a planned visit to the Dardanelles to assess the situation at first hand. Resistance to continuing the operation mounted. A further landing at Suvla Bay in August was a costly failure. Churchill stubbornly held out for one more push, but he was hardly listened to. It was only a matter of time before the whole operation would be abandoned.

Churchill could not bear being excluded from the war and now his mind turned increasingly to the

BELOW: *Although when he arrived at the front Churchill was only a major on attachment to the Grenadier Guards, generals treated him with the respect due to a famous politician. Here he visits the French 33rd Corps in December 1915; General Fayolle is on his left.*

possibility of serving at the front. He envisaged a senior command and asked the prime minister to make him a major general. Asquith refused, knowing that neither the Army nor public opinion would stand for it. Churchill legitimately held the rank of major in the Oxfordshire Yeomanry.

In early November, Asquith constructed a new, smaller Dardanelles Committee; Churchill was excluded. On 11 November he resigned. In his letter to Asquith, he wrote:

I could not accept a position of general responsibility for war policy without any effective share in its guidance or control. . . . Nor do I feel in times like these able to remain in well-paid inactivity. I therefore ask you to submit my resignation to the King. I am an officer, and I place myself unreservedly at the disposal of the military authorities, observing that my regiment is in France.

A week later, on 18 November, Major Churchill took leave of his family and set off for the front.

This was a gesture even Churchill's worst enemies found it hard to ridicule, although sceptics suggested he would immediately be installed in a safe and comfortable staff post, or promoted well above his proper rank and given precedence over officers with far greater experience. This almost happened. When Churchill arrived in France, Sir John French had him driven to General Headquarters and offered him the command of a brigade. Churchill accepted, but wisely requested first to spend a month gaining experience with a regiment in the trenches. He was sent to join the Grenadier Guards at the front near Laventie. The Guards officers were appalled to have a notorious politician imposed on them and made their hostility quite plain. The seriousness and energy with which he fulfilled his military duties soon won their respect, however. His only privileges consisted in the occasional use of the Admiralty messenger service for his letters to Clementine and the copious supply of brandy and cigars she was able to send him.

Quite fearless, Churchill found peace in the trenches after the complexities and frustrations of political life. He described the scene vividly to Clementine:

Filth and rubbish everywhere, graves built into the defences . . . feet and clothing breaking through the soil, water and muck on all sides; and about this scene in the dazzling moonlight troops of enormous rats creep and glide. . . . Amid these surroundings, aided by wet and cold, and every minor discomfort, I have found happiness and content such as I have not known for many months.

At the end of November came another of those incidents which made Churchill believe he was being preserved by a special power. He was summoned from the trenches to meet his corps commander who, in the event, never turned up; while he was off on this wild goose chase, the dug-out where he would otherwise have been sitting was completely destroyed by a German shell.

By mid-December Churchill felt his initiation into trench warfare was complete. He left the Guards and went back to GHQ in expectation of receiving the promised brigade. But the climate had changed. Sir John French was being forced out and his replacement, General Sir Douglas Haig, disliked Churchill and owed him no favours. Asquith, who had previously backed the offer of a brigade, now realized that such an unconventional promotion would be attacked by Tory MPs and the Tory press;

he suggested to Haig that he might give Churchill a battalion. Most of Churchill's friends in London, including Clementine, were relieved that he was not offered a brigade. They knew that his courageous service at the front was fast restoring his ruined public reputation and that any appearance of special favours would undo the progress that had been made towards rehabilitation. But Churchill longed for a command to match his talents and was for a time deeply depressed.

In January 1916 he was appointed colonel of the 6th battalion Royal Scots Fusiliers, taking with him as his second-in-command Sir Archibald Sinclair, a new acquaintance who was to become a lifelong friend. Joining the battalion at a section of the front known as 'Plugstreet' (Ploegsteert), Churchill flung himself into his new task with his habitual enthusiasm. The lowland Scots were less than happy to receive their new commander, whom they regarded with the deepest suspicion, but their hostility soon faded. Reading between the lines of the account later written by the battalion adjutant, it is obvious that Churchill's subordinates thought him wildly eccentric, with his bizarre projects for new earthworks (an obsession since his childhood), his unstoppable loquacity on every subject from lice to high strategy, and above all his revelling in the business of war. His remark, intended to boost morale, that 'War is a game to be played with a smiling face,' was hardly well adapted to the circumstances of the Western front. Yet all were impressed by his genuine concern for the wounded and his cheering courage under fire. By the end of his four months with the battalion, the Scots regarded him with genuine respect and affection.

RIGHT: *Field Marshal Sir Douglas Haig, who took over from French as commander of British forces on the Western Front in December 1915.*

LEFT: *Churchill and his second-in-command, Sir Archibald Sinclair, at Armentières in February 1916. The comradeship of war developed into a lifelong friendship – Sinclair later became leader of the Liberal Party and a member of Churchill's coalition government from 1940 to 1945.*

Although Churchill immersed himself in the exhausting detail of a battalion commander's task, he could not be content with such a lowly function. He longed to be back at the centre of power. Despite her fears for his safety, Clementine urged him to stay at the front and give his reputation time to recover. As usual, Churchill listened to her advice and ignored it. At the start of March he had ten days' home leave. Instead of devoting the time to his wife and family, he flung himself into discussions with a small circle of politicians and newspaper editors who urged him to speak out against the government's

mishandling of the war. Among those he met was Lord Fisher, whom he still counted among his friends.

On 7 March, Churchill spoke in the House of Commons for the first time since leaving for France the previous November. The subject of the debate was the naval estimates. Attacking the government's record in time of war is always a risky enterprise, since it can easily be portrayed as giving comfort to the enemy. But Churchill might have got away with his diatribes against the complacency and passivity of the Admiralty had he not concluded by

ABOVE: *Life in the trenches in 1916. Churchill's readiness to share such conditions, when he had the option of safety as a Member of Parliament, did much to restore his reputation with the general public and his peers.*

offering as a solution the restoration of Fisher as First Sea Lord. This suggestion was met with indignation and incredulity. It was one of the worst political miscalculations of Churchill's whole career. His friends were distressed and his enemies triumphant. The goodwill generated by his bravery at the front was dissipated at a stroke.

Despite this setback, Churchill remained determined to resume his political career. At the end of April, his battalion was fused with another as part of an Army reorganization and he had to make way for a more senior colonel. This offered a suitable pretext for a return to civilian life. In early May, Churchill resumed his seat in the House of Commons. Through the summer and autumn of 1916 he strove to clear his name of the many accusations made against him over the Gallipoli operation, preparing a meticulous statement of his case for the Dardanelles Committee of Enquiry. The final outcome was inconclusive. The committee's report made it publicly clear for the first time that Asquith and Kitchener had borne much of the responsibility for the operation – it had not been a personal whim bred out of Churchill's reckless adventurism. But he was far from being entirely vindicated and the stain on his reputation stubbornly persisted.

By the time the report appeared, Churchill had suffered another disappointment. In December Asquith was ejected from the premiership and Lloyd George took his place, forming a new coalition government. Churchill fondly expected his old

colleague would invite him back into office, but the new coalition was even more dominated by Tories than the old, and they would not stomach Churchill in any post. He felt bitterly his exclusion from the conduct of the war. He wrote to his wife in May 1917: 'Never for a moment does this carnage and ruin escape my mind.' He had lost none of his self-confidence and was fully convinced that, if he could but get his hands upon the levers of power, he would help direct the war to a successful conclusion.

In the House of Commons and in the press, he urged fresh strategic concepts upon the government. As at the time of Gallipoli, his main concern was to end the fearful attrition on the Western front. His new vision was of 'a war of Machinery.' The mass production and skilful deployment of tanks and aircraft would eventually lead to victory. Until then, there should be no more costly infantry offensives. As so often with Churchill, this view was humane and imaginative, but hopelessly unrealistic. The tanks and aircraft of the day were simply not up to the task he demanded of them. There was no alternative to Haig's unimaginative use of artillery and infantry, which would eventually win the war.

Churchill made himself a great nuisance with his sharp criticism of the conduct of the war. In May 1917 Lloyd George, who in any case had a genuine respect for Churchill's abilities, decided to silence him by bringing him into the government. Tory opposition was, however, still intense. It was not until July that the prime minister felt powerful

Page 2   THE DAILY MIRROR   March 9, 1916

MR. BALFOUR ACCUSES COLONEL CHURCHILL OF WEAKENING FLEET

TERRIBLE TALE OF A BLACK EYE!

Kaiser's Government on German Boy's School Adventure.

PHANTOM MURDER.

The very dreadful case of a German boy whose eye was blackened by another child at school is included in a communication received by the British Government from the German Government covering twenty-six affidavits relating to the treatment of German women and children in England since the outbreak of war.

These affidavits, says a Foreign Office statement issued last night, are by German subjects who have returned from England to Germany, and whose evidence has been collected by the German authorities.

"The twenty-six cases produced by the German Government," says the statement, "turn out upon investigation to afford no basis for the wholesale fabrications which have been founded upon them."

DIDN'T WANT TO GO HOME.

More convincing, says the Foreign Office, than any detailed examination of the particular instances brought forward by the German Government are the broad facts: first, that although some 7,000 men, women and children have returned to Germany and Austria, the actual cases of alleged ill-usage deposed to are no more than twenty-six in number; and, second, that over 18,400 Germans and Austrians, men over military age, and women, applied to the Home Secretary in May, June and July, 1915, to be allowed to remain in the United Kingdom.

In over 15,200 cases these requests, after careful examination of the circumstances, were granted, and those whose requests were refused departed in many instances only with the greatest reluctance and after repeated entreaties to the British authorities not to be obliged to return from British to German surroundings.

LUSITANIA DAYS.

After the sinking of the Lusitania, says the statement, (and the British Government has never sought to deny it) a spontaneous outburst of popular feeling which, especially in the working-class quarters of London and Liverpool, led to regrettable manifestations.

"Delay in Completion of Capital Ships Caused by Use of Guns and Mountings for Monitors."

LORD FISHER NOT TO BE RECALLED.

Colonel Winston Churchill was last night subjected to the most withering criticism of his parliamentary career.

It came from Mr. Balfour, the First Lord of the Admiralty, who denounced in scathing terms his predecessor's speech, urging the recall of Lord Fisher as First Sea Lord.

Colonel Churchill and his Board, said Mr. Balfour, in building monitors, had used guns and mountings for them which had been designed for capital ships.

The taking of these, he said, might have been right or it might have been wrong, but it deliberately prevented the strengthening of the Grand Fleet.

MR. BALFOUR'S THRUSTS.

The chief points of Mr. Balfour's speech were :—

'Mr. Churchill's speech is unfortunate in form and substance.

The Grand Fleet is more powerful than when Mr. Churchill left office, and as months go on it will be more powerful still.

The deliberate desire to suggest doubts, fears and alarms among the public, which could not intimately know the facts, is acting contrary to the public interest.

The cause of delay in completing Dreadnoughts is due to the construction of monitors and the fact that the guns and gun-mountings designed for capital ships were used for them.

It does not, therefore, lie in the mouth of those who had weakened the Grand Fleet by creating these monitors to say to their successors, "You have delayed the building of capital ships."

The six months to which Colonel Churchill had referred had indicated that bustle, hurry and push, and all the great qualities which might sometimes be pushed to an undue extreme.

Certain ships, built in a hurry, had proved faulty in design and had had to be re-modelled.

The House listened to Colonel Churchill's

garded it as the deepest insult that could be offered me.

"If it were true it is almost high treason. I do not believe for a moment that it is true."

NO CAUSE FOR ALARM.

Colonel Churchill stepped to the table, clenched the box with both hands and leaned forward.

Straight in front of him sat Mr. Balfour, his legs crossed, his eyes fixed on the ceiling.

Colonel Churchill admitted there was no reason to suppose that our margin of strength at the present time was not sufficient; and there was no cause at the present time for alarm.

"But I have tried to bring the House and the country to a feeling that the greatest efforts must be made to carry the programme forward with the highest speed.

"It is right that a note of warning should be sounded and sounded in time.

"So far from having gone beyond what the facts of the situation justified, I have been restrained only with the strictest regard to secrecy and the public interest from making my statement in a stronger form, and this is perfectly well known to those who sit on the Treasury Bench.

"The real fact is that if the Admiralty could associate the driving power of Lord Fisher with the carrying out of Lord Fisher's programme, great public advantage would result."

MARRIED MEN UP TO 35.

Eight New Derby Groups To Be Called on April 17.

The married men included in Groups 32 to 41, whose ages range from twenty-seven to thirty-five inclusive, it is understood, will be called up on or about Monday, April 17.

Proclamations to this effect will be issued early next week.

Exemption for three months was granted yesterday by the East Ashford (Kent) Tribunal to a hairdresser, named Huckstep, of Wye, who said he was the only barber in the town, and attended 300 to 400 soldiers.

The owner of a large Wold farm, appealing

CHILDREN'S CHANCE TO HELP US WIN.

Sir Robert Blair's Booklet of 'Don'ts' and 'Do's.'

HIS BREAD SUM.

How can children help to save and win the war?

Sir Robert Blair, the distinguished education officer of the London County Council, has issued a little booklet of "Don'ts" and "Do's," which is to help parents and teachers in economy talks to children. And grown-ups, too, can pay heed to this sage advice. Here are some of Sir Robert Blair's "Don'ts" and "Do's."

Don't go to picture palaces.
Don't throw away empty bottles or jam pots, but give or sell them to people who will use them.

Be careful not to waste bread or other kinds of food.

Do take the trouble to cook well, so as to make the food taste nice and go further.
Do be careful of your clothes, and mend them instead of buying new ones.
Do be careful of things at school—like paper, pencils, and even ink.

"These are just a few suggestions of the sort of things which you might save," says Sir Robert Blair, "but you will be able to think of many more.

BREAKFAST TABLE PROBLEMS.

Thirty thousand of the booklets, *The Daily Mirror* understands, are being distributed among the London County Council schools this week, but a copy should be in every home and in the hands of every teacher in the country.

Sir Robert Blair suggests that pupils should be asked to come to school with a list of things which they think they could do without and of ways in which they could avoid waste.

"As to our little bits of saving being not worth troubling about," says Sir Robert Blair, "we can easily get rid of this difficulty by doing a little sum in arithmetic.

"There are, roughly speaking, forty-five millions of us, so that a very little saving by each of us comes to a fairly big sum. If we each save a penny, that is £187,500.

"Here is a sum for you to do. If each of the forty-five millions of us wastes a piece of bread three inches square by half an inch thick, how big a bit of bread does that make altogether?"

ABOVE: *Churchill's dramatic return to political life in March 1916 was a total debâcle. He was trounced by his successor, Arthur Balfour, in debate, and his call for Lord Fisher's reinstatement as First Sea Lord was received with incredulity.*

LEFT: *Prime Minister Lloyd George on a tour of the Western Front. Juggling conflicting forces in a coalition cabinet, Lloyd George was in no hurry to bring Churchill back into the government, despite the claims of friendship from the past.*

NO "BUTTER"

'BUYING · A · HAT'

THRILLS

HIS GREAT
JUGGLING FEAT

MILITARY
IMPERSONATIONS

ABOVE: *A savagely hostile view of Churchill in February 1918, typical of much press comment at the time.*

enough to overrule his cabinet colleagues and bring Churchill back as Minister for Munitions. The hostility of press reaction to this appointment shocked Churchill and brought an access of unwonted humility. Kept under control by Lloyd George and by his watchful Tory colleagues, he concentrated almost

all his energies on the specific tasks of his ministry. He proved himself once more a masterful administrator. Supplies to the front improved, as even Haig was reluctantly forced to admit.

One of the most difficult problems Churchill faced was labour relations. Militant shop stewards in the munitions industry agitated against employers who were making huge profits out of the war while their workers sacrificed many hard-won rights in the patriotic drive for higher output. Churchill was highly critical of the employers and inclined to trust the patriotism of the workforce. He reinstated shop stewards dismissed for leading strikes, raised wages and pursued conciliation wherever possible. Only once, in July 1918, he reacted aggressively against a wave of stoppages, threatening strikers with conscription. It proved unnecessary to carry out the threat.

Churchill expanded production in three areas he considered vital to win the war: tanks, aircraft and poisoned gas (by the summer of 1918, one-third of all shells being fired by the British Army were gas shells). He wanted cavalry to abandon 'the obsolete horse' – 'Make catmeat of those foolish animals,' he wrote to the cavalry officer Sir Archibald Sinclair – and transfer to tanks, armoured cars and motorcycles. Haig rightly disapproved of Churchill's naive obsession with new, untried technology, but appreciated his success with munitions and welcomed his visits to France for consultations. He put at Churchill's disposal the impressive Chateau Verchocq near St Omer. From this base Churchill was able to tour the battle zone and witness some of the fighting in the desperate battles of 1918.

These trips to France involved considerable risk. Churchill had once more taken to the air, being flown back and forth by a Communications Squadron he had himself established. On 7 July his aircraft almost ran out of fuel before reaching the English coast and Churchill, in his own words, 'very nearly finished an eventful though disappointing life in the salt waters of the channel.' The tours of the front, often conducted in the Duke of Westminster's splendid Rolls-Royce, were equally hazardous. Churchill could never resist setting off in the direction of gunfire. On several occasions the car was shelled and once its occupants narrowly escaped being gassed. Evidently, this was all great fun.

The rapidity of the final German collapse took Churchill by surprise, as it did most Allied leaders. For the duration of the war, he had taken up residence in the Ministry of Munitions building in Northumberland Avenue, and it was from there that he watched the crowds pour into the streets on 11 November for the wildest outbreak of popular rejoicing ever witnessed in Britain. Clementine, pregnant once more as she had been when war was declared four years earlier, joined him and together they drove through the cheering throng to congratulate Lloyd George at Downing Street.

Although Churchill's political fortunes had recovered from the nadir of Gallipoli, the war had been a grave personal disappointment for him. In the public view he was confirmed as a gifted but irresponsible eccentric who could not be trusted with the highest office at time of crisis. Still only 44 years old, he had a past to live down and little prospect of fulfilling his highest aspirations.

ABOVE: *Shell-filling in a munitions factory. Churchill's efficiency and drive at the ministry of munitions achieved his political rehabilitation, although doubts about his character and his fitness for the highest office persisted.*

CHAPTER SIX

Back to the Tory Fold

LEFT: *Churchill in his early 50s, depicted by Walter Sickert. As a Conservative Chancellor of the Exchequer, his radical days were well behind him.*

Iɴ the general election held immediately after the end of the war, Churchill successfully defended his Dundee constituency as a Coalition Liberal. Most coalition candidates played upon the hysterical jingoism of the moment and whipped up a clamour for vengeance against Germany. Churchill resisted these popular sentiments. Until the moment of victory, no one had been more absolute for war. But once the armistice was declared, his thoughts turned immediately to helping 'the fallen foe.' He advocated rushing 'a dozen great ships crammed with provisions' into Hamburg to prevent starvation. He rejected the call to 'Hang the Kaiser' and suggested moderation in demands for financial reparations. It was essential to avoid reducing 'the mass of the working class population of Germany to sweated labour and servitude.' Only treating Germany according to the principles of justice, freedom and humanity, he argued, would guarantee peace and prosperity.

While rejecting the outcry for revenge, Churchill embraced the second great popular theme of the election, Lloyd George's pledge to make Britain 'a fit country for heroes to live in.' Churchill had not ditched radicalism. He advocated nationalization of the railways, confiscation of excess war profits, heavy taxation of unearned incomes and a guaranteed minimum standard of living for the masses. These were not, unfortunately, the policies of most of his political colleagues. A landslide victory for the coalition resulted in a House of Commons with a large preponderance of Conservatives. These were mostly, in Stanley Baldwin's phrase, 'hard-faced men who . . . had done very well out of the war.' They were not about to embrace a pre-war Liberal radicalism.

When Lloyd George formed his new government in January 1919, he appointed Churchill Secretary of State for War (and Air). Churchill grumbled about the uselessness of being war secretary without a war; the ever-hostile Bonar Law retorted that if they had thought there was going to be a war they wouldn't have appointed him. In fact, peace had not yet broken out everywhere. Postwar chaos offered plenty of scope for all of Churchill's most active tendencies.

He took up his new post in the middle of a major crisis over demobilization. The War Office had decided that only soldiers with skills needed in essential industries and those with definite offers of jobs would be released immediately. This decision caused great resentment among troops eager to return to civilian life. There were mutinies in camps at Calais and Folkestone and the Army commanders

BELOW: *At the end of October 1918, Churchill observes a march past of British troops in Lille, northern France. Behind him on his left, clutching a bowler hat, is the omnipresent Eddie Marsh.*

sweated at visions of Bolshevik revolution, a disaffected soldiery turning its arms against its officers. Churchill attacked the problem with unaccustomed calmness and common sense. He calculated that a million men were needed to fulfill Britain's widespread commitments during the peace negotiations. The other two and a half million troops were to be demobilized according to the universally understood principle of 'first in, first out' – all those who had signed up before 1916 would be released as soon as possible. Demobilization proceeded without further difficulty and was completed by October 1919.

The appendage of the air ministry to Churchill's responsibilities as Secretary for War was much criticized as overburdening a single minister, but Churchill naturally welcomed it. He appointed Sir Hugh Trenchard as Chief of Air Staff and between them the two men strove successfully to defend the independence of the Royal Air Force against the claims of the Army and Navy. Civil aviation was neglected in favour of military aviation, which Churchill saw as the key to an economical policing of far-flung outposts of Empire. A small number of air bases, defended by armoured cars, would maintain control of large underpopulated areas, carrying out swift punitive raids against restive tribesmen (with the use of mustard gas bombs, rather oddly described by Churchill as 'a scientific expedient for sparing life'). This policy was pursued most thoroughly in Mesopotamia (Iraq), where overall responsibility for defence was transferred from the Army to the RAF, allowing a substantial cut in expenditure.

Churchill's personal interest in flying was still lively and in the summer of 1919 he resumed his training for a pilot's licence, interrupted five years

ABOVE: *'Winnie' caricatured by Bert Thomas in December 1919 – a man in a hurry at odds with the world.*

earlier by his wife's pleas. At Croydon on 18 July, he lost control of his aircraft and nose-dived into the ground at 50mph. His instructor had the presence of mind to turn the engine off a split second before they crashed, otherwise both men would have been incinerated. The instructor was nevertheless seriously injured. Although Churchill escaped with cuts and bruises, this incident finally persuaded him to abandon his aerial ambitions for good.

Churchill's chief preoccupation throughout his period as Secretary for War was the situation in Russia. After the 1917 Bolshevik revolution Britain and its allies had hesitantly committed themselves to a measure of military intervention in support of anti-Bolshevik forces. This had initially been aimed at bringing Russia back into the war against Germany, but after the armistice it was pursued simply as an attempt to overthrow the revolutionary regime. Chastened by criticism of his hot-headed adventurism, Churchill was always careful to point out that he had taken no part in initiating British military involvement in Russia. But he took over the campaign against Bolshevism as his personal crusade.

Churchill was never a moderate man or restrained in the expression of his opinions, but there is a bitterness and extremism in his attacks on Bolshevism at this period that stands out from his habitual style. His turn of phrase was unusually coarse and brutal. Bolshevism was 'the Black Death or the Spotted Typhus,' a 'tapeworm,' 'baboonery.' The animal image Churchill used again and again, as if he was especially proud of it: for instance, the Bolsheviks 'hop and caper like troops of ferocious baboons amid the ruins of cities and the corpses of their victims.' Usually completely free of anti-semitism, he denounced 'the tyrannic government of the Jew

commissars' and alleged that Trotsky would establish a 'worldwide communist state under Jewish domination.' This was a line of argument Goebbels was to perfect.

It is quite understandable that Churchill should have hated Bolshevism, for it was against everything he believed in: rule by parliamentary democracy, individual freedom, humane restraint in the exercise of power, the established social order with its historic ruling class steeped in tradition. But Churchill's inflamed imagination took him far beyond the limits of balanced reason or common sense, aligning him on this issue with the reactionary right-wing of British politics. Worst of all, he completely misunderstood the nature of the forces at work inside Russia. His information on the situation there came from his contacts with the British Secret Intelligence Service and bizarre Russian anti-Bolsheviks such as the ex-revolutionary assassin, Boris Savinkov. These sources assured him the Bolsheviks had no popular support and that the White armies opposing Lenin were popular and democratic. Churchill believed them because this was what he wanted to believe. As at Gallipoli, he let wishful thinking undermine his judgment.

His persistence in pursuing military intervention in Russia, in the face of the indifference or hostility of the prime minister, most of his cabinet colleagues, the press and the British public, was folly on an heroic scale. Told that conscripts would not accept service in Russia, he called on volunteers. He advocated turning the German Army against the Russians – 'Kill the Bolshie, Kiss the Hun.' Ordered by the cabinet in March 1919 to withdraw British forces from north Russia, he pressed the case for an advance to protect the retreat. He handed over surplus war supplies worth £100 million to Admiral Kolchak in Siberia and General Denikin in the south. Elements of the RAF were sent in to help Denikin, with instructions only to stop short of bombing Moscow, and the Royal Navy supported anti-Bolshevik military operations in the Baltic and the Black Sea. Despite Denikin's notorious pogroms against the Jews, Churchill persisted in regarding him as a liberal democrat. When the Bolsheviks looked like being defeated in October 1919, Churchill sent a British general to supervise the occupation of Petrograd and planned a visit himself to direct the drawing up of a new Russian constitution. His friend Lord Riddell quipped that if he went to Petrograd he 'might become Tsar.'

The defeat and disintegration of the anti-Bolshevik armies at the end of 1919 did not deter Churchill from pursuing his obsession, but opinion was now so firmly set against any further military aid to anti-Bolsheviks that his fulminations had no effect. When

BELOW: *As Colonial Secretary, Churchill hosts the Commission on Mesopotamia. He played an important role in the reshaping of the Middle East after World War I.*

ABOVE: *A survivor of the massacre at Amritsar in July 1920, when 300 Indian demonstrators were killed by British troops. Churchill denounced the massacre as a sinister departure from 'the British way of doing things.'*

to recognize their legitimate claims to a measure of self-determination which his political principles should have led him to support. His vision of Empire was still the Liberal vision: in one of his finest speeches, in July 1920, he denounced the Amritsar massacre, in which British troops had killed some 300 unarmed Indian demonstrators, as 'an event which stands in singular and sinister isolation,' an aberration from 'the British way of doing things.' 'Our reign in India,' he correctly stated, 'has never stood on the basis of physical force alone.' But he failed to see that the only alternative to coercion in the future was to trust the nationalists.

In February 1921, Churchill moved from the War Ministry to become Colonial Secretary. At almost the same time, the death of a childless distant cousin in a railway accident in Wales brought him his first – and only – significant inherited wealth, giving him a reliable unearned income of £4000 a year. He found this dual change in his circumstances very much to his taste, and his wife rejoiced to receive a measure of relief from her constant worries about money. Clementine had been considerably worn down by the experience of the war and by the strain of running a household of four noisy undisciplined children – the youngest, Marigold, born in November 1918 – with little help from a husband who, although in principle devoted to his family, was always busy with work and preferred to spend much of his holidays with his aristocratic friends, painting, gambling and hunting wild boar in the south of France. It was in a mood of relief and celebration that Clementine arranged to accompany Churchill on an official visit to Cairo and Jerusalem in March 1921.

The trip was a public and private success. The Cairo Conference organized the large areas of the former Turkish empire acquired by Britain at the end of the war into three new states under British mandate – Iraq, Trans-Jordan (now Jordan) and Palestine. Churchill disliked Arabs, but advised by Colonel T. E. Lawrence, soon one of his greatest admirers, he installed members of the Sherifian ruling family of Arabia in power everywhere except Palestine. Here, Britain's commitment to a Jewish homeland, which Churchill faithfully upheld, was an insuperable bone of contention with the local Arab population. In between business, there was time for sightseeing trips, including a tour of the pyramids during which Churchill fell off a camel.

The Churchills returned from the Middle East in good spirits, but the rest of the year was blackened by a series of personal tragedies. In April, Clementine's brother Bill inexplicably committed suicide, shooting himself in a hotel bedroom in Paris. The next to be mourned was Churchill's mother, Jennie. After the breakdown of her marriage to Cornwallis-West in 1913, this indomitable woman had once more shown her superb disregard for social opinion by marrying an even younger man, Montagu Porch – he was in his early forties, she was 64. In the summer of 1921, precariously balanced on fashionable high heels, she fell down a staircase, injuring her leg. Gangrene set in and the leg had to be amputated. After courageously enduring great pain,

all hope of overthrowing the Bolshevik government was past, he still opposed every move to create normal relations with the Soviet regime. After the first Soviet trade delegation came to London in 1920, the unrepentant Churchill asked Lord Curzon contemptuously: 'Did you shake hands with the hairy baboon?'

Lloyd George was exasperated by Churchill's endless harping on the Bolshevik threat. In an irritable moment he described him as 'the only remaining specimen of a real Tory.' The impression made on the general public was worse. Churchill was confirmed as an irresponsible warmonger and an arch-reactionary. As Labour MP Emanuel Shinwell later remembered, 'Nobody in British politics during the early 1920s inspired more dislike in Labour circles than Winston Churchill.' But he was little better liked elsewhere. The chief of the imperial general staff, Sir Henry Wilson, wrote of Churchill in his diary: 'His judgment is always at fault, and he is hopeless when in power.'

Churchill's judgment of events throughout the Empire was biassed by his obsession with the international Bolshevik conspiracy. Everywhere there were nationalist movements – in Ireland, Egypt, India – he detected the hand of Bolshevism. This led him to underrate and disparage nationalists, failing

she died of a haemorrhage on 29 June. Churchill was still grieving for his mother when the family suffered an even more painful loss. In August the youngest child Marigold developed a throat infection which turned to septicaemia. Medicine had not yet devised a remedy and the little girl died while her parents looked helplessly on.

Churchill's political duties made small allowance for grief. The critical situation in Ireland demanded the lion's share of his time and energy throughout this tragic year. Since 1919 a Sinn Fein government in Dublin had claimed to rule an independent Irish Republic. The British authorities had fought an increasingly brutal war against the Irish Republican Army (IRA) in an attempt to regain control of Ireland. As Secretary for War during 1919 and 1920, Churchill was largely responsible for setting up the Black and Tans and the Auxiliaries, recruited from demobbed British soldiers, who earned a fearsome reputation as the scourge of the Catholic population. He publicly defended the punitive measures and indiscriminate reprisals which were the British response to IRA attacks, and as usual detected the hand of Bolshevism behind the Republican campaign.

As Colonial Secretary during 1921 and 1922, however, Churchill had the opportunity to demonstrate

ABOVE: *Churchill on camelback during his visit to Cairo in March 1921. On his right is Clementine, and on his left Gertrude Bell, traveller and archaeologist, and T. E. Lawrence – 'Lawrence of Arabia'.*

LEFT: *Churchill's mother at the age of 60. She died in 1921 after much suffering bravely borne.*

RIGHT: *The Black and Tans, tough ex-soldiers who instigated a reign of terror in Ireland during the struggle with the IRA in 1919-21.*

FAR RIGHT: *'The Big Fellow' Michael Collins (right) with other Sinn Fein leaders in 1922.*

BELOW: *The Black and Tans in action, arresting a Sinn Fein suspect. Churchill approved of their brutal methods, endorsing retaliatory murders as justified when combatting a guerrilla enemy.*

his skills as a peacemaker rather than a warmonger – to abandon what Clementine called 'the rough iron-fisted "Hunnish" way' to which he was sometimes too prone. He was an advocate of moderation in the summer of 1921, when the cabinet faced the stark choice between a full-scale military campaign in Ireland and negotiation with Republican leaders engaged in armed rebellion against the Crown. Churchill favoured a truce followed by negotiations, a view which carried the day. He then played a leading role in protracted talks with Sinn Fein representatives in London, including Michael Collins, the adjutant-general of the IRA. The personal trust established between Collins and Churchill was one of the most important elements allowing progress toward a settlement. Agreement on a 'Treaty between Great Britain and Ireland' was finally reached in December 1921. Ireland was to have Dominion status within the British Empire, as the 'Irish Free State.' Sinn Fein accepted the temporary *de facto* existence of a separate Northern Ireland; a neat formula was found to release them from the need to swear allegiance to the Crown. Churchill presented the treaty to the House of Commons in one of his finest speeches, both tactful in allaying the fears of Tory diehards and fervent in his plea for an end to 'implacable quarrels.'

Southern Ireland now came under the Colonial Office and Churchill had the task of overseeing the full implementation of the treaty by both sides. It was not at all evident at first that the settlement would succeed. Sinn Fein was split almost equally between supporters of Collins who accepted the treaty and supporters of De Valera who held out for a united Republican Ireland. Right-wing Tories at

Westminster and their Ulster Protestant allies refused to believe in Collins' good faith and looked forward to a further chance to crush Sinn Fein when the agreement collapsed. Churchill had to pilot all the necessary legislation through the House of Commons, deploying his highest rhetorical skills to convince the majority that vital British interests were not being sacrificed and that the new Irish government was capable of bringing order out of chaos. In Dublin, Churchill backed Collins to the hilt. He insisted that the Irish leader must take decisive action against the anti-treaty Republicans who were controlling parts of the country in armed defiance of the provisional government. When Collins went on to the offensive, Churchill provided him with ample supplies of armoured cars, shells and guns from British stores.

Churchill's performance on Ireland was not without blemish. He envisaged that Ireland would eventually be united under one government and he strove to bring Collins and the Northern Ireland Prime Minister, Sir James Craig, together. But he did nothing to stop the blatant gerrymandering in the North which denied many Catholics their democratic rights, and his response to the Protestant B Specials' campaign of assassination and intimidation of Catholics in Belfast was uncharacteristically feeble. Nevertheless, before his death in an ambush

in August 1922, Michael Collins left this message for Churchill: 'Tell Winston we could never have done anything without him.'

BELOW: *Chartwell, Kent, Churchill's country home for more than 40 years.*

ABOVE: *Lloyd George (seated, in the light suit) heads his cabinet in a meeting with French leaders in February 1922. Marshal Pétain is on the Prime Minister's left. Sitting next to Churchill is Arthur Balfour, one of the Conservative majority in the cabinet. Lloyd George's uncomfortable coalition was to collapse within seven months of this photo being taken.*

Involvement in Irish affairs, then as now, brought with it the risk of terrorist attack. After the assassination of Sir Henry Wilson by the IRA in London on 22 June 1922, Churchill took extensive precautions. He travelled around in an armour-plated car with bullet-proof windows, accompanied at all times by armed detectives. At home he kept his service revolver to hand day and night and had an armchair reinforced with metal plate to provide a shield in case of a shootout. One may suspect he was secretly disappointed that no would-be assassin ever came.

Churchill's performance at the Colonial Office won him many admirers, both for his powerful speeches in the House of Commons and his evident administrative ability, but the ghost of Gallipoli was still unexorcised. In September 1922 a storm blew up once more around the Dardanelles. Against Churchill's advice, Lloyd George had insisted in following an anti-Turkish policy since the war. The Greeks had been encouraged to attack the Turkish

nationalist forces of Mustapha Kemal and an Allied occupation force controlled a 'neutral zone' around the Dardanelles. Now the Greeks had been routed and Kemal's forces advanced on the small contingent of British troops at Chanak on the eastern edge of the zone. Lloyd George was spoiling for a fight and Churchill unwisely rallied to the cause of defending his beloved straits. All that blood had been shed to wrest this waterway from the Turks during the war: was it now to be handed back to them without a struggle?

Popular feeling in Britain and the Dominions was hostile to any new war. Once more, Churchill was denounced as a warmonger and lambasted for the irresponsible pursuit of a personal obsession. The 'war party' in the cabinet found themselves politically isolated and it was fortunate that the commander of the British troops on the spot, General Harington, ignored their instructions to fire on the Turkish troops.

The Chanak crisis was in the end resolved peacefully, but it destroyed the government coalition. The Conservatives had for some time been growing restive under Lloyd George's leadership and they now determined to force a general election that they would fight under their own banner. Churchill was left stranded. He owed little allegiance to either wing of the enfeebled Liberal Party, hopelessly split between supporters of Lloyd George and Asquith, and his relations with the bulk of the Conservative Party remained hostile. He desperately floated the idea of a National Party that would unite Liberal and Conservative elements against the reactionary right and the socialist left, but found no takers. He had to fight the election in no man's land – a Liberal appealing to Conservatives for support.

In mid-October, just as the election campaign got under way, Churchill was struck down with appendicitis. Clementine, who had given birth to her last child, Mary, only the previous month, was obliged to travel up to Dundee and make speeches on his behalf, in the face of some very hostile crowds. According to one observer: 'Clemmie appeared in a string of pearls. The women spat on her.' Churchill put in a convalescent but typically abrasive appearance before the end of the campaign, to no avail. He was humiliatingly beaten into fourth place, the two seats going to a socialist and a prohibitionist – a most thorough-going rejection of his deepest-held beliefs. His description of his fallen state is justly famous: 'In the twinkling of an eye,' he wrote, 'I found myself without an office, without a seat, without a party and without an appendix.'

In partial compensation for this comprehensive divestment, Churchill had acquired a country estate. His inheritance in 1921 had stimulated the search for a house in the country, and in July of that year an estate agent had shown him Chartwell manor, near Westerham in Kent. The rambling acres, looking out over a wide stretch of the Weald toward the North Downs, thrilled his ever-romantic imagination. Clementine, more practical and realistic by nature, recognized a poorly designed house in dilapidated condition. She baulked at the extreme expense of renovating an existing building riddled with dry rot and constructing new wings to remedy the defects of design. Churchill usually steamrollered opposition with a torrent of argument and obstinate persistence. In this instance, uncharacteristically, he stooped to cunning. For a while nothing more was heard of Chartwell and Clementine believed the project had been shelved. Then, in September 1922, Churchill suddenly announced that he had secretly bought the property for £5000. His wife had to bow to the *fait accompli*.

All her misgivings about Chartwell were fulfilled. It did prove astonishingly expensive both to reconstruct and to run. It was fortunate that Churchill's

YES, WE HAVE NO BANANAS

NO TINNED SALMON
NO CURRANTS
NO APPLES
NO LIME JUICE
NO HONEY
NO TOBACCO
NO SUGAR
NO TEA –

BUT WE HAVE
MORE TAXATION TO-DAY
STOP TAXING FOOD
VOTE
LABOUR

literary and journalistic output was so hugely profitable. In 1923, *The Times* began serialization of *The World Crisis*, his massive account of the recent historical events in which he had been so deeply involved (described by Balfour as 'a brilliant autobiography disguised as a history of the universe'). Paid at the rate of half-a-crown a word, it financed not only Chartwell but holidays in the south of France, dinners at the Ritz and a constant supply of champagne, brandy and cigars – but only just.

Although with his writing, his painting and the renovation of Chartwell, Churchill was hardly unoccupied, he could never be content outside of politics. *The World Crisis* was itself partly an exercise in self-vindication, a retelling of the past which would help resuscitate his own political fortunes. Whatever his personal reputation, however, the only path back to power lay in allegiance to a party. The ground base of Churchill's political attitudes was now anti-Socialism. He had notoriously described the Labour Party as 'unfit to govern.' His closest friends in politics were Tories, such as Lord Birkenhead (formerly F. E. Smith), who had been a member of Lloyd George's coalition government, and the newspaper tycoon Lord Beaverbrook (formerly Sir Max Aitken). The Conservative Party was his obvious future home.

In December 1923 the new Conservative Prime Minister Stanley Baldwin once more took up the cause of protection and called an unexpected election on the issue. As a dedicated Free Trader, Churchill had no choice but to stand as a Liberal. He fought the West Leicester constituency and lost again. When Parliament reassembled with no clear majority for any party, the Liberals allowed Labour to form its first ever government. Churchill could not tolerate this collaboration with the socialist enemy and broke off all links with the Liberal Party.

In February 1924 he made another attempted comeback, standing in Westminster for the Abbey

division as an independent anti-socialist candidate. He enjoyed the support of some prominent Conservatives, but an official Tory stood against him. After a barn-storming campaign conducted in a blaze of publicity, he lost by 43 votes. That summer, Baldwin effectively renounced protection. Nothing now stood in Churchill's way. Although he still insisted on calling himself a 'Constitutionalist,' he was adopted by the West Essex Conservative Association and, in

the general election of autumn 1924, was at last returned to Parliament with a handsome majority. He was to represent the constituency, later renamed Wansted and Woodford, for the next 40 years.

The 'Blenheim rat' was delighted to be back in the Tory fold. 'Anyone can rat,' he quipped, 'but it takes a certain amount of ingenuity to re-rat.' Accompanied by Clementine to a Conservative rally, he told his hosts: 'She's a Liberal, and always has been. It's

all very strange for her. But to me, of course, it's just like coming home.' He was even more delighted by the welcome he received. Baldwin felt, as Lloyd George had before him, that Churchill was too dangerous a man to leave outside the government. The general expectation was that he would be given some minor post to keep him quiet. When Baldwin told him he was to be Chancellor, Churchill assumed he meant 'of the Duchy of Lancaster.' 'No,' said Baldwin, 'of the Exchequer.' Churchill shed tears of gratitude. He still had his father's robe of office preserved in tissue paper and went off to unwrap it.

This extraordinarily generous appointment has never been fully explained; perhaps Baldwin believed that only a really serious post would ensure Churchill's loyalty.

Churchill is obviously open to the charge of opportunism. He had skipped from the Tories to the Liberals in 1904 just in time for a long spell of Liberal government. Now, as the Liberal Party fell irremediably into third place in the British political league, he hopped back to Conservatism. But the government in which he took his place in November 1924 could in most ways claim to be the direct inheritor of the pre-war Liberal tradition. It combined faith in a Free Trade and the free market economy with a commitment to ameliorating the conditions of the poorest members of society. It pursued peace at home and abroad. If anything, Churchill stood out as an old-fashioned Tory among these moderate Conservatives.

The difference was one of style, rather than substance. Asquith, himself a man of the Edwardian era, described Churchill as 'a Chimborazo or Everest among the sandhills of the Baldwin cabinet.' The placid pipe-smoking Baldwin, with his low-key 'fireside chats' on the wireless, epitomized the new unheroic politics of post-war British democracy. It was hard to believe that both Baldwin and the rising star of the cabinet, Neville Chamberlain, were

actually *older* than Churchill. With his high-flown rhetoric and his colourful persona, the 50-year-old Chancellor of the Exchequer seemed a survivor from an earlier age.

Churchill had always had a poor head for figures and knew nothing of economics. Chancellor from 1925 to 1929, he made his most dramatic gesture in his very first budget, when he returned sterling to the gold standard, abandoned since World War I. There is now a general consensus that maintaining the gold standard overvalued the currency, forced up interest rates and reduced exports, raising unemployment and lowering wages. At the time, however, almost all economists, apart from the maverick John Maynard Keynes, favoured it. Unable to follow the economic arguments, Churchill fell in with expert opinion. He could not avoid responsibility for the adverse consequences.

Overall, his performance as Chancellor was a curate's egg. He introduced contributory old age pensions, which almost doubled the income of the indigent elderly. He attempted to push through swingeing cuts in military spending (shades of Lord Randolph once more), but these were moderated by resistance from the service chiefs, backed by many of his Tory colleagues. As a magic formula to stimulate industry, he brought in a complex de-rating scheme that transferred most of the cost of local

BELOW: *The Chancellor of the Exchequer on his way to the House of Commons on Budget Day 1929. On his right are his parliamentary private secretary Robert Boothby and his personal detective; on his left a family group, Clementine, Sarah and Randolph.*

£10 off your tax!

THE Morris-Commercial light tonner is the *only* ton truck on the market coming within the £16 tax—all others are subject to £26. Thus the purchaser saves £10 on every vehicle annually—virtually a gift of £10 from the Chancellor of the Exchequer!

Thousands of these robust commercial vehicles are in daily use by leaders of British industry, and particularly by tradespeople, in all parts of the kingdom. It is impossible to get such value in any other commercial car. And special bodies are available for each individual trade. Ask for particulars.

There is a special body for every individual trade.

MORRIS-COMMERCIAL
Sold and Serviced— —all over the World.

government from businesses to private householders and taxpayers. He cut income tax to four shillings in the pound, but maintained death duties and supertax. For the rest, like most chancellors, he was a 'penny on, penny off' man, tinkering with the details of indirect taxes and duties in an attempt to balance the books and penalize frivolous luxury or anti-social hedonism (his betting tax, an especially unsuccessful example of this genre, provoked a bookmakers' strike). On the whole, his budget speeches were more memorable for their rhetoric than their substance. Churchill himself later had the last word on his Chancellorship, as on most things: 'Everybody said I was the worst Chancellor of the Exchequer there ever was,' he commented, continuing after a slight pause, '. . . and I am now inclined to agree with them.'

Compared with previous governments in which Churchill had participated, Baldwin's administration lived a very peaceful life. The tranquillity of the times was interrupted only once, by the eruption of the General Strike in 1926. At the beginning of May the mineowners locked out their workforce, who had refused to accept a cut in pay and longer hours.

The major national unions struck in support of the miners. Churchill sympathized with the miners' case, but regarded the general strike as a direct challenge to the existing order of society which must be resisted, with force if necessary. Once more his fighting spirit and his inflamed imagination carried him far beyond the bounds of reason or common sense. He cast the muddled and timorous leaders of the trades union general council in the unlikely role of red revolutionaries. He advocated putting machine guns and tanks on the streets to protect food convoys and he rejected compromise as weakness.

All Baldwin's instincts were for conciliation. In the hope of preventing Churchill causing too much harm, he put him in charge of producing a government newspaper, the *British Gazette*. Since Fleet Street had been closed down by the strike, the *Gazette* had an essential function to perform, keeping the public informed of new developments. Churchill chose to run it as an aggressive propaganda organ, denouncing the strikers (the majority of British trade unionists) as 'the enemy' and insistently demanding their 'unconditional surrender.' He refused to publish an appeal for conciliation from the Archbishop of Canterbury or a report of a football match between strikers and police. In the House of Commons he flaunted his bias: 'I decline utterly to be impartial as between the Fire Brigade and the fire.' Production of the newspaper, which after a week had achieved a circulation of over two million, was a considerable feat of improvisation, and Churchill revelled in his new-found role as press magnate. But in political terms the effect of his inflammatory publication was entirely negative.

Despite Churchill's best efforts, a compromise was negotiated with the trade union leadership after just over a week of strike action. With only the miners still locked out, he now (unsuccessfully)

LEFT: *An armoured car in central London during the General Strike of 1926.*

advocated putting pressure on the mineowners to compromise. This was in line with his unswerving principle: 'In victory, magnanimity.' But it won him no friends in the trade union movement. His aggression at the time of the general strike, much exaggerated in the public perception, confirmed his status as a blood-thirsty reactionary in the eyes of the left, just as it won him a strong following among diehard right-wing Tories who despised Baldwin's stolid moderation.

BELOW: *The first issue of Churchill's strike-breaking newspaper* The British Gazette. *He delighted in playing the role of press baron, if only for a week; the leading articles he dictated himself.*

Scenes from the Churchill family album. RIGHT: *Bricklaying at Chartwell with Sarah (left) and Mary.* OPPOSITE TOP: *In the garden with Mary.* OPPOSITE BELOW: *Entertaining a famous house guest, Charlie Chaplin (far right) at Chartwell in 1931.*

BELOW: *A comical picture of Churchill at play – scuttling across the sands at Deauville with the Duke of Sutherland in 1927.*

BELOW RIGHT: *Churchill in the role of 'old man of the sea,' having landed a 188lb marlin swordfish off Catalina Island, California, 1929.*

During his period as Chancellor, Churchill divided his time between No. 11 Downing Street and Chartwell. Although Clementine never grew to like their country estate, the children loved it, and so did Churchill. He found there an unbounded field for his favourite activities – painting, entertaining guests and dictating articles or books. He also discovered a new release in physical labour. In 1928 he wrote to Baldwin that he had spent a month 'building a cottage and dictating a book: 200 bricks and 2000 words a day.' There were few things he liked better than to be surprised by visitors with a bricklayer's trowel in his hand.

The staff at Chartwell usually numbered eight or nine indoor servants and about six outdoors, as well as Churchill's two secretaries (there had to be two because he was in the habit of dictating both early in the morning and late at night, so a shift system operated). Despite the expense of this establishment, Churchill threw himself into the development of the house and its grounds with a superb disregard for cost. The imperturbable optimism with which he pursued the most unrealistic projects, disregarding all practical obstacles, had the same infuriating effect on his wife as it had often had on his cabinet

SAFEGUARDING SHIELDS YOUR WAGES & YOUR JOB!

WORKERS !

VOTE CONSERVATIVE !

colleagues. In her exasperation, Clementine once threw a dish of spinach at his head, the sort of gesture denied to Asquith or Lloyd George by social convention. There were recurrent financial crises, during which Churchill would draw up elaborate schemes for economizing, rarely observed in the letter or the spirit. His enthusiastic projects for 'self-sufficiency' through livestock farming on the

estate were uniformly unsuccessful and only added to the costs. Yet in the end the family survived without the final often-threatened expedient of renting out or selling off the estate.

Visitors to Chartwell in the 1920s and 1930s ranged from the staple of family and close friends to such exotic birds of passage as Charlie Chaplin and Albert Einstein. T. E. Lawrence was at one time a frequent guest, arriving on his motorbike and changing into Arab dress for dinner. Another familiar figure was the financier, journalist and political adventurer Brendan Bracken: carrot-haired and voluble with thick bottle-glass spectacles, he encouraged the absurd rumour that he was Churchill's illegitimate son (his real origins, of which he was strangely ashamed, were lowly and Irish). More surprising was the constant presence of the physicist Professor F. A. Lindemann, known universally as 'the Prof.' A humourless vegetarian teetotaller, he might have seemed as out of place at Chartwell as a pacifist at a military review. But Churchill was grateful for his loyalty, admired his intelligence, and thrived on his ability to explain complex scientific ideas in layman's language.

Clementine rather liked 'the Prof,' but in general the tone of the court that assembled around Churchill at his country seat was not to her taste. She disliked not only newcomers like Bracken but old-established cronies of her husband such as Lord Birkenhead (a frequent visitor until his death in 1930) and Lord Beaverbrook. On more than one occasion she stormed from the dinner table, offended by the raffishness of their conversation or their arrogantly expressed Tory views, or both. Churchill loved the company of such men. He disliked dull respectability and moral hypocrisy, the

uniform views and uniform behaviour that he disparaged as a feature of modern democratic society. He craved aristocracy and extravagance. Increasingly, his thoughts turned to a romanticized past. At the end of the 1920s he wrote *My Early Years*, an autobiographical evocation of the lost world of his childhood and youth. Full of charm and self-deprecating humour, it is his most readable book and was published to general acclaim in 1930. But it is the work of a man looking back from the end of his life. He felt increasingly out of place in contemporary politics and at one point even contemplated leaving Parliament.

In May 1929 Baldwin's government had almost run its term and a general election was called. Baldwin campaigned under the slogan 'Safety First';

Churchill did not. He noisily denounced the Labour Party for its 'outrage' in supporting the General Strike and wildly misrepresented its mild reformist policies as 'the banner of plunder.' As reports of Labour gains flooded in on the night of 30 May, Churchill flew into a fury. According to Tom Jones, deputy secretary to the cabinet: 'His ejaculations to the surrounding staff were quite unprintable.' Churchill held his own seat, but Labour became the largest single party in parliament. Baldwin did not share Churchill's demonic view of his political opponents. He could have kept them out of government, but resigned because to stay would have been 'unsporting.' Thus Churchill was once more ejected from office. It would be ten long years before he came back in from the cold.

CHAPTER SEVEN

A Prophet in the Wilderness

LEFT: *Churchill at Chartwell in 1939, an anguished exile from power amid the gathering storm.*

THE poet W. H. Auden epitomized the 1930s as a 'low dishonest decade.' For Churchill this was a malign period of life, the locust years, eaten away by public and private misfortunes. It began with the Wall Street crash of October 1929 which plunged the world economy into depression. Churchill was on holiday in the United States at the time, and actually witnessed the traffic jams caused by a ruined stockbroker plunging to his death from a New York skyscraper. Unwisely, Churchill had himself invested a substantial portion of his hard-accumulated wealth in the transatlantic boom; most of it was lost. Over the next ten years he was engaged in a relentless struggle to rebuild his ruined fortune.

Luckily he could command large sums of money for his writings and public appearances, especially in North America where he was more honoured than in his own country. In the winter of 1931 he returned to the United States for a strenuous lecture tour which promised to be extraordinarily profitable. Again, misfortune struck. On 13 December he was knocked down by a car on New York's Fifth Avenue. 'I do not understand why I was not broken like an egg-shell or squashed like a gooseberry,' he later wrote. It seems to have been his thick winter coat

that saved him from serious injury. Nevertheless, although he eventually completed the lecture tour, his health and spirits were badly affected. During a visit to the sites of Marlborough's great European battles the following summer, he contracted paratyphoid fever; there were complications from which he took time to recover.

Churchill gave no outward signs of declining energy through the decade. His literary and journalistic output was titanic – admittedly based on a 'factory' principle, with teams of research assistants and secretaries to keep the production line going, but still requiring constant input from the man whose distinctive views and voice gave the operation its purpose. However many hands worked on a book like his *Marlborough*, a vast biography of the first Duke which appeared between 1933 and 1938, Churchill left his personal stamp on every page. No one could mistake it for the work of a committee. His journalism was protean and often shamelessly mercenary. Apart from expressions of his political views, sketches of famous people he had known and embroidered accounts of his personal experiences, he was quite prepared to turn his hand to such popular subjects as whether there was life on the moon

BELOW: *Churchill is moved from a London nursing home during his slow recovery from paratyphoid fever in October 1932.*

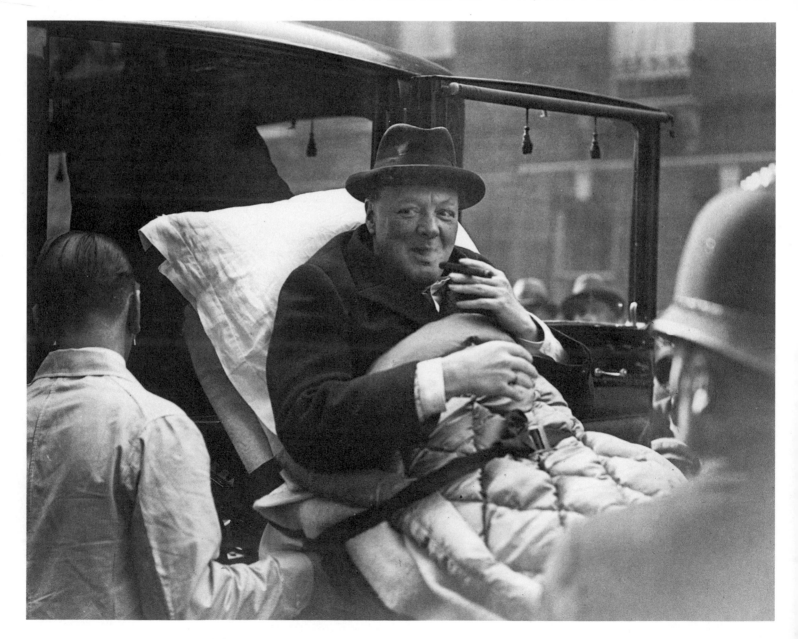

LEFT: *In October 1935, Diana arrives at St Ethelburg's church, Bishopsgate, for her second wedding, to the young Conservative MP Duncan Sandys. Her first marriage had lasted little more than two years.*

or, with the help of 'the Prof,' science fiction speculations on the shape of wars to come. He even accepted a commission from Alexander Korda to write a film script based on the life of George V, though this project never came to fruition.

Despite this ceaseless activity, Churchill nursed the feeling that his life was drawing to a close. At the end of 1931 he told Clementine that he thought 'he would never recover completely' from the blows he had suffered – the loss of his money in the Wall Street crash, his political isolation and the road accident. He had never expected longevity. Two of his close friends and contemporaries died around this time, Lord Birkenhead in 1930 and 'Sunny,' Duke of Marlborough, in 1934. Churchill was not given to expressions of morbidity, but we find in a letter to Clementine the casual suggestion that 'my life is in its final decade'; and Lord Beaverbrook described him as having 'reconciled himself to the part of a farewell tour of politics.' He even managed to look older than he was. As a schoolboy, future playwright John Mortimer witnessed a visit by Churchill to Harrow in 1939:

. . . his ancient head emerged from the carapace of his dinner jacket like the hairless pate of a tortoise, his old hand trembled on the handle of the walking-stick which supported him and his voice, when he spoke, was heavily slurred with brandy and old age. He seemed to us to be about 103.

Even Churchill's children had become a source of distress and anxiety. Determined to avoid his father's mistakes, Churchill had nourished the young Randolph on praise and affection. As a result, the boy was totally spoilt and grew into a handsome but thoroughly insufferable young bully. He could not be dissuaded from entering politics in support of his father, who suffered constant embarrassment from the ill-conceived interventions of his uncontrollable offspring. Churchill's eldest daughter, Diana, married in great style in 1932, only to divorce three years later. She quickly moved on to a second husband, the young Conservative MP Duncan Sandys, but her evident emotional instability was a source of worry to her parents. The second daughter, Sarah, caused the greatest uproar by first becoming a chorus girl – the Churchills disapproved of girls who 'went on the stage' – and then running off to New York to marry the leading man in her first show, the American comedian Vic Oliver. Her parents did everything in their power to try to stop the marriage and the subsequent reconciliation was slow and painful.

Through all these tribulations Clementine remained the rock on which Churchill's life was founded. Yet even this relationship suffered a distant tremor. Despite their deep mutual attachment, the Churchills frequently spent their holidays apart. Clementine could not tolerate the company of the rich and vulgar hosts who invited Churchill to the Cote d'Azur, where she was trapped in idleness while he painted by day and gambled through the night. Instead, she preferred to stay with more cultured friends or visit galleries and museums. In December 1934 she embarked on a far more adventurous voyage, when she was invited to join Lord Moyne for a zoological cruise on his yacht *Rosaura* around virtually unexplored islands of Indonesia. During this idyllic journey she fell romantically in love with a fellow voyager, the rich and cultivated Terence Philip. It was an escapist experience that did not overflow the bounds of the holiday, but the temporary happiness it brought does suggest just how much Clementine was sacrificing to the often rather grim and invariably uphill task of keeping Churchill afloat.

RIGHT: *Randolph's marriage to Pamela Digby, after the outbreak of war in 1939, was a glittering ceremonial occasion, but the relationship did not last. Of the Churchill children, only Mary satisfied her parents' ideal of contented monogamy.*

The basic issue, as always for Churchill, was not money, health or family, but politics. From the start of the 1930s he felt miserably out of place in the domestic political scene. As the economic indicators switched toward depression, any lingering hopes of resurrecting the values of the pre-war era vanished for good. The sacred cows of Free Trade and the gold standard were unceremoniously slaughtered. Churchill's romantic Edwardian patriotism, his invocations of 'this island race' and the glories of Empire, struck a false note, out of tune with the times. Retrospect had drained the Great War of all heroism; it was reviled as a shabby and senseless butchery. The Oxford Union declared they would never fight 'for King and Country.' It was vain for Churchill to dismiss this undergraduate vote as an 'abject, squalid, shameless avowal.' It represented, more than he did, the mood of the country.

RIGHT: *The grim face of unemployment in the 1930s, a desolation of shattered hopes and wasted lives.*

OPPOSITE: *Churchill painting in the south of France in 1933. He found great solace in his art, 'an unceasing voyage of entrancing discovery.'*

RIGHT: *A 1931 Conservative election poster. The Depression killed the nineteenth century ideal of Free Trade, as each country tried to protect itself from the effects of economic recession by blocking imports.*

BELOW: *On the election trail again, October 1931. Churchill shared in the Conservative triumph at the polls, but not in the fruits of victory.*

Churchill's bitter years in the political wilderness began with his resignation from Baldwin's shadow cabinet in January 1931. He was at loggerheads with his colleagues over their attitude to the Labour government, which they insisted on regarding as a legitimate and generally benign temporary alternative to their own administration, rather than as a subversive conspiracy against the majesty of the British Empire. The breaking point came when Labour approved the principle of Dominion status – in effect, limited internal self-government – for India and the Conservative leadership supported it in all but detail. Churchill resigned to become the leading light of the India Defence League and deployed his full oratorical powers to prevent Britain 'casting away that most truly bright and precious jewel in the crown of the King.' The general election of October 1931 initiated 14 years of absolute Conservative predominance in Parliament. Churchill was not invited to join the Conservative-dominated National government. He was left to fight the cause of British India from the back benches.

Churchill was convinced that the proposals for India were wrong, not only because they would harm the Empire, but because they would institute the rule of a minority of sophisticated Hindus over the 'untouchables' and the Muslims, leading

LEFT: *Churchill's conflict with his party leadership over policy on India occupied the lion's share of his time between 1931 and 1935. The pipe-smoking Baldwin looks distinctly uncomfortable sitting on the elephant's back.*

BELOW: *Indian nationalist leader Mahatma Gandhi, famously denounced by Churchill as 'a seditious Middle Temple lawyer . . . posing as a fakir.'*

ultimately to intercommunal violence and civil war. Like so many upper-class Englishmen, Churchill identified instinctively with the Muslim aristocracy in India and loathed the new urban educated middle class which presented a sharper racial challenge. His verbal onslaughts on the Indian nationalists were excessively violent and frequently offensive. One especially abusive attack on Mahatma Gandhi was long remembered in India:

It is alarming and also nauseating to see Mr Gandhi, a seditious Middle Temple lawyer, now posing as a fakir of a type well known in the East, striding half-naked up the steps of the Viceregal Palace . . . to parley on equal terms with the representative of the King-Emperor.

Churchill also abused the leaders of the British government. Very much in the manner of Lord Randolph, he found a woundingly comic epithet for Prime Minister Ramsay Macdonald: 'the Boneless Wonder.' He was no more flattering toward Baldwin.

For five years Churchill fought progress toward Indian self-government with his customary obsessive determination, against all the odds, predicting the most dire consequences for Britain if it should come to pass. He was the only prominent politician to oppose the India Bill. A small bloc of Tory backbenchers voted with him, although they were generally men who disliked him on many other grounds. Among Conservatives in the country he had more support, but could not muster it to any decisive effect: in 1933 the party membership narrowly but decisively voted to back the leadership. The following year Churchill suffered a severe rebuff when he alleged before a Parliamentary select committee that Sir Samuel Hoare, the Secretary of

State for India, and Lord Derby had used improper means to obtain submissions to parliament favourable to Indian reform. It is now known that he was right, but he could not prove his allegations and was publicly humiliated. Finally in 1935, after a quite staggering quantity of debate which was provoked by Churchill's verbose resistance to every clause, the House of Commons at last passed the India Act and he had to admit defeat.

At the time, most political observers were inclined to interpret Churchill's chosen position on India as a cynically opportunist manoeuvre, an attempt to unseat Baldwin and win the leadership of the Conservative Party for himself. In reality, it was a typical example of Churchill's failings as a political operator. He could not manipulate support or ease his way toward power. Inflexible and emotional in his advocacy of the causes he adopted, the only way he knew of dealing with an obstacle was to charge at it full tilt. Whatever the rights or wrongs of the India Act, Churchill's virulent and unflagging opposition to the measure was a political disaster. It made it unthinkable for him to be included in the National government. It confirmed his reputation as an arch-reactionary, further alienating him from all moderate or left-wing political opinion. Worst of all, by the violence of his speeches, in the words of historian Robert Rhodes James, he 'debased the coin of alarmism,' so that his prognostications about Hitler's

Germany were not at first heeded. Churchill's doom-laden prophecies became such a boringly familiar feature of the parliamentary scene that the MP Leo Amery was able to puncture one such oration with the simple quip: 'Here endeth the last chapter of the Book of the Prophet Jeremiah.' But Churchill's jeremiads on the gathering storm in Europe were, in the end, the salvation of his political career and the making of his destiny.

Churchill was not a consistent champion of freedom and democracy in the Europe of the Dictators. Like most Conservatives, he had welcomed Italian Fascism in the 1920s. He was attracted by its anti-Bolshevism, its martial spirit and its promise to redeem the people from the 'squalid materialism' of the age. He met Mussolini in 1927 and pronounced himself a wholehearted supporter of the Duce in his 'triumphant struggle against the bestial appetites and passions of Leninism.' Fascism, he declared, 'has rendered service to the world.' For many years a signed photograph of Mussolini, presented to Clementine during another visit to Rome, was prominently displayed at Chartwell. In 1932 Churchill extravagantly referred to the Italian dictator as 'the greatest lawgiver among living men,' and even as late as 1937 some of his comments on Mussolini were still flattering and respectful.

If Churchill's attitude to Hitler was, almost from the first, unequivocally hostile, this was because he

BELOW: *Churchill's future adversary, Adolf Hitler. The two men never met – a possible encounter in 1932 was abandoned when Churchill contracted paratyphoid fever, and the opportunity never arose again.*

saw in the German dictator a re-embodiment of the Prussian militarism that he had fought to defeat in World War I, only more hysterical in tone and more barbaric in behaviour. He first sounded the alarm over the rebirth of German militarism in 1932, before Hitler was yet in power:

All these bands of sturdy Teutonic youths, marching through the streets and roads of Germany, with the light of desire in their eyes to suffer for their Fatherland, are not looking for status. They are looking for weapons.

He observed the events of the following years with gloomy foreboding. His imagination was inflamed by the spectacle of Nazi tyranny and his speeches were replete with the most eloquent denunciations of 'the odious conditions now ruling in Germany.' He denounced the mistreatment of the Jews and the establishment of the first concentration camps, the abolition of democracy and individual freedom, the all-pervading secret police. His sympathy for those suffering under Nazi terror was deeply felt and sincerely expressed. But above all he feared for the peace of Europe.

Most of Churchill's British contemporaries, and almost all those of a younger generation, thought they had learnt the lesson of World War I. Wars happened because of a race for superiority of armaments accompanied by fixed alliance systems. To preserve peace, which was essential for the survival of civilization, it was necessary to reduce armaments and avoid dividing Europe into mutually hostile blocs. Old-fashioned in this as in most matters, Churchill believed World War I had been caused by German aggression. The way to prevent its recurrence was to keep Germany disarmed or, failing that, to build up strong armaments and create an alliance system to deter the potential aggressor. As he said in a 1934 radio broadcast: 'Peace must be founded on preponderance.' Also, although the pursuit of peace was his overriding aim throughout the

ABOVE: *Hitlerjugend on the march, the 'sturdy Teutonic youths' whose warlike enthusiasm inspired Churchill with such foreboding.*

LEFT: *Il Duce, Benito Mussolini, signs the Munich agreement in 1938. Churchill was for many years an admirer of Mussolini and never regarded him in the same light as Hitler.*

FOR PEACE

BETWEEN NATIONS

BETWEEN CLASSES

WAR

CLASS WAR

NATIONAL GOVERNMENT

1930s, he was convinced that there was something worse than war – dishonourable surrender. In the last resort, Britain must be prepared to fight for its interests and its beliefs.

At first Churchill was a voice crying in the wilderness. Britain was actively committed to international disarmament and was leading by example. Pacifist sentiment was widespread. Opinion

followed those who believed, in Churchill's phrase, 'that peace could be preserved by praising its virtues.' In political circles, Hitler's rise provoked contradictory responses. Many Tories welcomed the Nazis as a bulwark against Bolshevism; Labour denounced Hitler's crimes but continued to press for disarmament. Churchill was isolated not only by his unpopular theme but by his general political record. In the Conservative Party, his reputation for opportunism, irresponsibility and lack of judgment stood against him. A wider public, used to regarding him as a rash warmonger, dismissed his views on rearmament as a further manifestation of a dangerously bellicose temperament. There was no audience for the dire warnings of an old warhorse.

It was in 1935 that a shift in the mood of public opinion first brought Churchill a more respectful hearing. His prophecies seemed increasingly vindicated by events. He had claimed that Germany was re-arming contrary to the terms of the Versailles treaty: it turned out to be true. In November 1934 he asserted in the House of Commons that the Germans had achieved parity with Britain in the air; Baldwin, speaking for the government, estimated the Luftwaffe at 50 percent of the strength of the RAF. Five months later, Baldwin apologized and declared (quite erroneously, as we now know) that Churchill had in fact been right: the Germans had achieved parity after all. Churchill's stock rose sharply.

From this time forward he enjoyed a strangely privileged position in government circles. Baldwin gave him a seat on the recently established Air Defence Research Committee, yet explicitly left him free to continue attacking government air defence policy in public. The intelligence services,

government officials and officers in the armed services were authorized to pass him information on all issues affecting national defence. Desmond Morton, the head of the government's secret Industrial Intelligence organization, became one of his closest personal advisers. As biographer Martin Gilbert has written, Churchill enjoyed 'a unique position in British public life for someone without cabinet office.' To the general public, he appeared as a straightforward, outspoken critic of government defence and foreign policy. But in private he was a sort of unofficial adviser to the government, in close contact with ministers who kept him informed of state secrets and, although they rarely acted on his views, usually gave them a respectful hearing.

Churchill's specific contributions to the Air Defence Committee were not especially helpful. It was largely to the credit of Baldwin and his Secretary for Air, Lord Swinton, that Britain had the excellent air defence system which won the battle for survival in the summer of 1940. Churchill disagreed with Baldwin's emphasis on arming for defence, describing the principle of defensive war as 'the theory of the turtle, which is disproved at every Lord Mayor's banquet.' His insistence that his friend Professor Lindemann should have a place on the committee's scientific sub-committee, headed

by Sir Henry Tizard, was totally counter-productive. Although a few of Lindemann's ideas were fruitful, most were a crazy waste of time – such as his proposal for aerial mines or for 'a cloud of substance in the path of an aeroplane to produce detonation' – and his character-clash with the brilliant Tizard created chaos. Lindemann was eventually excluded from the sub-committee, although Churchill continued to rely on his advice.

While membership of the Air Defence Research Committee gave him some temporary outlet for his energies, Churchill itched to be back in government where he could exercise effective influence over policy. He fought the general election of November 1935 as a more-or-less loyal supporter of the Conservative leadership. With the India issue dead and buried, he hoped for high office – he wanted the Admiralty – and was cruelly disappointed to be left out again. Since he had been attacking Baldwin day in, day out for the previous five years, his aspirations were not perhaps very realistic. With notable prescience, Baldwin half-jokingly remarked: 'If there is going to be a war . . . we must keep him fresh to be our war Prime Minister.' Churchill later consoled himself with the thought that his exclusion from power had preserved him for his destiny – 'Over me beat the invisible wings' – but at the time

ABOVE: *Wearing imitation gas masks, women participate in a left-wing peace demonstration in London, May 1936. There was little common ground between those, like Churchill, who wanted stronger armaments to resist Hitler's warlike ambitions, and socialist anti-Nazis who seemed to believe that 'peace could be preserved by praising its virtues.'*

he merely sulked, sidling off to paint in the south of France.

In 1936 Churchill strove for the first time to create a unified national campaign to militate for resistance to Hitler's aggressive designs. It was known as the 'Arms and the Covenant' movement, because it advocated rearmament to uphold the covenant of the League of Nations against acts of aggression. This was the banner which, it was thought, could rally maximum support from all shades of the political spectrum. Unfortunately, Churchill's own obsession was with Germany. He had not denounced Japanese aggression in Manchuria in 1931, the first serious breach of the League of Nations covenant. Even more seriously, he was lukewarm in his opposition to Mussolini's invasion of Abyssinia in 1935, describing it as 'a very small matter' and expressing the view that 'no one can keep up the pretence that Abyssinia is a fit, worthy and equal member of a League of civilized nations.' Such attitudes were bound to alienate many potential sympathizers with 'Arms and the Covenant.'

Worse followed. General Franco's attempted coup against the Republican government in Spain in July 1936 struck Churchill as an unwelcome distraction. He wrote irritably: 'This Spanish business cuts across my thoughts.' As the attempted coup developed into civil war, he tended to favour Franco. But this cut him off from large areas of potential support for his campaign against Germany. Those left-wing anti-Fascists who saw the Spanish civil war – in which, after all, German and Italian forces took part – as the first round of the war against the European dictators, could not back a man who denounced Hitler but not Franco.

Still, through 1936, the Baldwin government writhed under the lash of Churchill's scornful philippics ('They are decided only to be undecided, resolved to be irresolute, adamant for drift, all-powerful for impotence'). Parliamentary opinion was swinging against the government's lack of decisive action on defence. Then, in December, Churchill's political reputation suffered a fresh blow from a quite unexpected direction. The new King, Edward VIII, decided to marry the American divorcee Mrs Wallis Simpson. Baldwin, with the support of politicians of all parties (but against the opposition of large sections of the press controlled by Lord Beaverbrook and Lord Rothermere), offered the King the stark choice between Mrs Simpson and the throne. Churchill's imagination was stirred by a romantic devotion to the monarchy. Twenty-five years earlier he had participated in Edward's investiture as Prince of Wales. Now he pleaded with the House of Commons for 'time and patience' to work out a solution, declaring, with what had become habitual hyperbole, that 'if an abdication were to be hastily extorted, the outrage so committed would cast its

RIGHT: *The news of the King's liaison with a divorcee breaks on the London streets.*

shadow forward across many chapters of the History of the British Empire.'

Churchill was widely suspected of attempting to create a 'King's Party' that would form an alternative government. His last-ditch appeal to Parliament on Edward's behalf was met with howls of derision, described by one witness, Lord Winterton, as 'one of the angriest manifestations I have ever heard directed against any man in the House of Commons.' A shocked Churchill stumbled from the chamber mumbling that he was 'finished.' His last act in the drama was to help Edward draught his abdication speech for the wireless. Many observers felt Churchill might as well have announced his own abdication from politics at the same time. Yet the damage was not as bad as might have been feared. Churchill was soon waxing lyrical over the pomp and splendour of the coronation of George VI. Dusting himself off, he returned to the fray as before, his knightly armour a trifle dented.

In 1937 Baldwin passed on the premiership to Neville Chamberlain. Whereas Baldwin had great respect for Churchill, Chamberlain dismissed him as 'a brilliant wayward child.' Vain and self-assured, the new prime minister believed he could do a deal with Hitler and set out to secure peace in Europe by an active policy of appeasement. Rearmament, begun under Baldwin, steadily gathered pace. But Chamberlain was admirably dedicated to peace. Unfortunately, this was a poor state of mind in which to approach Hitler, who was only too prepared for the threat or reality of war.

The events of 1938 were the turning-point of the decade. In March, Hitler annexed Austria. Churchill

ABOVE: *Prime Minister Neville Chamberlain, in the guise of an angel of peace, flies off to meet Hitler in September 1938, while the storm clouds of war gather in the background.*

LEFT: *Churchill leaves No. 10 Downing Street after discussing the Czech crisis with Chamberlain, 10 September 1938. The Prime Minister was determined to do a deal with Hitler and ignored Churchill's advice to make a firm stand.*

warned the House of Commons: 'Europe is confronted with a programme of aggression, nicely calculated and timed, unfolding stage by stage.' He pressed for a system of alliances to restrain Hitler. France was committed to defend Czechoslovakia, believed to be Hitler's next target. If Britain stood firm with the French and the Czechs, Germany would not dare to act. What is more, the Russians could be brought in. Since 1936 Churchill had been in touch with the Soviet ambassador in London, Ivan Maisky. Always prepared to concentrate on one issue at a time, the old anti-Bolshevik was ready to call on the Soviet Union to restrain the Nazis. Chamberlain was not. He preferred Nazis to Communists. He also regretted both Britain's alliance with France and France's commitment to Czechoslovakia. His ambition was to settle the future of Europe by personal negotiations with Hitler.

The Munich agreement of October 1938 was Chamberlain's triumph. Czechoslovakia was betrayed, Germany annexed the Sudetenland without firing a shot, and the British prime minister returned to public adulation, talking of 'peace with honour.' Churchill could only look on impotently while the country sold out its friends and its future. He spoke out against the Munich agreement – 'a defeat without a war' – and was one of 30 Conservative MPs who abstained when it was put to the vote. So unpopular was this stand that he only narrowly retained the support of his constituency party. In Parliament he was such a discredited figure that most of the anti-Munich Tories preferred to group themselves around Anthony Eden, the former Foreign Secretary. Churchill's own clique consisted of only three MPs, all members of his personal entourage: Brendan Bracken, Duncan Sandys and Robert Boothby.

The political disasters of 1938 coincided with the worst crisis in Churchill's financial affairs when a fall in American stocks left him with pressing debts of £18,000. Only the intervention of one of Brendan Bracken's rich friends saved him from ruin. During these sombre days of defeat and despair, Churchill sought solace in working at Chartwell on his monumental *History of the English-Speaking Peoples*, which would not be published until two decades later. He found in the past valuable perspectives on the present and themes that were to nourish his

BELOW: *Enthusiastic crowds acclaim Chamberlain the peacemaker after his return from Munich, 30 September 1938. Churchill denounced the agreement to hand over the Sudetenland to Germany as 'a defeat without a war.'*

LEFT: *Impotent to affect the course of events as the international situation deteriorated, Churchill worked through the winter of 1938-39 on his* History of the English-Speaking Peoples *at Chartwell.*

BELOW: *Many Europeans who were dismayed by Chamberlain's policy of appeasement established contact with Churchill during the late 1930s, inspired by his unwavering hostility to the Nazis. Here French premier Leon Blum visits the Churchills at Chartwell in 1939.*

rhetoric during the conflict ahead. It was not only the stories of Drake against the Armada or Nelson defying Napoleon that enthused him, but the Magna Carta and the tradition of English liberties. He envisaged the English-speaking peoples becoming 'the armed champions . . . of freedom and law, of the rights of the individual.' He was inspired to 'condemn tyranny in whatever guise and from whatever quarter it presents itself.' He had lost any leanings toward Mussolini or Franco, whose triumph in Spain he ultimately abhorred.

Shunned by British politicians and public, Churchill enjoyed a far higher reputation abroad. Exiles from Nazidom beat a path to his door. On visits to France he was welcomed as a leading statesman and hobnobbed with generals and ministers. He was equally famous in Germany. Hitler made personal attacks on him in speeches after Munich – an uninvited foreign intrusion into British political life which did much to restore Churchill to public favour. Although no one would have guessed it in the bleak winter of 1938-39, his desert years were almost over.

Within months of the Munich agreement the public mood of relief had given way to shame and disquiet. Churchill prophesied that Hitler would not be content with what he had been given, that his aggression would continue. In March 1939 German

troops occupied Prague; the prophet had been proved right again. A great shift was under way in the public's perception of Churchill. He was widely represented as the man who knew how to stand up to Hitler, the man who had been right all along. His obstinate persistence in his monomanic theme was no longer boring or absurd, it was heroic. He was no longer a warmonger, but resolute. There were calls in the press for his inclusion in the government. The *Daily Mirror* described him as 'Britain's most trusted statesman.'

Chamberlain steadfastly resisted the newspapers' clamour for Churchill to enter the cabinet. He still sought an accommodation with Hitler and did not wish to risk a gesture that the dictator might interpret as provocation. Also, he still regarded Churchill as hopelessly irresponsible and lacking in judgment. He was appalled when Churchill privately urged him to respond to the Italian invasion of Albania in April 1939 by seizing the island of Corfu. It is hard to see how two men so divided in their attitude to the European crisis could have worked together.

So Churchill continued to pressure Chamberlain from the back benches. He campaigned for the creation of a Ministry of Supply and for the introduction of conscription: both were conceded. Crucially, he insisted that Britain should back up

BELOW: *In July 1939, an anonymous supporter paid for this poster to appear in the Strand. Chamberlain, however, did not invite Churchill into the government until war forced his hand.*

its guarantee of Polish independence, hastily announced at the end of March, by an alliance with Moscow. 'There is no means of maintaining an eastern front against Nazi aggression,' he affirmed, 'without the active aid of Russia.' But Chamberlain's government did not want an alliance with the Communists – both because they disliked them and because they thought their armed forces useless – and nor did the Poles. Desultory negotiations dragged on in Moscow through the summer months until on 23 August, tired of British procrastination and distrustful of British intentions, Stalin did a deal with Hitler instead. The Germans were now free to invade Poland.

When the Nazi-Soviet Pact was announced, Churchill was on holiday in France – the French general staff had just taken him on a tour of the supposedly impregnable Maginot Line. He immediately hastened back to London, knowing that with the approach of war his inclusion in the government was almost certain. On 1 September, as German tanks rolled forward into Poland, Chamberlain informed Churchill he would be offered a post in the war cabinet. There for two days the matter rested. Chamberlain prevaricated, still clutching at vain hopes of peace, until a revolt by his own ministers finally forced his hand. On 3 September, with the upmost reluctance, the man of peace finally declared war on Germany, being resigned to the ruin of his life's work.

The rise of Hitler had saved Churchill's career from petering out in a political wasteland. But for the war crisis, he might have rumbled on, a half-extinct volcano on the reactionary edge of the Tory Party, through his declining years. Now he was to be granted an almost unhoped-for second chance to quash the verdict of Gallipoli and prove his true worth as a leader in time of war. His mood after the declaration of war, sitting for his last few hours on the back benches, was one of Olympian serenity. He later wrote, in his most elevated vein:

I felt a security of mind, and was conscious of a kind of uplifted detachment from human and personal affairs. The glory of Old England, peace-loving and ill-prepared as she was, but instant and fearless at the call of honour, thrilled my being and seemed to lift our fate to those spheres far removed from earthly facts and physical sensation.

Chamberlain offered him his old cherished wartime post as First Lord of the Admiralty. It was all that he could have wished for. At six o'clock in the evening he walked back into that same Admiralty building that he 'had quitted in pain and sorrow almost exactly a quarter of a century before.' Soon the famous signal was winging its way to the Fleet: 'Winston is back!'

BELOW: *The officers and men of HMS* Exeter *give a rousing three cheers for the First Lord of the Admiralty in February 1940.*

CHAPTER EIGHT

Walking with Destiny

LEFT: *Churchill in 1940, the symbol
of Britain's resistance to Nazi
tyranny – his finest hour.*

A<small>T</small> the start of World War I, it had taken just ten months for Churchill's conduct of the Admiralty to plunge him into political disgrace. In World War II, eight months sufficed to make him Prime Minister. Yet his character had not changed. Age had done nothing to temper his rashness or lend balance to his judgment. He was as fertile with madcap schemes for instant action as he had ever been. All the accusations made against him in 1915 could have been repeated in 1940, and perhaps with more justice. But his long absence from power was a great political strength. As he wrote in his war memoirs:

I had not held public office for 11 years. I had therefore no responsibility for the past or for any want of preparation now apparent. On the contrary, I had for the last six or seven years been a continual prophet of evils which had now in large measure come to pass.

Apart from Anthony Eden, his colleagues in the war cabinet were 'men of Munich,' advocates of peace at almost any price half-heartedly conducting a war they did not want. In their midst sat Churchill, eloquent, pugnacious, untainted by appeasement, his spirits rising at the scent of battle. If the war went badly, Chamberlain and his old colleagues would bear the blame; if the war went well, Churchill was likely to steal the credit.

RIGHT: *Admiral Sir Dudley Pound, the First Sea Lord, struck up an effective rapport with Churchill at the Admiralty.*

BELOW: *Chamberlain's War Cabinet, left to right, seated, Lord Halifax, Sir John Simon, the Prime Minister, Sir Samuel Hoare and Lord Chatfield; standing, Sir Kingsley Wood, Churchill, Leslie Hore-Belisha and Lord Hankey.*

At the Admiralty he found a First Sea Lord, Admiral Sir Dudley Pound, who could stand up to him. The two men developed a firm mutual respect. Churchill's habit of working at least 18 hours a day, with an hour's break for siesta in the afternoon, always put a strain on his colleagues; Pound learnt the knack of grabbing an occasional few minutes sleep in an armchair (even during cabinet meetings!) so that he could keep up the pace. Despite his age – he was 65 in November 1939 – Churchill's energy was apparently limitless. He made whirlwind visits to ships and naval installations, chatted to the officers and delivered morale-boosting speeches to the men. He bombarded the war cabinet with memoranda and bored them with rambling perorations. He deluged his staff with ideas good and bad, constantly interfered in operational matters and tormented Admiral Pound with impossible plans. Pound fought back with the tactics of Fabius Cunctator. Churchill's favourite scheme – and his craziest – was to send warships into the Baltic. These vessels would be specially modified to make them impervious to torpedoes and bombs. Pound fought a brilliant series of delaying actions to block this fantastic project, fortunately proving more than a match for Churchill at his most persistent.

Just as in World War I, British shipping proved embarrassingly vulnerable to German submarines and mines. Churchill shared the general expectation in naval circles that the U-boat menace would be relatively easy to counter because of the development of the Asdic underwater location device. This was a grave error of judgment. But when the *Royal Oak* was sunk by a U-boat at Scapa Flow, Churchill could correctly claim that this gap in the defences had been recognized as soon as he took over and

was being rapidly remedied when disaster struck. He made the right decision in choosing to build a larger number of small destroyers, rather than a smaller number of large ones, to fight the U-boat war, and also gave enthusiastic support to the naval scientists who, by the end of 1939, had devised a means of protecting ships against magnetic mines.

Whereas at the start of the previous war the Navy had stood idle while the crucial battles were fought on land, in 1939 only the Navy showed any sign of action while the bathos of the 'Phony War' reigned by land and in the air. The scuttling of the pocket battleship *Graf Spee* after the battle of the River Plate in December was the only cheering news of the year. Naturally, this reflected on the reputation of the First Lord of the Admiralty as the man who was ready to take the war to the enemy.

Churchill had no desire to see fighting break out between the armies in Europe; he anticipated that a land war would take the form of attritional trench warfare as in 1914-18. He accepted the war cabinet line that the Allies had time on their side and that Germany might even be defeated by economic blockade alone. But he saw scope for action to increase the economic pressure. From the first month of the war, he suggested mining Norwegian coastal waters, the winter route for exports of Swedish iron ore to Germany via the port of Narvik. This would be a breach of Norwegian neutrality, but Churchill had no time for neutrals (he had also advocated forcing neutral Ireland to open its ports to British warships). The Foreign Office thought differently and the plan was turned down by the war cabinet.

By December, however, the situation had been transformed by the Soviet invasion of Finland. Public sentiment backed the gallant Finns, and the

RIGHT: *Churchill addresses the crew of the cruiser HMS* Exeter *on its return from the battle of the River Plate, which had resulted in the scuttling of the pocket battleship* Graf Spee. *This welcome naval success confirmed Churchill's reputation as the man prepared to take the war to the enemy.*

French government, much keener on fighting the Communists than the Nazis, advocated Allied intervention against the Red Army. Neither Churchill nor his war cabinet colleagues wanted to take on Hitler and Stalin at the same time; indeed, Churchill had welcomed the Soviet occupation of eastern Poland the previous September. But, seizing a fresh opportunity to press for action to cut off Germany's iron ore supplies, he persuaded the cabinet that, under the guise of an expedition to help the Finns, a force should land at Narvik and advance across Scandinavia to gain control of the ironfields. Aware that Germany would almost certainly launch a counter-invasion, Churchill complacently asserted that 'we have more to gain than to lose by a German attack upon Norway and Sweden.'

While plans for an Anglo-French expedition to Scandinavia stumbled forward, Churchill found

BELOW: *Finnish troops with a captured Soviet tank during the Winter War of 1939-40.*

another opportunity to violate Norwegian neutrality. On 16 February he ordered HMS *Cossack* to capture the German prison-ship *Altmark* which had taken refuge in a fjord. We now know that it was this bold action, extremely popular in Britain, that provoked Hitler into preparing an expeditionary force to occupy Denmark and Norway. The Anglo-French plan, on the other hand, was aborted in March because the Finns surrendered, removing the pretext for action. The British now revived Churchill's original idea of mining Norwegian coastal waters, with a back-up plan for occupying Norwegian ports.

The Admiralty had warning from several sources of a German amphibious force preparing to invade Norway, but this information was misinterpreted or ignored. On the same night that the British at last laid their mines, 8/9 April, German troops marched into Denmark and German paratroopers and seaborne forces occupied Norwegian ports as far north as Narvik. The German ships were spotted by British aircraft, but the Navy failed to intercept them. Churchill believed that the Germans had placed their head into a trap; he was soon disillusioned. The attempted British counter-attack degenerated into a debacle. Newly appointed Chairman of the Military Coordination Committee, Churchill officially had control over the whole operation, but he found it impossible to impose his will on the War Office, which issued its own orders often contradicting those of the Admiralty. Divided counsels caused delay, and when British troops eventually landed they proved ineffectual. Meanwhile, the Navy could not sail in to stop the Germans ferrying reinforcements across from Denmark to Norway, since the risk of U-boat and air attack was too great. In early May the British forces around Trondheim were evacuated under fire. The ghost of Gallipoli walked again.

ABOVE: *Norway 1940, the campaign that brought down the Chamberlain government.*

LEFT: *British troops landing in Norway, 14 May 1940. They were not to stay for long, however.*

ABOVE: *Chamberlain walks with his wife in St James's Park on the morning of 10 May 1940 – the day of his resignation as prime minister.*

There were so many failings for which Churchill could have been censured over Norway. His was the original plan to breach the country's neutrality. He had failed to appreciate that Germany would be in by far the stronger position if battle for Scandinavia was joined. He had totally overestimated the value of British seapower in the face of German command of the air. His blithely optimistic imagination had led him to neglect difficulties and drawbacks and fatally underestimate his enemy. As he later wrote: 'Considering the prominent part I played in these events . . . it was a marvel that I survived and maintained my position in public esteem and parliamentary confidence.' Ironically, it was Chamberlain who paid the price of failure.

Churchill's reputation had risen steadily through the seven months of wartime. His rousing broadcasts and public speeches had made a powerful impression. For the first time in his life, he inspired confidence. Chamberlain inspired few positive sentiments. He was so evidently a man of peace, his manner gave no promise of an energetic prosecution of the war. He had made the fatal mistake of sounding complacent, announcing on 4 April: 'Hitler has missed the bus.' It was an unfortunately memorable phrase, impossible to live down. And the memory of Munich hung like an albatross around his neck.

On 7 May the House of Commons debated the Norway campaign. The anti-Munich Conservative Leo Amery summed up the angry mood of the House, addressing the government with a quotation from Oliver Cromwell: 'In the name of God, go!' Churchill loyally defended the government's record, to no effect. His old partner Lloyd George rose to

warn him 'not to allow himself to be converted into an air-raid shelter to keep the splinters from hitting his colleagues.' Labour forced a division and over 100 Conservatives voted against the government or abstained.

Conservative backbenchers informed Chamberlain that to restore confidence and unify the nation for war, there would have to be a coalition government. But Labour would refuse to serve under him; another prime minister would have to be found. Chamberlain favoured Lord Halifax, the mild Foreign Secretary, a 'man of Munich,' but acceptable to Labour. He was also the first choice of the King and most Conservatives. The only other possible contender was Churchill, popular in the country but with no following in Parliament. On 9 May, Chamberlain held a meeting with Halifax and Churchill, in the presence of the Conservative chief whip. Chamberlain said he was ready to serve under either of them. For once in a voluble lifetime, Churchill remained silent. After a long pause, Halifax modestly declined the premiership, on the grounds that the war could not be run from the House of Lords. Only then did Churchill speak. As Halifax later recorded: 'Winston, with suitable expressions of regard and humility, said that he could not but feel the force of what I had said.'

Chamberlain was in no hurry to draw the obvious conclusion. The following day, news came through that the Germans had invaded Holland and Belgium. Chamberlain hoped this crisis meant he could stay on. It did not. Labour stated plainly that they could serve only 'under a new prime minister who would command the confidence of the nation.' At 6pm on

THE DAILY MAIL, Saturday, May 11, 1940.

Daily Mail

FOR KING AND EMPIRE

LATE WAR NEWS SPECIAL

NO. 13,743   ✶ ✶   SATURDAY, MAY 11, 1940   ONE PENNY

NOT JUST A NAME— BUT A GUARANTEE
JUNIOR 2'-
CHUM 3'-
PLUS 5'-
SENIOR 10'6
PRINCE 15'6
SOVEREIGN 20'-

Culmak

AMSTERDAM BOMBED
A Page of Pictures —Page FIVE.

LATEST NEWS

ALLIES ADVANCING ON FRONT OF 200 MILES

B.E.F. Pour Across Belgian Frontier

VANGUARDS CLASH IN LUXEMBURG

BRITISH and French troops were last night advancing on a 200-miles front from the North Sea to the Moselle River. Britain's Mechanised Army—guns, tanks, armoured cars, and men—had reached points deep in Belgian territory.

The greatest air battle in history was still being fought over Belgium and Holland, and official announcements gave German losses at over 130 'planes.

The Dutch officially claimed to have destroyed 70, the French 44, and the Belgians "eight or nine." The R.A.F. destroyed "numerous" aircraft. At least 500 Allied 'planes roared over the Low Countries searching for enemy aircraft and troops.

Bitter Battle in Rotterdam Streets

GERMANS' CLAIM:

'Allied Bombs Killed 24 Civilians'

'We Will Reply'

THE official Nazi News Agency alleged last night that three Allied 'planes bombed the German town of Freiburg, killing 24 civilians.

The agency declared that

CHURCHILL IS PREMIER

All-Party Cabinet

By WILSON BROADBENT, Daily Mail Political Correspondent

MR. WINSTON CHURCHILL is Britain's new war Prime Minister. He took office last night after Mr. Chamberlain had handed his resignation to the King; until early this morning he was engaged in forming his War Cabinet of Conservative, Labour, and Liberal members.

He set about the task, with his customary vigour, immediately after exchanging places with Mr. Chamberlain.

Mr. Churchill's one object is to have the new War Cabinet at work to-day.

This, in order that there shall be no interruption in the continuance and conduct of the war in its further and more intensive stage.

Mr. Churchill's appointment to

WATCH FOR PARACHUTE

JUGO SLAV—GERMAN FRONTIER CLOSED

Belgrade, Friday.
The frontier between Germany and Jugoslavia at Maribor is reported to have been closed.—Exchange.

GERMANS INVENTED

---

10 May, Churchill was summoned to Buckingham Palace and asked to form a government.

This outcome surprised most politicians and government officials; some who distrusted or disliked Churchill were shocked and depressed. Yet with hindsight it is obvious that no other solution was possible. The man and the hour were matched. Churchill's lack of party ties, which denied him support in Parliament, ideally suited him for the role of national leader. His reputation as a prophet of doom made him a natural leader when doom befell. And he wanted the job more than anyone else. He had not conspired to become prime minister; he had supported Chamberlain to the last with scrupulous loyalty. But there was no doubt in his own mind that he was the leader the country needed. In his memoirs he described his feelings the night after his appointment:

. . . as I went to bed at about 3am, I was conscious of a profound sense of relief. At last I had the authority to give directions over the whole scene. I felt as if I were walking with destiny, and that all my past life had been but a preparation for this hour and for this trial.

Without a solid basis of personal support in the House of Commons, Churchill might have led a precarious life at the top. Events decided otherwise. In rapid succession, Britain faced the evacuation of the Expeditionary Force from Dunkirk (27 May–3 June), the surrender of France (22 June), the Battle of Britain, with the constant threat of German invasion (July through to mid-September), and the Blitz (September 1940–May 1941). To confront such a momentous challenge, Britain needed not a coalition

ABOVE: *Churchill's appointment as war premier fails to make the main headline, upstaged by the dramatic events in Belgium and the Netherlands. The Allied advance into Belgium was to prove a mistake.*

LEFT: *Lord Halifax, the only alternative to Churchill as prime minister in May 1940, did not really want the job – the mere thought of it apparently gave him a stomach ache.*

prime minister but a war dictator. Despite maintaining the forms of respect for cabinet government and parliamentary tradition, Churchill seized the controls with both hands, taking on more personal power than any British premier before or since.

He set out the immutable programme of his administration in his first address to the House of Commons as prime minister on 13 May:

I have nothing to offer but blood, toil, tears and sweat. . . . You ask, what is our policy? I will say: It is to wage war, by sea, land, and air, with all our might and with all the strength that God can give us; to wage war against a monstrous tyranny, never surpassed in the dark, lamentable catalogue of human crime. . . . You ask, what is our aim? I can answer in one word: Victory – victory at all costs, victory in spite of all terror; victory, however long and hard the road may be.

Churchill never contemplated any compromise with Hitler, even at the end of May when it seemed the greater part of the British Army might be forced to surrender at Dunkirk. The Führer's quite generous peace proposals in July were ignored. Chamberlain and Halifax, more reasonable men, were tempted by a possible deal. After all, it is normal for

a nation, once defeated in arms, to sue for peace, as the French did. But Churchill was unshakeable. Even if, as appeared likely in the late summer, Britain were overrun, he intended that the Royal Navy should retreat across the oceans and continue the struggle from the Dominions.

No one seriously doubted that Churchill's single-minded dedication to total war represented the will of the British people. Although many Conservatives still preferred Chamberlain, Churchill was politically unassailable. The deal for a coalition required that Chamberlain and Halifax should both remain in the war cabinet, where they were joined by the two Labour leaders, Clement Attlee and Arthur Greenwood. But the war cabinet counted for little. Two trusted Churchill appointees to ministries without war cabinet rank, men from outside Parliament – the trade unionist Ernest Bevin, now Minister of Labour, and Lord Beaverbrook, Minister of Aircraft Production – exercised much greater influence. In any case, the political compromise with the 'men of Munich' soon succumbed to the pressure of events. By the end of 1940 Chamberlain had died and Halifax had been sent off as ambassador to the United States; the war cabinet had expanded to include,

BELOW: *Men of the RAF wait to cross the Channel during the evacuation of British forces from France. It was Churchill's greatest achievement to maintain national morale after this debacle.*

LEFT: *Newspaper tycoon Lord Beaverbrook (left), a friend of Churchill since World War I, was installed as Minister for Aircraft Production in May 1940, with a brief to increase output by any means, however unconventional.*

BELOW: *Low's famous cartoon of 14 May 1940 was captioned 'All behind you, Winston.' The cartoonist's left-wing political sympathies are clear in the prominence given to Labour men – with Winston in the front row are, left to right, Clement Attlee, trade union leader Ernest Bevin, and Herbert Morrison.*

ABOVE: *Churchill visits the Allied generals in France, from left to right, Ironside, Gamelin, Gort and Georges. Despite the smiles for the camera, the military situation was desperate.*

RIGHT: *Churchill leaves Downing Street for the House of Commons on 18 June 1940 after the French surrender, carrying the text of his speech, in which he would inform the nation that 'the Battle of Britain is about to begin' and call on them to make this 'their finest hour.'*

among others, Eden, Bevin and Beaverbrook. In October, Churchill took over the leadership of the Conservative Party. The spirit of Munich was dead.

The changes Churchill brought to government were, as he later wrote, 'more real than apparent.' His most decisive formal act was to appoint himself Minister of Defence. He intended to run the military side of the war in person, through direct liaison with the Chiefs of Staff via the military wing of the war cabinet secretariat, headed by General Ismay. The ministers heading the War Office, the Admiralty and the Air Ministry were by-passed, becoming mere functionaries with little influence on policy-making. Because of his interest in the application of science to warfare, Churchill brought Professor Lindemann with him from the Admiralty, where he had continued his pre-war role as personal scientific adviser. Although officially only head of the Prime Minister's statistical section, Lindemann was often to have a crucial effect, for better or for worse, on the conduct of the war.

Churchill's leadership had an immediate impact on morale in the urgent struggle for national survival. A new vigour ran through the war effort from top to bottom. The message was quickly transmitted downward that formal hierarchies and normal procedures were no longer sacred. Anything that advanced the war effort was good; anything that

stood in its way must go. Financial orthodoxy was thrown out the window and Britain went for broke. Limits on working hours in factories were ignored in the race for arms production. Over a million men joined the Local Defence Volunteers (later renamed at Churchill's insistence 'the Home Guard') to fight the invader with pitchforks and broomsticks. After the passage of the Emergency Powers Act on 22 May, the government had the legal power to do almost anything it liked with its citizens or their property. The nation uncomplainingly entrusted its fate to 'the man with the big cigar.'

Churchill's courage was unquestionable. During May and June he flew to France five times for meetings in which he vainly strove to overcome the defeatism of the French high command. Once his aircraft was almost 'jumped' by German fighters over the Channel, and on his last visit he had to land on an airfield cratered by recent German bombing. The terrible spectacle of the disintegration of the French government and the collapse of the French will-to-resist made a stark contrast to the unity and resolve that Churchill had nurtured in Britain. After the French surrender, he also showed his ruthlessness by ordering the sinking of the French fleet at Oran. This gesture may not have been strictly necessary, but it certainly made its point in no uncertain terms. Britain would fight on alone.

Issued by the Ministry of Information *in co-operation with the War Office* **and the Ministry of Home Security**

Beating the INVADER

A MESSAGE FROM THE PRIME MINISTER

IF invasion comes, everyone—young or old, men and women—will be eager to play their part worthily. By far the greater part of the country will not be immediately involved. Even along our coasts, the greater part will remain unaffected. But where the enemy lands, or tries to land, there will be most violent fighting. Not only will there be the battles when the enemy tries to come ashore, but afterwards there will fall upon his lodgments very heavy British counter-attacks, and all the time the lodgments will be under the heaviest attack by British bombers. The fewer civilians or non-combatants in these areas, the better—apart from essential workers who must remain. So if you are advised by the authorities to leave the place where you live, it is your duty to go elsewhere when you are told to leave When the attack begins, it will be too late to go ; and, unless you receive definite instructions to move, your duty then will be to stay where you are. You will have to get into the safest place you can find, and stay there until the battle is over. For all of you then the order and the duty will be : " STAND FIRM ".

This also applies to people inland if any considerable number of parachutists or air-borne troops are landed in their neighbourhood. **Above all, they must not cumber the roads. Like their fellow-countrymen on the coasts, they must " STAND FIRM ". The Home Guard, supported by strong mobile columns wherever the enemy's numbers require it, will immediately come to grips with the invaders, and there is little doubt will soon destroy them.**

Throughout the rest of the country where there is no fighting going on and no close cannon fire or rifle fire can be heard, everyone will govern his conduct by the second great order and duty, namely, " CARRY ON ". It may easily be some weeks before the invader has been totally destroyed, that is to say, killed or captured to the last man who has landed on our shores. Meanwhile, all work must be continued to the utmost, and no time lost.

The following notes have been prepared to tell everyone in rather more detail what to do, and they should be carefully studied. Each man and woman should think out a clear plan of personal action in accordance with the general scheme.

Winston S. Churchill

STAND FIRM

I. What do I do if fighting breaks out in my neighbourhood?

Keep indoors or in your shelter until the battle is over. If you can have a trench ready in your garden or field, so much the better. You may want to use it for protection if your house is damaged. But if you are at work, or if you have special orders, carry on as long as possible and only take cover when danger approaches. If you are on your way to work, finish your journey if you can.

If you see an enemy tank, or a few enemy soldiers, do not assume that the enemy are in control of the area. What you have seen may be a party sent on in advance, or stragglers from the main body who can easily be rounded up.

Churchill always longed to be as close to the fighting as he could. His frequent visits to military establishments, his tours of the south coast defences and his famous walkabouts in recently bombed streets were not just morale-boosting exercises; they were the indulgence of a personal desire to get the smell of war in his nostrils. During the summer months when Britain stood in daily expectation of invasion, he practised with rifle and bayonet, ready to follow his own instruction 'to take one with you.' On 15 September, the climax of the Battle of Britain, he drove down from Chequers to the Group Operations Room at Uxbridge, so he could follow the progress of the crucial aerial conflict minute by minute on the display boards. Fighter Command lost 27 fighters but destroyed 56 enemy aircraft.

When the bombers started to arrive over London, on one occasion shattering the kitchen windows at No. 10 Downing Street, Churchill moved to safer accommodation at nearby Storey's Gate, normally known as 'the Annexe.' There he occupied a flat with Clementine above the underground War Rooms – private accommodation squeezed in between public offices, so that, according to Mary Soames, 'embarrassed officials would often encounter Winston, robed like a Roman emperor in his bath towel, proceeding dripping from his bathroom to his bedroom.' But although Churchill's entourage were at some pains to confine him to secure cover during air raids, nothing could restrain him from climbing on to the roof of the building to watch the action during a spectacular attack. He was invig-

ABOVE: *Churchill was frequently portrayed as a bulldog, as in this Strube cartoon of June 1940. His features and build suggested the comparison, as did his pugnacity and fighting spirit.*

OPPOSITE: *Churchill was as often caricatured by his enemies as by his friends. This Nazi poster was distributed in occupied Belgium in the autumn of 1940; 'Madame la Marquise' was a popular song.*

orated by the feeling that Whitehall, badly battered in the Blitz, had become like 'a battalion headquarters in the line.'

During those desperate days when Britain's fate hung in the balance, Churchill forged a bond with the British people through the power of words. Broadcast on the radio, his speeches reached almost everyone at home and a large audience overseas. They were calculated political acts, scrupulously prepared and rehearsed, intended to boost morale, scotch defeatism, secure maximum effort from workers and soldiers alike, and convince the outside world that Britain really did intend to fight on in the face of defeat. They were also intended to resound through the ages, for even at the most critical moments of conflict Churchill never forgot that he was an actor on the great stage of history.

Professional broadcasters were surprised at the success of the speeches. Churchill's style of oratory was at the very least 20 years out of date and was considered most unsuitable for the intimacy of radio. He addressed not the real British people, with their habitual scepticism and comfortable materialism, but an heroic British people of his own imagination, the living embodiment of a great historical tradition. He drew on a sense of English history – the tradition of Agincourt and Trafalgar – that meant little or nothing to most of his listeners, evoking as if it were alive a pride in Imperial glory and national destiny that for most people had died long ago, if it had ever

existed at all. Yet the speeches worked, with their archaic language, their occasional colloquialism amid the high-flown phrases, their flashes of cheeky humour, delivered by that rich, strangely compelling voice, unmistakable but not inimitable as every barrack-room wit soon discovered.

They were speeches resonant with high emotion at a time when high emotions were widely felt. The grimness of tone was strangely reassuring when coupled with the expression of implacable determination. Each great moment in the developing drama called forth its appropriate expression. The powerful crescendo of defiance after the evacuation of Dunkirk was perhaps the most effective in its dramatic simplicity:

We shall fight in France, we shall fight on the seas and oceans, we shall fight with growing confidence and strength in the air, we shall defend our island, whatever the cost may be, we shall fight on the beaches, we shall fight on the landing grounds, we shall fight in the fields and in the streets, we shall fight in the hills; we shall never surrender.

The fall of France brought out Churchill's epic historical vein, plus the inspired journalist's knack of coining a single unforgettable phrase:

. . . the Battle of France is over. I expect that the Battle of Britain is about to begin. . . . Let us therefore brace ourselves to our duties, and so bear ourselves that, if the British Empire and its Commonwealth last for a thousand years, men will still say, 'This was their finest hour.'

And for the Battle of Britain there was the famous tribute to the pilots of Fighter Command: 'Never in the field of human conflict was so much owed by so many to so few.'

Churchill's speeches were backed up by press photos, newsreels and personal appearances that all presented the prime minister to his people as an attractively idiosyncratic character. His flare for self-publicity was a powerful asset in war. The cigar and the V-sign, the 'bull-dog' look, the variety of clothing – from military uniform to the famous 'siren suits,' designed for air-raid wardens – marked him out as something very different from a run-of-the-mill politician. Of his popularity there can be no serious doubt. The London Civil Defence chief has described one of Churchill's many visits to the East End during the Blitz. The homeless poor dropped their pitiful bundles of possessions and cheered him among the ruins. 'Putting his hat on the end of his stick, he twirled it round and roared, "Are we downhearted?" and they shouted back "No!" with astonishing gusto.' In his manner and appearance, Churchill did nothing to hide the gulf that separated his life – brandy and cigars, a personal physician, a valet, a clean shirt three times a day – from that of a slum-dweller cowering every night in an insanitary public shelter. But at the time it occasioned no apparent resentment.

Angus Calder, author of the best study of the Home Front, *The People's War*, plausibly concludes it was Churchill's eccentricity that won the nation's admiration:

. . . all classes were clear that there nowhere was, nor ever had been, anyone quite like this man they were cheering. Such singularity, in such a high position, could only amount to greatness, and it was profoundly reassuring to suppose that Britain was led at this moment by a great man.

Those who worked with Churchill saw another side of the man. Once established as leader, he was consciously self-indulgent. He allowed himself to be rude, overbearingly loquacious or moodily silent, insulting or arbitrary. After he had been in office for two months, Clementine felt moved to warn him: 'there is a danger of your being generally disliked by your colleagues and subordinates because of your rough, sarcastic and overbearing manner.' Desmond Morton, for long a trusted adviser, was horrified by the 'depths of selfish brutality' revealed in Churchill's sudden rages against those who crossed him. Yet a remarkable number of Churchill's 'colleagues and subordinates' have since recorded their admiration and affection for the man who so often bullied or abused them. General Sir Alan Brooke, who as CIGS from mid-1941 onward had to put up with as much of his ill-humour as anyone, later wrote of his 'uncanny faculty for inspiring respect, admiration, loyalty and deep affection in the hearts of all

those fortunate enough to work in close touch with him.' In the long run his warmth, courage and humour made a deeper impression than his egotism and his irascible temper.

Churchill always led by example. His own phenomenal workrate justified his otherwise unreasonable demands on those who worked with him. He woke at around 8am to be presented simultaneously with a copious breakfast and dispatch boxes full of telegrams and memoranda. He then worked in bed for most of the morning, dictating to his secretaries or receiving visitors. The first bath of the day and a working lunch were followed by the inevitable siesta. Refreshed, he resumed at a furious pace until his second bath and expansive dinner. Then the most demanding work of the day could begin, apparently interminable meetings and discussions that went on into the early hours, often degenerating into Churchillian monologues as exhausted ministers and generals, in desperate need of sleep or with other vital tasks to attend to, nodded off in their chairs and longed for the moment when the inexhaustible old man would finally go to bed. Throughout the day, the prime minister's intake of alcohol was almost continuous, but it seemed to have little effect on his thought processes. His own observation on the subject seems to have been correct: 'I

ABOVE: *Twirling the hat on the stick was an infallible crowd-pleasing gesture. Churchill used all his innate showmanship to win the hearts and minds of the hard-pressed British people.*

LEFT: *No doubt Churchill's arrival on the scene was sometimes viewed with scepticism by tired men at grips with the appalling aftermath of an air attack, yet his presence seems to have been genuinely welcomed by the vast majority.*

have taken more out of alcohol than alcohol has taken out of me.'

His conduct as prime minister was essentially no different from his behaviour in previous ministerial posts. He harried his subordinates with queries and instructions on every subject under the sun, often with the threatening injunction 'Action this Day' and a request for information 'on one sheet of paper.' He dominated committee meetings with his unstoppable flow of words. He simultaneously directed grand strategy and intervened to determine the size of the jam ration or demand an increase in the output of playing cards.

Some of his initiatives were masterpieces of simple common sense – ordering lookouts to be placed on the roofs of factories, for instance, so that work could continue after the air-raid sirens sounded until a bomber actually threatened the plant itself. Others showed his grasp of practical psychology: he insisted that 'Communal Feeding Centres' be renamed 'British Restaurants' on the grounds that 'Everyone associates the word "restaurant" with a good meal, and they may as well have the name if they cannot have anything else.' His generosity stimulated by visits to bombed areas – easily moved, he often had tears in his eyes as he walked through the rubble – he forced a reluctant Treasury to provide more adequate compensation for loss of

property through air attack. But the work of a ministry could be seriously disrupted for days by one of his sudden importunate demands for information or action. It sometimes appeared to hard-pressed officials as if they were fighting a war against Churchill, rather than Hitler.

The most dubious aspect of Churchill's premiership was, from the first, his direction of the military side of the war. He summed up his method in a single witty phrase: 'All I wanted was compliance with my wishes after reasonable discussion.' The Chiefs of Staff and senior officers were free to oppose his plans or propose their own. Decisions were analysed in exchanges of memoranda, thrashed out at interminable committee meetings, debated through exhausting working weekends at Chequers. If the military men were stubborn enough and forceful enough in their arguments, they could resist the more outlandish of Churchill's plans of attack. But in the end they often gave way against their better judgment.

Churchill brought to the war an ex-hussar's obsession with 'fighting spirit,' the sometimes naive inspirations of an amateur strategist, and a small boy's enthusiasm for secret weapons and secret intelligence. His fascination with the 'Wizard War' was the most useful – or least harmful – of these Churchillian peculiarities. Through Lindemann

LEFT: *An American poster by Henri Guignon uses the familiar bulldog image for the resolute British war leader.*

HOLDING THE LINE !

BELOW: *A bomber crew waits as a Stirling is prepared for a raid on Germany. Churchill allowed himself to be convinced that Bomber Command might win the war and committed resources to the bombing offensive that could have been better used elsewhere.*

ABOVE: *French resistance fighters prepare to go into action. Despite Churchill's injunction to 'Set Europe ablaze,' the British SOE was unable to galvanize national resistance groups into a serious threat to Nazi power.*

(elevated to the peerage as Lord Cherwell in 1941), Churchill was directly in touch with the latest developments in war technology and the controversies that raged around them. He was always persistent in urging new devices and techniques on the services, especially the Army which he regarded as particularly hidebound in its orthodoxy. Scientists would unquestionably have played a large part in the war under any leadership, but the knowledge of his support, and sometimes his direct intervention, encouraged those at work in the research laboratories, gave them access to resources and undermined the resistance of the military professionals to cooperation with the 'boffins.'

Churchill's special fascination with secret intelligence led to a vigorous shake-up of the intelligence system during his first few months in power. It is doubtful whether much would have been achieved, however, had not the Government Code and Cypher School (GC & CS) at Bletchley Park cracked the German Enigma codes. The intelligence available from decryption of German radio messages has been described as the best ever obtained by a country at war. Churchill was delighted with GC & CS and gave it his full support; the cryptographers were his 'geese who laid the golden eggs and never cackled' (although he was somewhat startled, when he visited Bletchley Park in 1941, by the collection of undisciplined eccentrics assembled there: 'I know I told you to leave no stone unturned to find the

necessary staff,' he huffily commented, 'but I did not mean to be taken so literally').

Churchill insisted on being given a selection of the Ultra Secret decrypts every day and took an almost childish delight in opening the secret yellow dispatch case, often delivered by the head of MI6, Sir Stewart Menzies, in person. Eager to curry favour, Menzies always tried to make sure there was at least one juicy item to suit the prime minister's palate. Churchill loved to spring this secret information on the uninitiated to clinch an argument, thus triumphing in debate from an unassailable position of strength – it would have been a breach of security to query the source of his intelligence.

Valuable as Ultra was, Churchill's love of secrets led him to put too much faith in it. He succumbed to the common fallacy of believing that a conversation overheard or a stolen document would necessarily reveal the truth. His interpretation of the Ultra intercepts was generally naive. It never seems to have occurred to him that when Rommel communicated with his superiors in Rome or Berlin, he might exaggerate his weakness in order to extort more supplies, or lie about his future plans to protect them from interference. Churchill's unshakeable confidence in Ultra unfortunately made his relationship with commanders in the field more difficult, because it encouraged the assumption that, sitting in London, he was as well placed to judge the risks of an offensive as they were. This was not always so.

To the rational side of Churchill, it was obvious once France fell out of the war in 1940 that only the entry of new allies into the war – above all the United States – offered any hope of victory. Until that happy event, Britain and its Empire stood under threat, requiring heroic efforts simply to survive. Apart from the defence of Britain and its trade routes across the Atlantic, there was a need to resist the Italians in the Mediterranean (Mussolini had declared war on 11 June) and to prepare against a possible Japanese attack in Southeast Asia. In fact, Britain lacked the capacity even to fulfil all these defensive tasks simultaneously.

But psychologically, Churchill was incapable of standing on the defensive, let alone making a strategic retreat to avoid being overextended. On the same day that the Dunkirk evacuation was completed, he began considering new designs for landing craft to carry British tanks back across the Channel. In August 1940, with Britain thinly defended and in daily expectation of invasion, he sent an armoured brigade to Egypt. This sublimely imprudent act was a statement of one priority from which he was never to waver. At the same desperate moment, the Chiefs of Staff were under orders to come up with a plan for overthrowing Hitler's rule in Europe. By September they had produced a scenario for the defeat of Germany: its economy, supposedly already near breaking point, would collapse under the twin effects of blockade and bombing, and an uprising of the conquered peoples of Europe would throw off the Nazi yoke. The British Army would then walk in to pick up the pieces. In pursuit of this fantasy, Churchill pushed forward a campaign of strategic bombing, sabotage and subversion.

Churchill had authorized Bomber Command's first raids on the industrial areas of the Ruhr only five days after taking power. By September he was convinced that Britain must prepare 'to carry an ever-increasing volume of explosives to Germany, so as to pulverize the entire industry and scientific structure on which the war effort and the economic life of the enemy depend.' In no other way could Germany's military power be overcome. The official objective was to hit military and industrial targets, but Churchill was not averse to taking revenge for the Blitz by terrorizing German civilians. A very high proportion of Britain's scant resources was henceforth devoted to strategic bombing. But the bomber offensive of 1940-41 was a fiasco. The night attacks were costly and inaccurate; they had no effect on German war production and killed more

BELOW: *Italian prisoners in the Western Desert after the fall of Tobruk in January 1941. Easy successes against Mussolini's poorly equipped and demoralized forces created an illusion of British prowess that the Germans soon dispelled.*

British fliers than German civilians. Churchill began to have doubts about the campaign through observing the limited effect of the Blitz on Britain. In the autumn of 1941, the first objective analysis of aerial reconnaissance photos revealed the abject truth that the raids were totally ineffectual. In November 1941 they were halted.

The proposed campaign of sabotage and subversion proved equally ineffective. The basic premise was that conquered Europe – and possibly Germany too – was only waiting for the chance to rise up against the Nazi oppressor. Britain would provide arms, organization and propaganda to spread guerrilla war. Churchill as usual supplied the memorable slogan: 'Set Europe ablaze.' It might have been supposed that Churchill would have little enthusiasm for subversion – he certainly had no desire to see the war turn into a socialist revolution – but he was ready to use any means to achieve victory. And he loved the Richard Hannay-style daring of the Special Operations Executive (SOE) set up to put sabotage and subversion into effect. Indeed, any irregular or 'élite' force could be sure of his active support. He bullied the War Office into backing the Commandos, for example, despite stubborn resistance from conservative officers. It was Churchill's influence that ensured World War II would become a spectacular playground for 'special forces.'

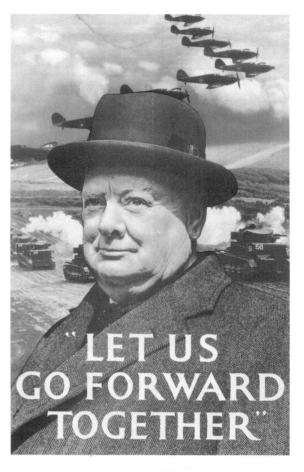

LET US GO FORWARD TOGETHER

BELOW: *Churchill's bedroom in the underground complex. He more often slept in the Annexe, a flat immediately above the War Rooms.*

But SOE was not a success. The premise behind its activities was at fault. Most Europeans (although not Germans) would have preferred to be freed from Nazi rule, but few were prepared to take the risk of doing anything about it in the face of SS terror. The German economy was not near breaking point – it was not even on a full war footing – the German people were not demoralized and ready to turn against their rulers under pressure from Bomber Command, and the rest of Occupied Europe was not just awaiting the signal to rise up against the oppressor. Despite Churchill's strong desire to the contrary, the war could never be won without a costly orthodox military campaign in France.

It was perhaps because they shared Churchill's aversion to recreating the Western Front – memories of 1914-18 were indelible – that the Chiefs of Staff did not resist his obsession with the Mediterranean theatre, which absorbed such a disproportionate share of the energies of the British Empire throughout the war. Churchill dreamed of a successful re-run of Gallipoli. He was ever to be tempted by the prospect of a thrust upward into Germany from below – either the Balkans or Italy could function as 'the soft underbelly.' He overrated the importance of the Suez Canal, for so long considered the hub of the British Empire. His amateur strategist's eye made too much of a possible enemy thrust through Egypt to the oilfields of Persia – more tempting on the map than in reality. He fantasized about the chances of Turkey entering the war on Britain's side. Perhaps above all, in the short term, he just longed for action and easy victories.

For a while the Mediterranean theatre obliged. In November 1940, aircraft from the *Illustrious* crippled the Italian fleet at Taranto. General Wavell's outnumbered forces in Egypt then routed the Italians in the Western Desert. This was heartening stuff for the hard-pressed British public battered by the Blitz. Churchill harried the impassive Wavell to take more action. But the moment the Germans turned their attention southward, in the spring of 1941, illusions of victory were swiftly dispelled. The Luftwaffe and the U-boats easily established their dominance over the Mediterranean sea and air. Betrayed into an unwise move by Churchill's insistent demand for a show of 'fighting spirit,' Wavell landed troops in Greece to face Hitler's forces advancing through the Balkans. They had to be withdrawn almost as soon as they arrived, leaving all their equipment behind. This adventure cost 12,000 men. It also fatally weakened British forces in North Africa, which were sent reeling back across Cyrenaica by General Erwin Rommel's newly arrived Afrika Korps. In late May there followed the loss of Crete to a German airborne assault. These were bitter defeats.

The Greek adventure brought Churchill's political authority into question for the first time since he had taken power. Memories of Gallipoli were suddenly re-awoken. It was as if people had for a time forgotten who this man was who was running the war. Now they remembered. Churchill was the same as he had always been, a gambler who played for high stakes, given to rash decisions that might well be wrong. He survived a critical House of Commons debate on 7 May without difficulty, demanding a vote of confidence and getting it, with an ovation thrown in. But his reputation would never quite stand as high again as it had in the first year of his war leadership.

Churchill's displeasure fell upon Wavell. He was the first general to fall victim to the prime minister's obsession with offensive spirit. His responsibilities spread far and wide – Iraq, Abyssinia, Syria – and his resources limited, Wavell wished to stand on the defensive in Egypt. This was also the advice of the Chief of the Imperial General Staff (CIGS), Sir John Dill, who argued that the defence of Britain and Singapore should take precedence over the Middle East. Churchill dismissed these arguments. Wavell was ordered to attack in mid-June; codenamed Battleaxe, the offensive was premature and failed totally. Churchill transferred Wavell to India in virtual disgrace.

BELOW: *The first meeting between Churchill and Roosevelt, on board the battleship* Prince of Wales *in August 1941. Churchill relied heavily on his personal rapport with the American president, already nurtured through a lengthy correspondence.*

But at this bleak period in Britain's military fortunes great changes were afoot. On 10 May, a year to the day after Churchill had come to power, London was subjected to its heaviest bombing of the war. In a single night 1436 Londoners were killed. Churchill wept over the ruins of the House of Commons, where so many dramatic moments of his life had been lived. Then the nights went strangely silent. The Blitz was over; the Luftwaffe had shifted to the east. On 22 June, the day after Wavell's public disgrace, Germany invaded the Soviet Union.

Churchill had long ago decided that Stalin would be an acceptable ally. He had not changed his attitude to Communism, as he made clear in his broadcast on the day of the invasion, but he was prepared to interpret Soviet resistance to Hitler as a war for national freedom: 'the cause of any Russian fighting for his hearth and home is the cause of free men and free people in every quarter of the globe.' This was the public line. In private, Churchill was more candid: 'If Hitler invaded Hell I would make at least a favourable reference to the Devil in the House of Commons.' Whatever his reservations, the embracing of the Soviet Union was a momentous act.

At the time, although there was psychological reassurance in no longer standing alone, it was not clear that any practical advantage would accrue. In July Churchill agreed to supply Stalin with arms and equipment, despite Britain's own shortages, but military experts believed the Soviet Union would be quickly defeated. Germany would then have plentiful raw materials at its disposal, ending any chance of economic blockade, and would be poised to attack Britain's Persian oilfields. Churchill did not accept these gloomy prognostications, but he looked west rather than east for real hope of eventual victory.

RIGHT: *Erwin Rommel, commander of the Afrika Korps, in the Western Desert. Still clinging to the romantic image of warfare as a chivalrous contest, Churchill was fulsome in his praise of Rommel – 'May I say across the havoc of war, a great general.'*

Perhaps mindful of his own Anglo-American ancestry, before the war Churchill had developed his thesis of 'the English-speaking peoples' as the privileged custodians of a noble tradition of freedom. It was therefore not only for practical reasons that he looked to the United States as an ally for Britain in the war against tyranny. His sentiments and his sense of history were involved. He worked tirelessly on American opinion. His every speech and action was angled to win the United States' support. During his period at the Admiralty, he had been in correspondence with President Franklin D. Roosevelt; the exchange of letters was continued, Churchill signing himself 'Former Naval Person.' In this personal relationship lay Britain's best chance of drawing the United States out of its neutrality.

The cordiality between the two leaders and Roosevelt's personal sympathy for the British cause at first produced little by way of concrete help. During the summer of 1940 all the president could provide in response to Churchill's desperate pleas were old rifles 'surplus to requirements' for the Home Guard. In September he agreed to hand over 50 ageing destroyers in a hardnosed exchange for British bases. These were mere crumbs from America's well-stocked table. A British purchasing commission was set up in Washington, but everything had to be paid for in cash and Britain was desperately short of dollars. Churchill begged Roosevelt to 'give us the stuff all the same' when the money ran out; in December 1940 the 'Lend-lease' legislation was introduced that waived the demand for immediate cash payment. In February 1941 Churchill delivered his famous appeal: 'Give us the tools and we will finish the job.' The United States was prepared to become the 'arsenal of democracy' – slowly and at a profit – but Britain needed much more.

At the start of August 1941 Churchill sailed on the battleship *Prince of Wales* to meet Roosevelt for the first time at Placentia Bay, Newfoundland. The voyage was the first break he had had from working seven days a week since becoming prime minister – a period of 15 months. The encounter was a personal success; the pen-friends liked one another in the flesh. But in practical terms it achieved little. The United States agreed to join Britain in aid to Russia and to step up arms production. They would go no further. A vague statement of principles, the Atlantic Charter, was produced for propaganda

purposes. Churchill came home virtually empty-handed. The United States was stretching the concept of neutrality a long way; in the late summer of 1941 the US Navy extended its patrols into the west Atlantic, soon clashing with German U-boats. But Hitler did not oblige by declaring war.

Salvation finally came from the Far East. On 7 December Churchill was dining at Chequers when the butler respectfully informed him that, according to the radio in the kitchen, the Japanese had attacked Pearl Harbor. Churchill rose from the table and walked calmly out of the room, excusing himself with the satisfied comment: 'I am going to declare war.' With Britain and the United States allied against Japan, they were bound to become allies against Germany also. Hitler prevented any delay

by gratuitously declaring war on the United States. For Churchill, the implications were clear: 'So we had won after all.'

The great danger, from the British point of view, was that the United States would choose to concentrate its main effort against Japan, instead of Germany. On 12 December Churchill set off across the U-boat infested Atlantic on board the battleship *Duke of York* with a bevy of military and political advisers to persuade Britain's new ally to put Europe first. In fact, Roosevelt was already agreed. The 'Arcadia' conference proceeded to lay the foundations for the extraordinarily close military coordination between Britain and the United States that would last until the end of the war. Churchill put his faith in his personal rapport with Roosevelt, best symbolized by a perhaps apocryphal anecdote: Roosevelt is supposed to have entered the principal guest room at the White House to encounter the startling sight of Churchill stark naked; unabashed, Churchill reassured his embarrassed host: 'The Prime Minister of Great Britain has nothing to hide from the President of the United States.'

Publicly Churchill bathed in the warm glow of personal triumph. He was rapturously received by Congress. He flew to Ottawa to address the Canadian Parliament, then returned to Washington to sign the United Nations pact at the New Year. Everywhere he was feted. But the long strain of the war had taken its toll. One night he suffered a slight heart attack, not sufficient to interrupt his routine, but a warning sign. Before returning to his post, he allowed himself five days' holiday in Florida.

It was a well-earned rest. Churchill had made his great contribution to history. Had Britain sued for peace or succumbed to German invasion, Nazi rule would surely have been consolidated over the whole of Europe and the future of the continent might have resembled, in George Orwell's phrase, 'a boot stamping on a human face – for ever.' Now the German armies had halted in front of Moscow and the immense resources of the United States were to be hurled into the conflict. Hitler's defeat was only a matter of time and 'the proper application of overwhelming force.' By his single-minded determination, his courage, and resolution, Churchill had contributed mightily to the survival of his country. His own estimate, given in much later, more peaceful times, was untypically modest: 'It was the nation and the race dwelling around the globe that had the lion's heart. I had the luck to be called upon to give the roar!'

BELOW: *From the deck of the* Prince of Wales, *Churchill watches Roosevelt steam away aboard an American destroyer, August 1941. Churchill based his hopes for Britain's future on the 'special relationship' with the United States and his personal relationship with the president.*

CHAPTER NINE

The Fortunes
of War

LEFT: *On the path to victory, the
warlord visits the Normandy
bridgehead. He is flanked by the two
commanders who best coped with his
demanding personality – Field
Marshal Sir Alan Brooke (left) and
General Montgomery.*

BY the time Churchill flew back from the New World to a frost-bitten London in mid-January 1942, he had been out of Britain for five weeks. In his absence, discontent with his management of the war had grown acute. Even in friendly political circles it was felt that he was carrying too much responsibility – that he could not at the same time conduct international diplomacy, run military strategy and coordinate war production. A wider public was restless at the failure to achieve a more vigorous prosecution of the war.

To silence his critics Churchill badly needed a military victory. But disasters, often of his own making, rained upon him. His sense of priorities and his grasp of military realities were constantly at fault. In his enthusiasm for a successful offensive in North Africa he had failed to provide adequate forces, particularly of aircraft, to defend Southeast Asia. Instead he sent two of the navy's best ships, the *Prince of Wales* and the *Repulse*, as a gesture to deter the Japanese from attack – a futile gesture in the absence of adequate air cover. On 10 December 1941 both ships were sunk by Japanese bombers. As the Japanese Army advanced through Malaya, Singapore lay in their grasp. Churchill thought it invulnerable; it was, in fact, indefensible. As he later

wrote: 'My advisers ought to have known and I ought to have been told, and I myself ought to have asked.' On 15 February 1942 the 60,000 British troops at Singapore surrendered, the greatest capitulation in British history and a blow from which British prestige in Asia never recovered.

Meanwhile in North Africa, the theatre for the benefit of which Southeast Asia had been denied the aircraft and supplies it required, another Churchill-inspired premature offensive, conducted by Wavell's replacement, General Auchinleck, had been driven back to Tobruk by the end of January. The Battle of the Atlantic was also going through one of its worst phases. There was a desperate need of more airpower to help in convoy defence and submarine-hunting. But Churchill allowed himself to be persuaded by Lord Cherwell and the new head of Bomber Command, Sir Arthur Harris, to devote resources to a renewed night-bombing offensive over Germany instead. The bombing failed to dent German war production; sinkings in the Atlantic reached a critical level.

Military failure was not the only problem. Churchill was increasingly out of step with popular feeling on the Home Front. In 1940, when Britain stood alone, he had seemed to possess a direct line

BELOW: *The surrender at Singapore, perhaps the most humiliating military defeat in British history. It destroyed at a stroke the twin myths of racial superiority and imperial invincibility.*

to the hearts and minds of the British people. Now his broadcasts were listened to, if at all, without great enthusiasm. The impact of total war had radicalized political and social attitudes, and the entry of the Soviet Union into the war had driven opinion further leftward. The hammer and sickle was a common sight throughout Britain. The news of continual heavy fighting in Russia provoked ignominious comparisons with Britain's feeble military performance. The demand for a Second Front, an immediate invasion of Europe to take the pressure off the Soviet Union, was insistent. Churchill did his best to harness this popular enthusiasm – Clementine was put in charge of an Aid to Russia Fund – but there would always be doubts about the sincerity of his commitment to the Soviet cause. His own enthusiasm for the United States was not widely shared at this stage of the war.

Popular discontent found expression in the newspapers, especially the *Daily Mirror*. Enraged by attacks on government policy, Churchill wanted to close the *Mirror* down; his cabinet colleagues persuaded him to settle for a severe warning. In any case, news of by-elections could not be suppressed. An electoral truce was in force between the three parties participating in the government, but independents could stand against coalition candidates. In quick succession four independents opposed to government policies were elected in widely differing constituencies.

Churchill tried to head off opposition by shifting his cabinet leftward in February 1942. Notably the Labour leader, Clement Attlee, received the title of Deputy Prime Minister and Sir Stafford Cripps, formerly Ambassador to Moscow, was brought into the war cabinet. The personification of austerity, and associated in the public mind with the heroic Soviet Union, Cripps was the man of the moment, tipped by some to replace Churchill at the top. He expressed the popular mood with his insistence that 'personal extravagance must be eliminated altogether.' Churchill found Cripps both personally and politically uncongenial. He swiftly undermined his popularity by sending him off to India with the thankless task of negotiating with hostile nationalists. Later, when the Cripps cult had faded, Churchill manoeuvered him out of the war cabinet again.

There was never much chance that Churchill would be replaced while the war lasted. Apart from Cripps the only possible alternative leader was Foreign Secretary Anthony Eden, but he was too young and lightweight to mount a serious challenge. Churchill's command of the House of Commons in debate was magisterial. It was after the fall of Tobruk in June 1942 that the most serious parliamentary assault was launched. Faced with a motion of 'no confidence in the central direction of the war,' Churchill defended himself with a familiar mixture of humour and contemptuous scolding. Rubbing his hands up and down over his waistcoat in a familiar gesture of self-satisfaction, he jollied the MPs along with a joke about a new tank: 'As might be expected, it had many defects and teething troubles, and when these became apparent the tank was appropriately rechristened the "Churchill."' The next minute, he was lecturing them in the tones of an angry headmaster: 'the duty of the House of Commons is to sustain the government or to change the government. If it cannot change it, it should sustain it.' Still, although the motion was feebly moved, 25 MPs voted against Churchill and about 40 deliberately abstained.

For most of 1942 Churchill was depressed, extremely bad-tempered and less than fully fit. Yet he

still managed to impose his own strategy on the United States. Like the British people and the Soviet government, the American Chiefs of Staff were keen on the Second Front. They wanted an invasion of France at the earliest possible opportunity, believing that to win a war you must engage your enemy's major forces. Churchill and his military chiefs, on the other hand, were agreed in opposing any direct confrontation with the Germans in northern Europe, at least until other forms of attack had worn down German strength. In June Churchill flew to the United States to urge this view on his Allies, taking with him the gift of Britain's work on the atomic bomb as a sweetener. The effect of the visit was somewhat undermined by its coinciding with the fall of Tobruk, hardly likely to persuade the US military leaders that the right place to begin fighting was in the Mediterranean. By the end of July, however, Roosevelt had persuaded his generals to prepare for a landing in French North Africa. The Second Front was postponed until 1943.

At the start of August, Churchill embarked on a delicate mission to Moscow, to break the news of

ABOVE: *A Churchill tank and its crew. Churchill quipped that the tank had been named after him because of its 'many defects and teething troubles.'*

the postponement to Stalin. On the way he stopped off at Cairo to shake up the British command in the desert. Auchinleck had just won the first battle of Alamein, the turning point in the desert war. But it had been a defensive victory. Victorious defence meant nothing to Churchill. Judged lacking in 'offensive spirit,' Auchinleck followed Wavell into disgrace. He was replaced by General Sir Harold Alexander and, as commander of the Eighth Army, by General Bernard Montgomery (in fact the second choice for the job). Churchill was disturbed by Montgomery's abstemious eating habits and his obsession with physical jerks, but recognized a man with much of his own flair for self-publicity and morale-boosting gestures. Oddly, he was a general to be noted for his cautious, methodical approach to battle. The great merit of Alexander and Montgomery is not that they possessed 'offensive spirit' but that they could stand up to Churchill and resist his constant 'prodding.'

The first meeting between Churchill and Stalin in Moscow did not run smoothly. Churchill was in a foul mood – the British ambassador felt 'he was at his bloody worst and his worst is really bloody.' He offended the Russians by turning up for an official banquet in his siren-suit; they were not impressed by this egalitarian dress. Stalin was in any case not well disposed toward bearers of bad tidings and made Churchill feel the full brunt of his displeasure

LEFT: *General Alexander, successor to Wavell and Auchinleck as British commander in Cairo.*

RIGHT: *Trucks come under artillery fire during the battle of Alamein. This single victory was enough to guarantee Churchill's political position for the duration of the war.*

BELOW: *An ebullient Roosevelt and a thoughtful Churchill answer questions from the press during the Casablanca conference.*

over the postponement of the Second Front. At one point Churchill declared his intention of leaving Moscow early in protest, but in the end a certain rapport was struck between the two men. Stalin kept a well-stocked table and could, when he wished, fabricate a ponderous geniality. The champagne and the vodka flowed. After a lavish midnight banquet Churchill convinced himself that he would be able to work with the Bolshevik dictator after all.

On his return journey Churchill stopped off at Cairo again and was impressed by the improvement in Army morale. But he was made to wait for his desert victory. Montgomery would not be hurried; he bided his time, building up an overwhelming superiority of forces. It was not until 23 October that the general was ready to launch his great offensive at Alamein. While Churchill fumed and fretted, the Eighth Army ground away at its enemy for almost a fortnight, until Rommel broke and ran. On 7 November Anglo-American forces landed in French North Africa. At long last, here was a taste of victory. In his joy and relief Churchill had the church bells rung in Britain for the first time since the start of the war. It was only, as he said on 10 November, 'the end of the beginning'; but his own hold on power was now secure for the duration.

The turning of the military tide during the winter and spring of 1942-43 – the German defeat at Stalingrad, the conclusion of the North African campaign and the taming of the U-boats in the Atlantic – ushered in the era of the great conferences. As the most mobile of the Big Three, Churchill roved the world, from Washington to Yalta, from Casablanca to Teheran, working tirelessly to hold together the Grand Alliance through personal contacts with Roosevelt and Stalin. Not surprisingly, under the strain his health began to fail. The apotheosis of Churchill as a world leader coincided with the onset of his physical decline.

On 12 January 1943 he set off on the first journey of a peripatetic year, flying to Casablanca for a meeting with Roosevelt. Because clearing North Africa of German troops was taking longer than expected – it was not completed until May – there was now no chance of opening the Second Front in 1943. Denied a crack at northern Europe, the American military chiefs wanted to transfer their main effort to the Pacific. Churchill fought for his Mediterranean strategy instead and the Americans eventually agreed to the invasion of Sicily. Other decisions included the stepping-up of the strategic bombing of Germany and an offensive in Burma. At the final press conference, Roosevelt announced the principle of 'unconditional surrender.' Churchill later claimed not to have been consulted about this decision, although he certainly did not oppose it as applied to Germany.

BELOW: *Visiting the desert on his return journey from Moscow in August 1942, Churchill in siren suit and topee chats with the newly appointed Eighth Army commander General Montgomery, with Alexander (left) and Brooke in attendance.*

There were considerable strains during the conference, not least from the presence of two mutually hostile French generals, de Gaulle and Giraud, competing for control of liberated North Africa. But Churchill enjoyed the winter sunshine, a welcome escape from the grim austerity of wartime London. Harold Macmillan, one of the British party at the conference, described the event as having elements of a cruise and a summer school for its privileged participants. Churchill even insisted on taking Roosevelt to savour the beauty of Marrakesh and painted a picture there, an uncommon self-indulgence during the war.

From Casablanca, Churchill flew on to Turkey for a meeting with the Turkish president in pursuance of his stubborn, futile fantasy of bringing that country into the war. Then, wandering apparently more or less on impulse, he travelled to Libya, witnessing a march past of the Eighth Army in Tripoli, and finally descended unexpectedly upon General Eisenhower, the Allied commander in North Africa, at Algiers, before flying back to London. Travelling by air under wartime conditions was a demanding experience for a 68-year-old. Apart from the risk of interception by enemy aircraft, the discomfort of long flights in often unheated Liberator bombers was extreme. One night Churchill's personal doctor, Sir Charles Wilson (later Lord Moran) witnessed the disconcerting spectacle of the prime minister, dressed only in a silk vest, crawling bare-arsed around a freezing bomb bay trying desperately to block out the draughts. By the time Churchill arrived back in England in mid-February, he had contracted a bout of pneumonia from which it took him a full month to recover.

Two further conferences with the Americans followed in May (Washington) and in August-September (Quebec). Churchill harried his Allies into pushing forward in the Mediterranean one step at a time – first Sicily, then Italy. But the Americans were determined to pin him down on a Second Front. He was forced to accept a definite date for the cross-Channel invasion, 1 May 1944, cede overall command of the invasion to an American general, and accept that landings in southern France would take place at the same time. Churchill probably still hoped at heart that some miracle would obviate the need for a full campaign in northern Europe, that the collapse of Italy and the eventual entry of Turkey into the war would allow a thrust up into the 'soft underbelly' of the enemy. But even the Italian surrender in September 1943 brought final victory no nearer, and Churchill's Balkan fantasies ended in a small fiasco. He insisted on British troops seizing Italian islands in the Aegean, although the Americans refused to have anything to do with the project. Rather than prodding Turkey into declaring war, this foolish initiative simply provoked a

BELOW: *Churchill gives his famous 'V for victory' sign as he disembarks in the United States for one of many conferences in 1943. His constant travels under wartime conditions were sometimes uncomfortable, often dangerous and always demanding for a man in his late 60s.*

LEFT: *Cairo, 1943. The Big Two are flanked by Chinese leader Chiang Kai-shek and his wife. Roosevelt is speaking to British Foreign Secretary Anthony Eden; behind the president, in the back row, stands a future prime minister, Harold Macmillan. Churchill seems cut off from the general good humour, perhaps feeling his isolation as Roosevelt deliberately distances himself from the British diplomatic position – or simply showing his habitual discomfort in the presence of women.*

German counter-attack which retook the islands, capturing most of the British troops involved.

In appearance, through 1943 Churchill was still exercising a predominant influence over Allied strategy. But this was an illusion. If the British got their way up to a point, it was because Roosevelt agreed with Churchill that Europe must come first and overruled his own military chiefs' Pacific bent. As early as December 1942 Churchill had been obliged to tell the House of Commons that Britain was 'neither militarily nor politically controlling the course of events' in North Africa. The United States, with its immense resources of manpower, money and productive capacity, was in command.

Churchill gambled everything on the special relationship with the United States. He gave the Americans valuable British secrets of science and technology; he put Britain's finances into their hands. So strong was his personal sense of identification with the United States that he once proposed the adoption of a common British/American citizenship. In return, he counted on the United States to maintain Britain as a world power. It was all very well for Churchill to declare, in November 1942, that he had 'not become the King's First Minister to preside over the liquidation of the British Empire.' Exhausted by the pursuit of victory at any cost, Britain no longer had the power to sustain an Empire without American support.

But Roosevelt and his advisers did not share Churchill's vision. They were concerned to further their own interests, both material and idealistic. No sentiment about a supposed bond between 'the English-speaking peoples' clouded the president's pursuit of his objectives. Specifically, he sought the application of the principle of self-determination to all peoples, not just Europeans. He wanted the abolition of the Empire that Churchill cherished.

The fragility of the personal rapport with the president on which Churchill counted so much first became clear at the Teheran conference at the end of November 1943, when the Big Three met together for the first time. Churchill arranged to meet Roosevelt first in Cairo, intending that the British and American delegations should coordinate their strategy before confronting the Soviets. But Roosevelt would have none of it. He avoided Churchill by spending his whole time in discussions with the Chinese leader, Chiang Kai-shek. Once in Teheran he immediately agreed with Stalin on the overwhelming importance of an invasion of northern France. Churchill saw his own stubbornly held views on the importance of the eastern Mediterranean and the Balkans swept aside.

With the grand outlines of strategy settled, the Big Three turned to discussion of a post-war settlement. Poland was already a potential stumbling-block. Churchill was aware of a special obligation to the country for which Britain had initially gone to war, but he was also conscious that the liberation of Poland from the Nazis would depend on the Soviet Army. The Polish government-in-exile in London was bitterly anti-Russian – even more so after the revelation of the Katyn massacre of Polish officers, probably a Soviet atrocity. Churchill refused to treat Katyn as a serious issue: 'There is no use prowling around the three-year-old graves of Smolensk.' He was inclined to regard the Poles as difficult

RIGHT: *Churchill celebrated his 69th birthday in Teheran – 'On my right sat the President of the United States, on my left the Master of Russia. Together we controlled . . . 20 millions of men engaged in the most terrible of wars that had yet occurred in human history.'*

troublemakers bent on disturbing the vital Grand Alliance. He and Roosevelt accepted Stalin's proposal that Poland should be shifted westward, taking a chunk of Germany as compensation for the loss of land to the Soviet Union in the east. The question of the nature of a future Polish government was left vague. On the future of Germany there was also general agreement. It was decided that the country

was to be dismembered and left in such a state that it could never again wage war.

The most striking aspect of the Teheran conference was the degree of trust and understanding achieved by the three main participants. The professionals of the British diplomatic corps hated Churchill's amateur handling of diplomacy, but even they had to admit that he got on with Stalin better

RIGHT: *Churchill's daughter Sarah accompanied him to Teheran as a personal aide. Here she is introduced to Marshal Stalin.*

LEFT: *A convalescent Churchill, clad in an eye-catching dressing gown over his siren suit, poses for photographers with Generals Eisenhower and Alexander at Carthage on Christmas Day, 1943.*

than expected. Evenings spent exchanging toasts – Churchill drinking to the 'proletarian masses,' Stalin toasting the Conservative Party – may have been a superficial ground for agreement, but it was better than rancour and suspicions that could have severely hampered the war effort. Whatever their differences the three men could always agree on the overriding priority of defeating Germany. There is no question, though, that Churchill was made to feel the odd man out. This was symbolized by one strange incident. At a certain moment, discussing the future of Germany, Stalin suggested, possibly as a joke, that 50,000 German officers and officials should be executed; Roosevelt facetiously replied with a counter-bid of 49,000. Outraged, Churchill stomped from the table and stood with his back

LEFT: *Churchill watches the Allied landings in the south of France from the bridge of HMS* Kimberley *on 15 August 1944 – to his mind, a poor consolation for having been forced to miss the Normandy landings.*

Churchill visits Normandy after the landings. RIGHT: *Crossing the Channel.* BELOW: *Disembarking at the Mulberry harbour.* BELOW RIGHT: *Poring over maps with his generals.*

turned, refusing to sit down again until the suggestion was withdrawn.

Returning with Roosevelt to Cairo, Churchill was exhausted and ill. His concentration was poor; he oscillated between a vacuous loquacity and sullen silence. Against medical advice he set off from Cairo to visit the Italian front before returning to England. At Tunis, where he stopped off for talks with Eisenhower, he was struck down with chronic pneumonia. His doctor feared for his life and Clementine was flown out from London to be at his side. Under strict discipline – no smoking, and alcohol consumption restricted to whisky and soda – Churchill made a slow recovery. As well as Clementine, Sarah was in attendance, having accompanied her father to Teheran as a personal assistant, and Randolph flew in on leave from the SAS.

At the end of the year Churchill retired to Marrakesh for two weeks' convalescence, staying at a villa described by Clementine as 'a mixture of Arabian Nights and Hollywood.' The patient was still very weak but enjoyed picnics in the foothills of the Atlas mountains in the cool winter sunshine. There were plenty of visitors – Generals Eisenhower, Montgomery, Alexander and de Gaulle for business, Lord Beaverbrook and the Duff Coopers for pleasure. Even in his invalid condition, Churchill forced through one of his pet projects, for an amphibious landing behind the German lines in Italy. It was

carried out at Anzio on 22 January, only for a mixture of inadequate resources and timid command to annul any advantage gained. 'I had hoped that we would be hurling a wildcat ashore,' Churchill later wrote, 'but all we got was a stranded whale.'

By the time of the Anzio landings Churchill was back in London, though still far from well. The war was slipping out of his grasp. As the preparations for D-day went ahead he played his usual role, prodding commanders, querying decisions, visiting troops and installations, and pursuing his own taste for clever gimmickry – it was largely at his instigation that the famous deception plan, designed to make the Germans believe the invasion would take place in the Pas de Calais instead of Normandy, was executed in such fanatical detail, complete with inflatable imitation tanks. But over the main course of events he had less and less control. He opposed the bombing of communications in France, because it would cause heavy French civilian casualties. The Americans disagreed and the bombing went ahead. He opposed a landing in the south of France, proposing an alternative blow at the 'armpit of Italy' in the Adriatic. The Americans insisted that the invasion of southern France should be carried out. Even in his own house, he was not obeyed. The British Chiefs of Staff, hardened now by years of resisting such favourite Churchillian projects as the invasion of northern Norway, held off his most ferocious

pressure for offensive action in Burma and Sumatra. The Great Man raged, but to no effect.

Churchill sought consolation in action: he was determined to witness the Normandy landings in person. 'A man who has to play an effective part in taking grave and terrible decisions of war,' he argued, 'may need the refreshment of adventure.' The pleas of his family and political colleagues were in vain. He finally desisted only when directly ordered by the King. As D-day approached he was disconsolate and bad tempered as a child denied an outing. It was not until 12 June, six days after the initial landings, that he was finally allowed to sail across the Channel; he cheered himself up by inducing the commander of the ship to shell the enemy-held French coast, so he could enjoy the sound of gunfire.

Shortly after D-day, Hitler's V-weapons brought London back into the front line of the war. But in Whitehall Churchill now felt too far from the centre of the action – the real decisions were being taken elsewhere. He had to be constantly on the move. In August he set out for Italy, mixing political discussions with sightseeing at the front. As a consolation for missing D-day he got to watch the landings in southern France from the deck of a ship

(a poor consolation since these were landings he had to the very last moment tried to stop). He met the Pope, the Yugoslav guerrilla leader Josef Broz Tito, Italian politicians and the Greek prime minister. By the time he arrived back in London, at the end of August, he had again contracted pneumonia. He emerged from the aircraft 'crumpled and feverish' and was rushed directly to hospital.

Rest was the obvious prescription, but a week later Churchill was away again, crossing the Atlantic with a large entourage for the second Quebec conference with the Americans. One issue in the forefront of his mind was the perilous state of the British economy. With the end of the war in Europe in sight, Britain might face the abrupt termination of Lend-lease. This would be catastrophic, since the country no longer had either the currency reserves or the level of exports to pay for the imports it needed to survive. One answer was to prolong the war. Churchill offered Roosevelt full British participation in the Pacific War once the war in Europe was over – on the understanding that American credits would then be continued until the defeat of Japan, expected to take at least another two years.

It was also for economic reasons that Churchill welcomed the American-initiated Morgenthau plan, which advocated the total de-industrialization of Germany. Lord Cherwell persuaded Churchill that if Germany was reduced to an agricultural country, British industrial exports would fill the gap left by German industry, thus saving the economy. Churchill and Roosevelt officially approved the Morgenthau plan on 15 September, but most of their advisers were appalled. Once the leaders returned to their respective capitals the plan was quietly dropped.

Churchill's attitude to the post-war fate of Germany vacillated along with his attitude to the Soviet Union. It was by now obvious that the defeat of Germany would leave Stalin with an overwhelming preponderance of military power in Europe. At one moment Churchill thought in terms of the dismemberment or humiliation of Germany; but at the next he talked of the need to reconstruct Germany as a bulwark against the Soviet Union. He could not get Roosevelt interested in the question of the future balance of power in Europe. Neither the American president nor his generals wanted to race to Berlin. Churchill decided he must try to settle the future shape of Europe with Stalin instead.

Less than a fortnight after returning from Quebec, Churchill set off for Moscow. The British party was received with the utmost cordiality, treated to banquets and entertainments. Churchill wrote home to Clementine: 'I have had very nice talks with the Old Bear [Stalin]. I like him the more I see him.'

LEFT: *During his visit to Italy in August 1944, Churchill watches an artillery bombardment from a forward observation post near Florence. He felt a constant need to be close to the military action and receive 'the refreshment of adventure.'*

RIGHT: *Churchill and Clementine arrive back from the Quebec conference of September 1944 on board the* Queen Mary. *Clementine's headdress was an imitation of the style of head scarf worn by women factory workers, a concession to the egalitarian spirit of the times.*

During one of these 'nice talks,' Churchill scribbled on a scrap of paper a plan for the division of Europe into spheres of influence. It read: 'Rumania 90% Russian; Greece 90% British; Yugoslavia and Hungary 50-50; Bulgaria 75% Russian.' Stalin looked through the list and ticked it with a blue pencil. Churchill then suggested burning the paper, because it would in all probability be thought 'rather cynical if we seemed to have disposed of these issues, so fateful to millions of people, in such an off-hand manner.'

Back in London at the end of October, Churchill reported to the House of Commons: 'Our relations with Soviet Russia were never more close, intimate and cordial than they are at the present time.' In private his attitude was less complacent and more complex. He did believe that his relations with Stalin were based on personal friendship – Uncle Joe's less friendly moments were put down to the influence of hostile elements in the politburo – and he admired the Soviet dictator as the leader of a fighting people in a great war. But he still loathed the Soviet system and wished to limit its influence in Europe. He never really trusted Stalin – as Stalin knew very well, since his spies in the West kept him informed of all the secrets his Allies were keeping from him.

Despite a growing sense of foreboding about the future of Europe, Churchill's overwhelming priority – shared by Stalin and Roosevelt – was still victory over Germany. To this end he was certainly prepared to back communists if necessary. In Yugoslavia, acting partly on the advice of his son Randolph who was there liaising with the resistance, he decided to channel supplies to Tito's communist Partisans instead of the alternative monarchist movement, the Chetniks. Challenged on this policy by a British diplomat with close knowledge of Tito's politics, Churchill resorted to total cynicism: 'Are you going to live in Yugoslavia after the war? No? Neither am I.' As far as he was concerned, the Partisans were prepared to fight the Germans and the Chetniks were not. That was all.

Churchill was only too aware that his power over the shape of the political settlement emerging in 1944-45 was limited. In liberated France, for instance, General de Gaulle took control despite the hostility of the Americans and the ambivalence of the British. Churchill was asked along after the event, invited to Paris in November 1944, a gesture which must have given de Gaulle immense satisfaction, after the often bitter disputes and humiliations of the previous four years in exile in Britain. It was only after the war that the two men would develop a retrospective mutual admiration.

Increasingly impotent to control major political and military events, Churchill enthusiastically seized an opportunity to intervene in a small country where British forces might prevail: Greece. Stalin had agreed that the cradle of democracy should come in the British sphere of influence and faithfully instructed the Greek communists to join a coalition government after the German withdrawal. But the communist-led Greek resistance movement, ELAS, which had fought heroically against the German invaders with British arms, would not desist and intended to install its own leftist republican government. Churchill sent a British force of 60,000 men to quell the resistance fighters and preserve the Greek monarchy. His instructions to the British commander, General Scobie, were unequivocal: 'Do not hesitate to act as if you were in a conquered city where a local rebellion is in progress.'

Churchill's action provoked an outcry in Britain, but he was unrepentant. The fact that they had fought the Nazis did not, in his view, give a resistance group the natural right to run their country after the war. As he cryptically expressed it: 'Democracy is no harlot to be picked up on the street by a man with a tommy-gun.' But ELAS was strong and determined; British troops proved incapable of maintaining control of Athens and by late December the situation was precarious.

Churchill convinced himself that only his personal intervention could bring a successful conclusion. On Christmas Eve, to the distress of his wife who set great store by the family's yuletide festivities, he flew off to Greece, taking a reluctant Anthony Eden with him. It was, as Harold Macmillan commented, 'a sort of super Sidney Street.' Mortars exploded around the cruiser *Ajax* where Churchill took up

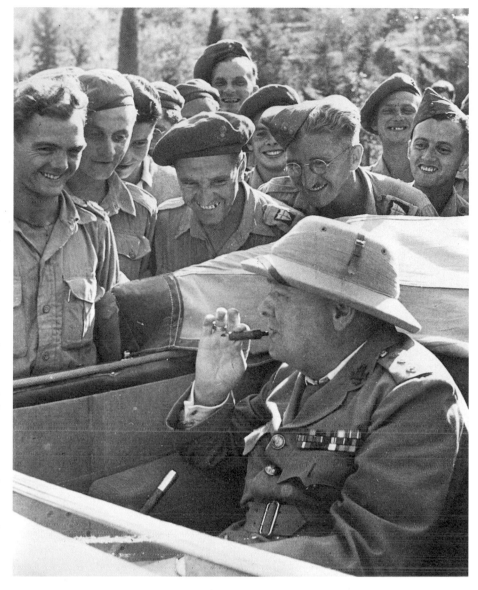

ABOVE: *Cheering-up the troops at Siena, 24 August 1944.*

LEFT: *Tough Soviet soldiers on the Eastern front. Whether the Western Allies liked it or not, victory in Europe depended on such men.*

residence off-shore. An armoured car bore the distinguished guests from the port into Athens to meet political leaders, through streets so dangerous that the visitors all carried small arms to fight off any ambush. Churchill insisted on standing out in the garden of the British embassy having his photo taken, while nervous soldiers covered the surrounding windows in case of snipers. At one moment a burst of machine gun fire struck a wall above the prime minister's head. Of course, he enjoyed all this immensely. A deal was struck for a provisional government under Archbishop Damaskinos, described by Churchill with relish as 'a scheming medieval prelate.' The resistance agreed to lay down their arms. Churchill returned to London refreshed by his exhilarating jaunt.

The simplicity of danger was a welcome release from the impenetrable complexities of imminent victory in Europe. With very little influence over events, Churchill was gnawed by fear and indecision. He foresaw confrontation with the Soviet Union: 'I fear increasingly that new struggles may arise out of those we are successfully ending,' he wrote. Yet he was impressed by Stalin's loyalty and dedication to the war effort. In January 1945, with British and American forces hard pressed after the German Ardennes offensive, Churchill telegraphed a personal appeal to the Soviet leader to advance the date of his planned offensive in the east; Stalin responded immediately, at great cost to his Army, relieving the pressure on his Western Allies. Churchill was also much impressed by the way Stalin had kept to his bargain over Greece – even when the Soviets took their *quid pro quo* by installing a communist government in Romania.

Churchill thus went to meet Stalin and Roosevelt at the Yalta conference (4-11 February) possessed by an uneasy mixture of goodwill and pessimism. He

ABOVE: *Churchill with General de Gaulle in Paris, Armistice Day, 11 November 1944. Relations with de Gaulle were often abrasive or downright hostile during the war, probably not helped by the misunderstandings engendered by Churchill's appalling French.*

RIGHT: *This photo session in Athens at Christmas 1944 was menaced by sniper-fire. With Churchill are Archbishop Damaskinos and Anthony Eden.*

ABOVE: *The Yalta conference in February 1945 was the last meeting between the Big Three – Roosevelt had only two months to live.*

was installed in a fine villa overlooking the Black Sea and feasted on caviar and champagne. A relaxed, almost euphoric atmosphere surrounded the talks. Yet Churchill's private mood was bleak. One night he commented gravely to his daughter Sarah, who had accompanied him to the conference: 'Tonight the sun goes down on more suffering than ever before in the world.' Such thoughts were frequently with him as the war drew toward its close.

At Yalta relations were most strained between the British and American delegations. The ailing Roosevelt, suspicious of Churchill's anti-communism and imperialist sympathies, tended to side with Stalin, especially when the Soviet leader gave the Americans what they most wanted – a promise to join in the war against Japan. There was general agreement on the division of Germany into zones of occupation, and Soviet influence over Romania, Bulgaria and Hungary had already been ceded. But for Churchill Poland was now a critical issue. He had agreed with Stalin that the country must accept new borders, but agreement on a future Polish government posed insurmountable difficulties. The brave uprising of the Polish Home Army in Warsaw in August 1944, and the refusal of the Russians to

support it, had swung Churchill's sentiments back in favour of the Poles. Yet there was no way round the reality of power: Poland was being liberated by the Soviet Union, and the Soviet Union would decide its future. At Yalta Churchill accepted the installation in Warsaw of a slightly diluted version of the Soviet-selected 'Lublin' government and tried to believe Stalin's assurances that democratic elections would follow.

Returning to London by a roundabout route – via a triumphant reception in pacified Athens and a last meeting with Roosevelt in Egypt – he presented the cabinet with a determinedly optimistic view of the Yalta conference. 'He was quite sure that [Stalin] meant well to the world and to Poland. . . . He had a very great feeling that the Russians were anxious to work harmoniously with the two English-speaking democracies.' Some MPs were not so easily convinced of Stalin's good intentions. Events in Greece had brought a motion of censure in Parliament from the left; over Poland, Churchill was attacked from the right. He took a certain bitter amusement in observing that the right-wing Tories who castigated his 'appeasement' of Stalin in eastern Europe were the same ones who had most fervently supported

RIGHT: *Crossing the Rhine on board a US landing craft at the end of March 1945.*

BELOW: *Churchill made friends with Monty's dog, Rommel, as well as with the general himself. The walking stick, prominent in so many photos of Churchill, was a wedding gift from King Edward VII in 1908.*

the appeasement of Hitler at Munich. As usual he was at his best in the Commons when on the counter-attack, reserving his most memorable insult for the elderly Lord Winterton: 'He will run a very grave risk of falling into senility before he is overtaken by old age.'

As victory in Europe drew closer, Churchill's mood was far from triumphal. After Bomber Command's devastating raid on Dresden in mid-February, he turned against the practice of area bombing that he had supported for so long – although as his minute on the subject shows, his motive was not so much moral as practical:

the moment has come, [he wrote], when the question of bombing of German cities simply for the sake of increasing the terror . . . should be reviewed. Otherwise we shall come into control of an utterly ruined land.

His thoughts on the Soviet Union in the last months of the war could only be regarded, from his ally Stalin's point of view, as treacherous. He urged Eisenhower to race for Berlin, since if the Russians got there first they might present themselves as 'an overwhelming contributor to our common victory.' Eisenhower preferred to let the Soviet Union have the prestige and the heavy casualties. Churchill relieved his frustration by visiting the conquered Siegfried Line and urinating upon it. He also spent two days at Montgomery's headquarters during the British crossing of the Rhine. Witnessing Churchill cling resolutely to an exposed position among the girders of a ruined bridge under bombardment from enemy artillery, General Brooke was sure the great war leader had visions of an heroic death at this climax of the world struggle.

But it was Roosevelt who died. Churchill's loss was both personal and political. He had counted on Roosevelt to guarantee American support for Britain in the difficult post-war period. The new president, Harry S Truman, was an unknown quantity. In fact, although he had no intention of propping Britain up as a Great Power, Truman was more sympathetic than Roosevelt to the anti-Communism that was increasingly predominant in Churchill's mind as victory approached.

Churchill's main fear was that the Red Army would not stop with the defeat of Germany, but roll on across Europe. He instructed Montgomery to capture as much German equipment as possible intact, since it might be needed against the Russians. He suggested the use of air power for 'striking at the communications of the Russian armies should they decide to advance further than is agreed.' In the event, only Tito overstepped the mark, occupying the Adriatic port of Trieste; Churchill advocated the use of force to turn him out and eventually the Partisans withdrew, unwillingly but peacefully. Elsewhere, the Yalta agreement held. Soviet and Anglo-American forces met in amity and, after the German surrender, took up their pre-planned zones of occupation. In this matter at least, Stalin had been trustworthy and Churchill's fears unjustified.

LEFT: *On VE Day, 8 May 1945, Churchill salutes an ecstatic crowd in Whitehall. He told them: 'This is your victory. It is the victory of the cause of freedom in every land.'*

In London, victory in Europe was celebrated on 8 May with appropriate scenes of popular rejoicing. Churchill broadcast to the nation from Downing Street and later addressed a rapturous crowd from a balcony in Whitehall. According to his bodyguard he enjoyed himself 'like a schoolboy on an outing.' But his underlying mood remained sombre. The news from Poland was bad, auguring ill for the future of Europe; the British economy was in ruins; and, of

BELOW: *The celebrations at the end of the European war in 1945, although enthusiastic, were considerably more restrained than in 1918.*

course, the Japanese remained to be beaten. Churchill hoped to keep his coalition government in being to cope with these heavy problems, but the Labour Party rank-and-file, overriding their leaders who were quite happy to stay in office, demanded a return to peacetime party politics. On 23 May, Churchill re-formed his government excluding Labour, and a general election was called for July.

The Conservatives were certain that the mass of the people would vote for their prestigious war leader. But the great issues of the election lay in domestic policy – housing, social security, education, health care, employment. There was an overwhelming demand for a new society to be built on the ruins of the old. Public attitudes had shifted sharply to the left in the course of the war and policies that would have been considered wildly socialist in 1939 now had the support of a large consensus. Even the majority of the Conservative Party accepted that the state must provide extensive social welfare and play a large role in the economy alongside private enterprise. They did not differ in this from Labour.

Although Churchill had not much occupied himself with domestic policy during the war, he should have been well placed to appeal to voters inspired by this new consensus. Following the guiding principle

'Everything for the war, whether controversial or not, and nothing controversial that is not needed *bona fide* for the war,' he had presided over the introduction of war socialism. Since 1940 the individual and private enterprise had been almost entirely

ABOVE: *Churchill on a visit to defeated Germany in July 1945. He was the first British prime minister ever to wear military uniform while in office.*

OPPOSITE AND LEFT: *A tale of two cities – victory celebrations in London and the ruins of Berlin. Churchill went to visit Hitler's bunker and to view the spot where the Führer's body had been burned.*

CONFIRM YOUR CONFIDENCE IN CHURCHILL

PUT IT THERE !

insurance . . . from the cradle to the grave,' full employment, a National Health Service, equal opportunity in education and a vigorous house-building programme. His government had proceeded to act on these lines, issuing proposals for legislation in a series of White Papers and carrying through at least one major reform, the Butler Education Act of 1944.

But the public impression was, not altogether unfairly, that these measures had advanced more in spite of Churchill than because of him. He was bored by the irritating distractions of social reform when a great war was in progress, and he had let it show. His failure to welcome the immensely popular Beveridge Report when it was published in late 1942 had revived memories of his earlier role as a right-wing Tory and scourge of the working class. Wise advisers in 1945 would have counselled Churchill to emphasize his commitment to social reform and his responsibility for the state control measures introduced during the war. But Churchill did not receive wise counsel. His closest advisers were Beaverbrook and Brendan Bracken (who had been Minister of Information since 1941). Instead of encouraging Churchill to bid for the middle ground, they urged him to fight an aggressive campaign against socialism.

Churchill's first election broadcast on 4 June was a disaster. It included a vicious, ill-judged attack on Labour: 'no socialist system can be established without a political police.' The Labour leaders 'would have to fall back on some form of Gestapo, no doubt very humanely directed in the first instance.' This was entirely the wrong note to have struck. The public was shocked by such vehemence after the years of national unity. Churchill once wittily

subjected to the state, which dictated the pattern of consumption and production, sometimes in minute detail. Churchill had occasionally resisted what he regarded as an unnecessary extension of state control – he prevented the nationalization of the coal mines, for instance – but on the whole he had gone along with it. And in March 1943 he had, if somewhat reluctantly, proclaimed a programme for post-war reconstruction that included 'national compulsory

HELP THEM FINISH THEIR JOB!
Give *them* homes and work!
VOTE LABOUR

described Attlee as 'a very modest man – but then he has much to be modest about.' But the Labour leader was no mean tactician and knew how to adopt the sober, moderate tone the electorate wanted. He carefully distinguished between Churchill the great war leader, for whom he was all respect, and Churchill the Tory politician, unfit to lead his nation in peace.

Churchill was uncomfortably aware that in his radio broadcasts he was losing his touch – 'I have no message for them now,' he grumbled – but he was greatly reassured by the delirious reception he received on a tour of northern England and Scotland at the end of June. It was a triumphal progress without precedent in British political life. Yet there were warning signs. At Walthamstow on 3 July he was booed and heckled; Clementine noticed that while the front rows at his speeches were filled with enthusiastic supporters, further back were often silent and distrustful faces. Still, all the political pundits were agreed that Churchill would win.

There was a three-week delay between polling day, 5 July, and the declaration of the result, because of the need to collect the Service vote. During this interval, after a short holiday in France, Churchill set off to meet Truman and Stalin at Potsdam, taking Attlee with him as a sensible precaution

in case the government should change. While electioneering, Churchill had of course continued to determine questions of strategy and diplomacy. On 2 July he had given the American government his

BELOW: *Churchill meets the new president, Harry S. Truman, during the last wartime summit meeting at Potsdam in late July 1945.*

"Large and powerful" British forces will be fighting in the Pacific war theatre this year

formal consent for the use of the atom bomb against Japan. He arrived in Potsdam most keen to establish a personal relationship with Truman and soon convinced himself that here was indeed another Roosevelt. But Truman did not share the sense of wartime camaraderie that had bound his predecessor to both Churchill and Stalin, through all differences and difficulties. Above the din created by the usual high-spirited junketing, at Potsdam the first sharp notes of the Cold War were clearly audible.

In the middle of the conference, on 25 July, Churchill flew back to England to await the election results. That night he experienced a dark premonition of defeat:

just before dawn I woke suddenly with a sharp stab of almost physical pain. A hitherto subconscious conviction that we were beaten broke forth and dominated my mind.

He could not have guessed the scale of the disaster. As news of Conservative defeats rolled in through the following day, Churchill strove to cope with the terrible blow. Even in his own constituency, where he was opposed only by an eccentric independent, over 10,000 people voted against him. It was the biggest landslide since 1906, giving Labour an absolute majority of 146 in the House of Commons. At seven in the evening Churchill tendered his resignation to the King. He proved that he could be magnanimous in defeat, as in victory. When his doctor, Lord Moran, spoke of the 'ingratitude' of the British people, he protested: 'Oh no, I wouldn't call it that. They have had a very bad time.'

The shock of the great leader's defeat in the hour of victory reverberated around the world. Its supreme irony was never better expressed than by Churchill himself in the first volume of his war memoirs, *The Gathering Storm*:

At the outset of this mighty battle, I acquired the chief power in the State, which henceforth I wielded in ever-growing measure for five years and three months of world war, at the end of which time, all our enemies having surrendered unconditionally or being about to do so, I was immediately dismissed by the British electorate from all further conduct of their affairs.

CHAPTER TEN

The Dying of the Light

LEFT: *The grand old man, heaped with honours, but defenceless against the cumulative infirmities of old age.*

Iᴺ July 1945 Churchill was 70 years old. The election defeat offered him a graceful pretext for retirement from the political fray. He could have taken up the safe yet prestigious role of elder statesman, heaped with honours, devoting himself in a leisurely fashion to his writing and painting. The King discreetly offered a knighthood. But Churchill had no intention of retiring. He smarted at defeat. Being torn away from the busy excitements of the premiership was a terrible deprivation. The role of leader of the opposition offered at least some compensation. He refused to be put out to grass.

Exhausted by the war, Clementine was aghast at his decision to carry on. She could not contain her irritation at his stubbornness and there were some flaming marital rows. Many of his Conservative colleagues were also less than enthusiastic about the decision – especially Eden, the eternal understudy – but there was no prospect of a Conservative revolt against the war hero who quite possibly offered their only chance of ever being elected to office again. Most believed that, in any case, age and illness would force him to retire in the not too distant future. Few would have credited the Great Man with the stamina to remain in the saddle for ten more years.

Churchill clung on partly out of a sense of responsibility. He felt that he understood the international situation better than any other world statesman; it was his historical mission to complete the work of the war years by helping to create a just and lasting peace. But more fundamentally he refused to retire because he feared the emptiness of old age, the blankness of simply waiting to die. After so many years, he could not relax the will-to-power.

Yet Churchill's life outside politics could hardly be described as empty – indeed, he could often find little time for his duties as leader of the opposition. His major project was to write his own version of the origins and conduct of World War II. The first part of this six-volume historical epic appeared in 1948. More of an autobiography than a true history, Churchill's account of the war remains immensely readable, with its highly charged narrative flow and its powerful sense of personal involvement. There are inaccuracies and omissions, but no more perhaps than in any other necessarily selective account of such wide-ranging events. It was altogether a fitting consummation of his life as a writer and earned him the Nobel Prize for Literature.

His war memoirs made Churchill a rich man. Any of his writings could now command fabulous sums. He bought two adjoining houses in Hyde Park Gate, and kept a suite of rooms in the Savoy as more convenient for Parliament. Even the rich could not evade the austerity of post-war Britain, however,

BELOW: *Churchill keeps an eye on work at Chartwell farm in 1950. Standing is Christopher Soames, who managed the farm for his father-in-law; Anthony Eden squats beside Churchill's chair.*

OPPOSITE: *Churchill as photographed by Karsh – the sombre postwar statesman.*

RIGHT: *Three generations of Churchills at Chartwell in 1951. On the right is Randolph and on the left Diana with her husband, Duncan Sandys. Grandchildren were always welcome at the house.*

and once deprived of the privileges of the prime minister's office, Churchill found himself irritated by many petty deprivations from which he had previously been sheltered – petrol rationing, lack of meat, shortage of materials to restore Chartwell from the decay into which it had fallen through the war years. In 1946 a group of the Churchills' friends bought Chartwell and handed it over to the National Trust, on condition that the present occupants should be allowed to remain in residence for their lifetime. This step ensured that the estate would become a carefully preserved memorial to Churchill after his death.

Churchill's family were as much a source of trouble as support during the post-war years. Relations with Clementine were perhaps more acerbic

RIGHT: *A triumphant reception for the war hero in Zurich in September 1946. Churchill was feted everywhere he went, but he found this little solace for the loss of political power.*

than at any time in their marriage. Her conviction that he was wrong to continue in politics stood as a block between them, and ill-health did nothing to improve her temper. As for Churchill, his childish tantrums and spoilt moodiness perhaps not unnaturally worsened with age.

The children continued to be, on the whole, a disappointment. Randolph's argumentative, blustering temperament was very trying to his parents, as it was to most other people. Not surprisingly, his successive marriages ended in divorce. Sarah also failed to satisfy the Churchills' ideal of a successful marriage. Having divorced her first husband during the war, she married again in 1949 without telling her parents – much to their distress – but this again proved only a temporary liaison. Diana's neurotic instability increased over the years. She was often difficult and distressed, and in 1953 suffered a complete nervous breakdown. Her marriage to Duncan Sandys broke up shortly afterward. Only the youngest child, Mary, gave her parents full satisfaction, marrying a young Tory, Christopher Soames. The couple settled down on the farm next to Chartwell, which Churchill had bought to expand the estate. Soames and Churchill got on exceptionally well, and the young man inspired his father-in-law with a new

enthusiasm – horse racing. From 1949, adopting a version of his father's colours, Churchill bought a number of horses and raced them with considerable success. Soames also provided a welcome link with the younger Conservative MPs, for whom Churchill was a remote, if revered, figure.

During his period as leader of the opposition, Churchill was frequently abroad. This was partly for health reasons. The British winter was considered too dangerous and Churchill spent the worst months of the year in sunnier climes, painting and writing. There were also honours to receive. Invitations flowed in from European cities and countries wishing to demonstrate their gratitude to the great war hero. Everywhere Churchill went he was accorded a rapturous welcome by the populace and the highest official accolade.

But his travels also had a grimmer purpose. Despite his election defeat, he was determined to continue to influence world events. Exploiting his immense international prestige and his personal acquaintance with world rulers, he pursued his own independent foreign policy. During the 1930s he had raised the alarm against Hitler; now he felt the same fear of Stalin. Europe was in ruins, 'a rubble heap, a charnel house, a breeding ground of pestilence and

BELOW: *Churchill became interested in horse-racing through his son-in-law Christopher Soames. Here he is photographed with 'Gibraltar.'*

hate.' It was incapable of defending itself against the encroachment of Soviet power. Churchill set himself a twin goal: to counteract American isolationism, persuading Washington to throw its weight into the balance against the Soviet Union, and to promote West European unity as a defence against the spread of communism. In 1946, in the presence of President Truman, he made the famous speech at Fulton, Missouri, that is often interpreted as the first salvo in the Cold War:

From Stettin on the Baltic to Trieste on the Adriatic, an iron curtain has descended over the continent . . . there is nothing they [the Russians] admire so much as strength and nothing for which they have less respect than military weakness.

It was an unpopular theme at a time when the Soviet Union was still regarded as an ally of the West, and it drew much adverse criticism. But within two years events in Eastern Europe had swung public opinion completely around and Churchill was once more being praised for his prophetic insight. His aim was not, as his critics alleged, to stir up war, but to preserve peace. It was the same argument as in the 1930s: only adequate force could restrain a potentially aggressive power.

His advocacy of a 'United States of Europe,' including Germany, was inspired by the same considerations of collective security. He played a prominent role at the first meeting of the Council of Europe at Strasbourg in August 1949, stealing the limelight from the official British government representative, Foreign Secretary Herbert Morrison. Churchill enjoyed himself immensely baiting Morrison and hearing himself declared 'the first citizen of Europe.' But his attitude towards Britain's relationship with the continent always remained confused. He saw Britain as an essential part of the new united Europe, but only in association with its Empire (now redubbed the Commonwealth). And he continued to insist on the prime importance of the link between the English-speaking peoples, seeking a privileged relationship with the United States. These were incompatible priorities. In practice Churchill would sacrifice a place in Europe to the preservation of the Empire and the 'special relationship.'

It was immediately after the Council of Europe meeting that Churchill's health underwent its first serious deterioration since the war. He suffered a stroke while playing gin rummy at two o'clock in the morning at Lord Beaverbrook's villa near Monte Carlo. Recovery was swift, but the warning was clear. Churchill's Conservative colleagues were already asking themselves how long he could continue. His performance as leader of the opposition had provoked much private criticism within the party. It is hard to say whether there was more objection to his long absences from Parliament or to his often ill-judged attacks on the government when present. He was no more of a party man as leader than he had been on the back benches. He pursued his own policies and expressed his own views with little or no reference to his colleagues. They found him unpredictable and often infuriating. But he was

OPPOSITE: *Churchill speaking at a Conservative Party conference in 1947. Although some of his parliamentary colleagues would have preferred him to retire, his hold on the party members was unshakeable.*

BELOW: *Always inclined to be lachrymose, Churchill sheds tears of emotion at the warm response to his speech to the Congress of Europe at the Hague in May 1948.*

ABOVE: *Everywhere Churchill went, he was the object of curiosity as well as admiration. Despite the efforts of the local police, this painting expedition on the Italian riviera attracted a swarm of photographers.*

RIGHT: *By 1950 Churchill was becoming very hard of hearing, as this tell-tale gesture during a press conference betrays.*

still both immensely popular and personally formidable. No one had the courage to attack him openly.

It must be said that leading the opposition during 1945-50 was not an easy task. Most of the reforms carried out by the Labour government had been initiated by Churchill's wartime coalition and enjoyed the support of a broad popular consensus. Despite his use of anti-socialist rhetoric to berate the government, Churchill could not wholeheartedly denounce many of its specific policies. The measure he most ardently opposed was, not surprisingly, the precipitate granting of independence to India and Pakistan in 1947. He fulminated against this policy of 'scuttle and run.' But here, as in the 1930s, he found himself out of step with most of his own party, all of whom had long ago resigned themselves to the loss of the Raj.

At the time of the 1950 general election, Churchill's leadership was still energetic enough – he countered Labour sniping about his age by publishing an official denial that he was dead. The cutting down of the great Labour majority to a mere six seats was a great triumph and held out the prospect of an imminent Conservative government. Churchill longed to win a general election and return to Downing Street. He made it privately known that he would continue to lead the Conservatives until they were returned to office and then, after a decent interval, hand over to his successor designate, Anthony Eden.

With the scent of power in his nostrils, Churchill launched himself into the parliamentary fray with renewed enthusiasm. The government was abused in his best rhetorical style, harassed with all-night sittings, impeded by every trick of procedure. Labour's best counter was to exploit Churchill's reputation as a warmonger. The Korean War was at its height and there was a general fear that the conflict might spread. By suggesting that Churchill could not be trusted in the atomic age, that he might indeed precipitate World War III, the Socialists succeeded in minimizing their losses in the election of October 1951. But the Conservative majority of 17 was sufficient. On 26 October Churchill was summoned to Buckingham Palace and asked to form a government.

This was a sweet revenge for the humiliation of 1945. But Churchill's second administration was not to prove a distinguished or memorable one. Those Conservatives who hoped for a wholesale reversal of Labour legislation were disappointed. Churchill still aspired to be a national, rather than a party leader – he even floated the idea of a renewed national coalition with Labour and the Liberals. He refused to dismantle the welfare state and accepted the existence of a large state sector in the economy. Living standards continued to rise and the austerity regulations were lifted as they must inevitably have been under any government. But Churchill, as ever, took little interest in domestic affairs. He dreamed of crowning his career with a last magnificent gesture that would ensure him his place in history as a great peacemaker: he would reconcile East and

ABOVE: *Campaigning in the 1950 general election. Despite the patriotic bulldog, the Conservatives were once more defeated, although by a relatively narrow margin.*

LEFT: *The election of October 1951 at last returned Churchill to Downing Street. His colleagues thought that, having won, he would soon resign – but once back in office, he was not inclined to step down.*

West in a final settlement that would lift for ever the shadow of war from the world. In this project he found justification for holding on to power for almost four years, despite his physical decline and the evident desire of his colleagues that he should go.

Unfortunately, Churchill's diplomatic efforts were almost wholly unsuccessful. He backed the agreement that ended the Korean War and helped persuade the Americans not to intervene to rescue the French from Ho Chi Minh's guerrilla army at Dien Bien Phu (there was some pique in Churchill's attitude – Britain had lost India, so why should the French be allowed to keep Indochina?). But his major objective, to organize a summit meeting at which the United States, Britain and the Soviet Union would resolve outstanding differences, remained unattainable. He even failed satisfactorily to confirm the 'special relationship' with the United States. President Eisenhower, taking over from Truman in 1953, was never especially amenable to Churchill's advances and his Secretary of State, John Foster Dulles, could be positively offensive ('dull, duller, Dulles,' Churchill quipped). Churchill still believed that Britain, standing at the head of the Commonwealth and developing its own nuclear weapons, was a Great Power that could influence world events. He was wrong, and the Americans knew it.

Churchill found another motive for postponing his retirement in February 1952 when George VI died and was succeeded by his young daughter Elizabeth. Churchill conceived for himself the role of guardian and protector of the new monarch; his deepest sentiments of loyalty and devotion were stirred. The Queen had the highest regard for her Prime Minister and welcomed his support. In April 1952 she invested him with the Order of the Garter and he was knighted the following year. Sir Winston reciprocated by taking a pedantic interest in every detail of the Queen's coronation, a ceremony in which he cut a striking figure accoutred in the archaic uniform of a Lord Warden of the Cinque Ports.

Up to this time Churchill's health had held up moderately well. He was partially deaf and his concentration sometimes flagged, but apart from a brief period in 1952 when he was inflicted with aphasia, impairing his ability to speak and write, he had always been able to sustain the many demands of his office. Then, on 23 June 1953, three weeks after the coronation, he suffered a major stroke during an official dinner in honour of the Italian prime minister. He insisted on chairing a cabinet meeting the following morning, but his speech was slurred and he hardly knew where he was. He was quickly smuggled away to the privacy of Chartwell and a soothing press release was issued stating that the prime minister was in need of rest. His family believed that his career was at an end.

Ironically, at this same moment Eden was recovering from a major operation and was in no condition to assume power. Churchill remained the titular head of a leaderless government. By the time Eden was back on his feet, so was Churchill. As his strength returned through the late summer, he steeled himself to resume his duties. With a supreme effort of will, in October he made a successful speech at the Conservative Party conference. His cabinet colleagues were informed, to their total dismay, that he intended to stay on at least until the following summer.

There was no way Churchill could be forced to resign. Eden, now a member of the family – he had married Churchill's niece – would not conspire against him. The Conservative Party faithful would never vote him out. By July 1954 the cabinet had been reduced to the extraordinary expedient of sending the housing minister, Harold Macmillan, to talk to Clementine, in the hope that she might be able to persuade her husband to retire. But it was all in vain. Churchill clung to power like a limpet, finding excuse after excuse to postpone the inevitable day.

On his eightieth birthday, in November 1954, both Houses of Parliament met together in Westminster Hall and presented Churchill with a specially commissioned portrait by Graham Sutherland. Churchill was delighted with the ceremony and celebrations, the mountain of telegrams from well-wishers and the numerous presents. But the portrait struck a sour note. He had always loathed modernism in art and, on stylistic grounds alone, he was bound to dislike Sutherland's work. Worse were its implications about the sitter. The portrait showed a man ravaged by time, stripped down to his mere mortality. Clementine had long appointed herself the guardian of Churchill's image. The Sutherland portrait was hidden away at Chartwell where, sometime in 1956, presumably with Churchill's approval,

OPPOSITE: *The procession for the coronation of Elizabeth II, 2 June 1953. Churchill's mounted escort was provided by 4th Queen's Own Hussars, his first regiment.*

OPPOSITE BELOW: *Churchill arrives at Washington airport for talks with President Eisenhower in June 1954. Looking on are Eden, Foster Dulles and future president Richard Nixon.*

LEFT: *A family occasion in November 1954 – the grandparents attend the christening of baby Charlotte Soames in Westerham church. The other Soames children are, left to right, Nicholas, Emma and Jeremy.*

she destroyed it. It was not the first time she had destroyed a picture that she felt did not properly reflect her husband's greatness. But this was both a public gift and a major work of art. Its destruction was an act that compounded philistine arrogance with gross ingratitude – explicable only as a sad consequence of the bitterness of age.

At the end of 1954 Churchill remained defiant. In one extraordinary outburst he silenced his horrified cabinet colleagues with his childish obstinacy: 'I know you're trying to get rid of me,' he snapped, 'but it's up to me to go to the Queen and hand her my resignation and yours – and I won't do it.' Yet he knew he had to do it. His efforts to arrange a summit meeting with the Soviet and American leaders were coming to nothing. And a general election was in the offing. He had to agree that he could not lead his party to the country again, and that his successor must be given time to establish himself before an election was faced. In March 1955 he reluctantly took the decision to resign the following month.

The resignation was deliberately handled with the minimum of publicity (aided by a fortuitous newspaper strike). On 4 April the Queen and the Duke of Edinburgh came to dine at No. 10 Downing Street, along with a selection of Churchill's family, friends and colleagues. The next day he presented his resignation. On 6 April, cheered by his staff, he left Downing Street to drive down to Chartwell. For the press he had a cheerful comment: 'It's always nice to come home.' But Clementine knew how he really felt: retirement was his 'first death – for him a death in life.'

ABOVE: *Churchill gives his best wishes to his successor, Eden, who had waited so long for the old man to go.*

RIGHT: *Retirement with Clementine amid the beauty of the Kent countryside.*

OPPOSITE ABOVE: *A family group assembled for the wedding of Churchill's eponymous grandson in 1964. Almost 90, Churchill was too weak to go to the ceremony, but the wedding party visited him afterwards at Hyde Park Gate.*

OPPOSITE BELOW: *Churchill on his 87th birthday.*

Churchill left not only the premiership but all active involvement in political life. He was not invited by his party to play any significant role in the election campaign of May 1955. Although he officially remained the MP for Woodford until 1964 and occasionally occupied his seat in Parliament, he never again addressed the House on a political issue. His constituents were in practice represented by another Tory MP from a neighbouring constituency. Churchill's last significant political act came after Eden's resignation in 1957, when he advised the Queen to invite Macmillan, rather than Butler, to form the next government. Otherwise, his role was reduced to that of a prominent symbolic figure at ceremonial occasions.

He continued to write for several years, completing his *History of the English-Speaking People*, begun before World War II. Painting remained a solace and cards a pleasure. Most of his time was divided between Chartwell and the Riviera. He was a constant guest at La Pausa, the villa of his foreign literary agent, Emery Reves, and Lord Beaverbrook's villa, La Capponcina, was always at his disposal. A new friend was the Greek shipping millionaire Aristotle Onassis, and Churchill enjoyed many luxurious cruises on board his yacht *Christina*. He also frequented the Hotel de Paris at Monte Carlo. But often neither sunlight nor luxury could lighten his gloom. He was at times apathetic, lethargic and withdrawn. His silences increased with age.

In his biography of Marlborough, Churchill had written: 'It is foolish to waste lamentation upon the closing phase of human life.' There was nothing cheering in the spectacle of his own decline. He lived the full agony of old age – accident and illness, failing powers, the deaths of friends ('the Prof' in 1957, Brendan Bracken in 1958), with before him only the prospect of the inevitable end. Despite his famous quip on his 75th birthday – 'I am ready to meet my Maker; whether my Maker is prepared for the great ordeal of meeting me is another matter' – he had no belief in an afterlife. He at times looked forward to death as 'sleep, endless, wonderful sleep.'

Until 1959 he was still capable of conducting a measure of public life. He went to Paris to receive the Croix de la Liberation from General de Gaulle and visited Eisenhower in the United States. But a series of minor strokes progressively weakened his mental powers. In 1960 he suffered a serious fall in Monte Carlo, breaking a bone in his neck, and in 1962 he broke his thigh. Surrounded by the attentions of nurses and protected from public inquiry by his personal secretary, Anthony Montague Browne, he sank into hunched silence and immobility. In 1964 his daughter Diana committed suicide; but by then he had lapsed into a senile insensibility that shielded him from all suffering. Nothing could reach him any more.

After a final stroke, Churchill died at his London home in Hyde Park Gate on the morning of Sunday, 24 January 1965, the 70th anniversary of the death of his father. The Queen had made it known some years earlier that she intended Churchill to be honoured with a State Funeral, the first since the

ABOVE: *Churchill with Greek tycoon Aristotle Onassis, who he had first met in 1956.*

RIGHT: *On board Onassis's luxury yacht* Christina *in the Mediterranean, summer 1959.*

OPPOSITE: *Fragile but benevolent, Churchill appears at the window of 28 Hyde Park Gate on his 90th birthday. It was to be his last public appearance.*

CHRISTINA
Y. C. M.

ABOVE: *Mourners queue in the snow to file past Churchill's body, lying in state in Westminster Hall.*

Duke of Wellington. Over 300,000 people queued in freezing winter weather to file past his body lying in state for three days in Westminster Hall. Uncounted millions witnessed, either in person or on television, the magnificent ceremonial of the funeral on 30 January – the procession to St Paul's, the solemn service, the ferrying of the coffin by barge down the Thames to Waterloo. Churchill had desired to be buried alongside his parents in Bladon churchyard, within sight of his birthplace, Blenheim Palace. The journey by train from Waterloo to Oxfordshire was remembered by Churchill's daughter Mary as the most touching part of the day:

The winter fields had little groups of people – families with their children and dogs, a farmer taking his cap off; children on shaggy ponies – all waiting in the chill of a winter's afternoon, to watch Winston Churchill's last journey home.

After the burial, two wreaths were left on the grave, one from Clementine, inscribed 'To my Darling Winston. Clemmie'; and one from the Queen: 'From the Nation and Commonwealth. In grateful remembrance. Elizabeth R.'

It has often been said that the mass of people who filed past Churchill's coffin were mourning a symbol – the loss of Empire, the passing of Britain's greatness. But this is surely wrong: most were mourning an extraordinary human being. Of course, long before his death, Churchill had become a public monument; he had been adopted as the patron saint of right-wing patriots nostalgic for Empire and fearful of a socialist future. Yet even many of his political opponents, who loathed what Churchill had come to represent, could not help but feel a deep affection for him as a man.

Churchill's writings are less read now than in his lifetime; in retrospect he appears an inspired journalist and autobiographer, but not a true historian. The value and significance of his political career remains a subject for detailed historical controversy.

RIGHT: *The coffin is borne on a gun carriage from Westminster to St Paul's, past hushed crowds lining the streets.*

Unlike his hero Napoleon, he left no great body of legislation behind to confirm his stature. After 1911 he contributed little to the changing shape of Britain – indeed, the country in which he died, with its dedicated materialism and egalitarian manners, was quite alien to him. Only in the defeat of Naziism was he supremely successful; this alone is enough to guarantee his reputation for all time. In the pursuit of his other main objectives – to preserve the British Empire and limit the influence of Soviet communism – he was singularly unsuccessful.

Yet the extraordinary richness of the life he carved out for himself, his overwhelming vitality, still shine out undimmed by the passage of time. What most impresses in so many anecdotes of Churchill is his lovable, anarchic eccentricity: Eleanor Roosevelt, the president's wife, witnessing him walking through Buckingham Palace singing 'Roll out the Barrel' with immense gusto; or General Brooke remembering coming upon him at three o'clock in the morning, in the depths of the war, clad in a flamboyant dressing gown over his siren suit, skipping around his room in time to a gramophone record, a sandwich in one hand and some watercress in the other. Although like most men of power, he could be brutal and cruel in his uglier moods, another abiding impression from the memoirs of those who knew him well is of his personal warmth and his humane concern for suffering. And most endearing of all in retrospect is his mischievous wit, a few examples of which have graced these pages.

To have wielded the power Churchill did, and yet have remained a full human being, capable of pity, humour, courage and tenderness, was a remarkable achievement. It is rare for a Great Man to be loved, as well as admired. The memory of the man will outlive his works.

OPPOSITE: *The day after Churchill's interment in Bladon churchyard, thousands queued in the winding village street to pay their last respects.*

LEFT: *'In war, resolution; in defeat, defiance; in victory, magnanimity; in peace, goodwill.'*

INDEX

ACKNOWLEDGMENTS

The publisher would like to thank Martin Bristow who designed this book; Mandy Little, the picture researcher; Adrian Gilbert, the editor; and Ron Watson who compiled the index. We would also like to thank the following agencies and individuals for providing the illustrations:

Archiv Gerstenberg, page: 178(bottom)
Australian Associated Newspapers, page: 200(top)
Broadwater Albums/Churchill Archives, pages: 8, 20, 36(both), 37, 109(top), 115(both), 116(top), 120(bottom), 121(top), 194(bottom), 195(top), 206(top), 211(top).
Bundesarchiv, pages: 132, 133(both)
Camera Press, pages: 2, 12, 60, 161(both), 192(top), 194(top), 202(Karsch of Ottawa), 205, 207, 210(top), 214(top), 215(top), 221
Conservative Party Archives/Bodleian Library, Oxford, pages: 61(top two), 122(top), 130(top), 134(top), 198(top).
Express & News Features, page: 158
John Frost Historical Newspaper Service, pages: 16(top), 21, 28(bottom), 32(top), 35(left), 50(right), 55(top), 64, 99(top), 100, 118(top), 119(bottom), 131(top), 151(top), 156
Hulton-Deutsch Collection, pages: 65, 126, 130(bottom), 141(bottom), 146(bottom), 147, 169, 180(bottom), 183, 199(top), 201, 206(bottom), 209, 212(both), 213, 215(bottom), 217, 218
Hulton Picture Company, page: 17, 18, 25(both), 26, 27, 34(both), 41(top), 45(top), 47, 49, 50(left), 51, 54, 61(bottom), 63, 66(top), 67(both), 68, 69(bottom), 71(bottom), 76, 78, 80, 92(both), 93, 97, 105(top), 106(bottom), 108, 109(bottom), 110(both), 111(top), 114(top), 116(bottom), 117, 118(bottom), 119(top), 120(top), 127,

128(both), 131(bottom), 134, 138, 139(bottom), 140, 141(top), 142, 143, 146(top), 148(top), 150, 151(bottom), 153(top), 155, 177, 200(bottom), 208, 210(bottom), 211(bottom), 214(top)
Robert Hunt Library, pages: 85, 88(top), 89, 91, 96, 99(bottom), 106(top), 111(bottom), 163(bottom), 173, 176, 185(both), 187(top), 198(bottom), 218-9
Hoover Institution Archives, page: 106(bottom)
Angelo Hornak, page: 11(top)
Imperial War Museum, London, pages: 9, 12, 22, 33(bottom), 40, 69(top), 70(bottom), 71(top), 72, 79(bottom), 82, 83(top), 84(both), 86, 88(bottom), 90(both), 94, 98, 101, 104, 149(bottom), 152, 154, 157, 159, 162(bottom), 163(top), 164, 165, 166(both), 167(both), 168, 172(bottom), 174, 178(top), 179(both), 180(top), 181, 182, 184(bottom), 187(bottom), 188, 190, 193, 195(bottom), 197(bottom), 199(bottom)
Mansell Collection, pages: 10, 11(bottom), 13(both), 14(both), 15(both), 19, 21, 28(top), 32(bottom), 33(top), 35(right), 38, 41(bottom), 42, 43, 45(bottom), 46(both), 48, 52, 56, 57, 58(both), 59, 70(top), 73, 75, 77, 79(top), 83(bottom), 87, 105(bottom), 123, 139(top), 160, 162(top), 186(top), 192(bottom)
National Army Museum, page: 30
National Portrait Gallery, pages: 6, 16(bottom), 102
National Trust/Dick Makin, page: 95
Peter Newark's Military Pictures, pages: 24, 29, 31, 62, 189
Solo Syndication, page: 153(bottom)
Syndics of the Fitzwilliam Museum, Cambridge, page: 66(bottom)
Topham Picture Library, pages: 44, 55(bottom), 74, 112-3, 114(bottom), 120(bottom), 121(bottom), 122(bottom), 124, 129, 135, 136(both), 137, 144, 148(bottom), 186(bottom), 191(top), 196, 197(top), 204, 216(both), 220